P9-AGE-609

THE COMPLETE BOOK
OF
CANOEING & KAYAKING

THE COMPLETE BOOK
OF
CANOEING & KAYAKING

Paul Fillingham

DRAKE PUBLISHERS INC., NEW YORK

Published in 1974 by
Drake Publishers, Inc.
381 Park Ave. South
New York, New York 10016

Library of Congress Cataloging in Publication Data

Fillingham, Paul.
    The complete book of canoeing and kayaking.

    1. Canoes and canoeing.   I. Title.
GV783.F54   797.1'22   74-6214
ISBN 0-87749-698-6

CONTENTS

INTRODUCTION

The most difficult thing about writing a comprehensive book about canoes and kayaks is terminology. There are too many different types of boat around that come under the heading of canoe that we ought to broaden the term to mean a vessel propelled by a crew with an instrument which is not part of the vessel or the crew and which can be--both vessel and instrument--carried by the crew.

The term canoe of necessity include kayaks, Polynesian outriggers, what the Europeans call Canadian canoes (i.e. American Red Indian open--no deck--canoes) and so on. The instrument by which you move it can be a pole or paddle--most usually the latter. Sometimes it is a pole to the ends of which are two paddles. And sometimes you even attach a sail...these days to the boat, not the paddle.

Canoes, which thus encompass a miriade of ideas, are the basic water transport of humankind. You can find them in the upper latitudes, meeting the ice. You can find them at equatorial levels too. You will also find them in mountain rivers, high gorges, and estuaries where the tides of the sea meet the insistent down-pouring of the land. They are a ubiquitous creation of human mind.

Canoes are for having fun, for going places, and especially for going places you wouldn't normally be able to get to. They are not as speedy as a seaplane, but they can get to a lot more places than a seaplane can. Come to think of it, if you couple your canoe with a seaplane you can go almost any place on earth--if you want to.

So this book is for people who think they might like to canoe, or think they want to know more about the whole thing. How do you paddle your own canoe: how do you decide what you want? The book's a starting point from which to venture. You'll find information about camping and cruising--inland and coastal, about how to include canoeing (or kayaking) as a safe yet exciting part of living in your life. You can even find how to build your own canoe.

A writer is very much like a computer--he/she processes experience and writes a result. I'm extremely grateful, therefore, for the help given me in this work by Ed and Bonnie Bliss--a very beautiful husband and wife team. Both of them work at the national level in canoeing in the United States, and Ed--with Bonnie's brother Richard Church--has been national champion in C-2s.

Another thank you goes to the American Whitewater Affiliation who have very generously permitted me to list their members and publish their Safety Code, revised this year by Jim Sindelar, Executive Director of AWA. Thanks is also due to Iris, his wife, who edits *American Whitewater,* the excellent journal of AWA.

Across the water, thanks too to Bernard Apps, who does legion service with the British Corps of Canoe Lifeguards, an offshoot of the British Canoe Union which is their equivalent of our American Canoe Association. Interestingly, the Corps has developed its own rescue kayak for its work in saving lives.

Canoeing is an international recreation and sport and the people involved are generous, warm and outgoing. If you've never thought of paddling your own canoe you should try it; you'll meet some wonderful people along the way.

Have a *good* time! Most of what you need to know is here. The rest can only be learned from experience.

THE COMPLETE BOOK
OF
CANOEING & KAYAKING

Chapter 1

BACKGROUND & HISTORY

The Ancestors of today's canoes and kayaks are very likely lost deep in prehistory. But some clues remain. The Eskimo in Greenland and the Amerindian of South America still make some of their vessels in a manner which suggest a tribal art perfected across oceans of time. And in parts of Europe, too, some hints may be discerned.

The word *canoe* was borrowed from the Spanish, who in turn had borrowed it from their Carib captives—an Amerindian tribe which took the tropical islands of the eastern Caribbean by storm during the late Middle Ages. The Carib *canoa* was a less sophisticated boat originally developed by the Arawaks, whom the Caribs displaced (killing the men and keeping their women), for the Arawaks had been the earlier settlers of these isles from South America.

In parts of Brazil and elsewhere, it is still possible to see descendants of the Caribs and Arawaks constructing their dugouts. And in appearance these are not too dissimilar from similar craft to which outriggers are attached in the Pacific. First a tree of suitable length is selected. Then, after careful inspection, a ritual is performed to propitiate the spirit of the tree and to ensure the safety of those who will ultimately use the boat. Once felled, the tree is trimmed and moved nearer to the water where it will be launched. Depending on how much contact the Amerindians have had

with white people, more (or less) ritual will again be used so that the spirit of the water will deal kindly with the boat and its users. Finally the builders are ready to start.

The trunk is prepared by removing the bark and tracing an outline of the area to be hollowed. In earlier times, stone axes were used to create the "fireline," but most Amerindians today have access to that all-purpose bush tool, the machete. The fireline is an indentation along the top center of the trunk, where the cockpit will be. Hot charcoals are placed to burn away the wood, hollowing it out—and incidentally drying out the sap from the center to impregnate the hull. The process is carefully controlled, and calabashes of water are kept around to dampen areas where the fire may be burning too hotly or too freely.

The exterior of the dugout is roughly drawn when the bark is removed. After a clearly defined cockpit has been shaped, the next task is the trimming of the exterior lines. Finally, the cockpit is completed. The dugout is next tested for balance in water, and final adjustments are made if needed. The result is a vehicle that is fast, moderately stable, and capable of carrying a considerable load. It is normally crewed by two men, a bow person and stern person; because of its length, both assist in steering the craft in a manner quite similar to steering a tandem canoe.

The word *kayak* comes from the Eskimo word *quaja*

and refers to the canoes developed by those other Indian tribes who settled Greenland, the Arctic, and the Hudson Bay coasts of North America; the Labrador coast; Alaska; and the northeastern tip of Asia. *Eskimo* is derived from a Labrador-Algonquin Indian word, *eskimantik,* which means "raw flesh eater," apparently referring to the fat of sea mammals, from which these tribes obtain a rich and nutritious oil.

These days, of course, when the Eskimos have dumped their huskies in favor of automobiles, the making of kayaks has slightly changed. But traditionalists still prefer to make their own kayaks from frameworks constructed of driftwood or animal bones and bound together with gut. The frame is covered with sealskin—waterproof, obviously—and the boat is finally balanced and tested.

The similarity between these two designs, evolved so far apart geographically, is an extremely interesting one, for the kayak and dugout both share length and narrowness of beam. A quick look at the development of the indigenous North American Indian canoe gives us a chance to see a little of the evolution of boats. (Parenthetically, it may be noted again that the same sort of shape has found favor throughout the Pacific.)

But first let us go briefly to the Celtic tribes of Europe. The Celts appear to have had much in common with the Amerindians of America: they were resourceful, adventurous, and had a better understanding of mankind's relationship with the planet than we seem to have ourselves. Because of geophysical conditions, they were responsible for the development of two types of water transport: the Viking-type ship (a considerably more ambitious version of the Amerindian dugout, built with frames and keel, and developed independently from Phoenician, Egyptian, and Roman design), and a more simple, framework boat covered with hide.

The wood-surrounded ancient Briton made his coracle of a size that would take a cured horsehide without joints. The Irish followed the same pattern with the curragh, though they worked out a system for joints.

It is easy to imagine a scenario from time past. The women of the tribe take creeper and strip it down so that it can be woven into a frame. The men skin the animals and stake out the hide for curing. Someone knows about sewing, and the medicine man, who knows something about clays, collects the materials which will make the outer covering watertight. Farfetched? Not really, for this is much the same technique we employ ourselves when we use canvas as the outer covering of our canoes, except that we use a waterproof paint, and may even lay on a fiberglass sheath.

The point about using a fabric skin is that it permits the building of a round-bottomed hull without any fancy joinery work. Primitive man simply didn't have the tools to form curves and achieve a watertight hull.

The American Indian, it seems, was faced with similar problems as the European Celts, except that he was confronted by greater distances and, for some of his river work, by whiter waters than the Europeans. Presumably, centuries of experiment occurred, and it was probably determined that part of the resistance met when driving a machine through the water was actually caused by the bow wave itself. (In brief: resistance of water is the factor which controls speed, the bulk of which—between 80 and 90 percent—is simply friction caused by hull movement versus the water. It is highest at the lowest speed. To reduce frictional resistance, you play around with hull shapes. The ideal would be a hull which is a true semicircle below the waterline, rather short and deep at its widest point. The difficulty is that such a boat would have zero stability. More later.) The longer a canoe (or boat), the faster it can go—unless it has a planing hull, which means that it will ride on its own bow wave. But canoes are displacement vessels, which means they displace water rather than ride on it. And next, there really isn't sufficient power in human arms to get a planing machine on the step, which is the term used for getting (and staying) on the bow wave.

To solve this problem, the American Indian looked for a certain amount of length, plus a certain amount of beam, since it was obviously easier to paddle a loaded boat—once it was moving, there wasn't that much friction in keeping it going—than to walk with a load. Consequently, a more beamy vessel than the dugout or kayak was developed. But although in length slightly shorter—not so for transport and war canoes—in relative terms, the canoe wasn't shortened as absolutely as the coracle and curragh, where shape was dictated by animal skin. For according to tradition, the North American Indian had discovered that birchbark could be used as a covering.

The birchbark canoe was discovered by European settlers who decided to colonize this continent. They decided it was a convenient form of transport. It was also quiet, which made it an excellent vehicle for exploration and stalking both food and enemies. Indeed, as manifested in the war canoe, it could be said to be an early American (and New Zealand Maori) forerunner of high-speed torpedo boats and chasers of today.

The first two hundred years of European colonization of what is today the United States was achieved by canoe. But the real conquest occurred as a result of the development of communications techniques. First came the paddlewheel steamboat, and then the railroad. It is worth remembering that it is only a hundred and fifty years ago that the first state established beyond a river was the "steamboat state" of Missouri in 1821. Modern communications systems are a direct result of the need for people to communicate at long distance with each other—and so we have jets and telephones, and corporations and so-called utilities making the few rich out of the many's need to communicate. (Sigh!)

The American Indian canoe's design used a frame of more substance than either a kayak, coracle, or curragh, and was covered over with birchbark, whence it derives its name. It seems quite probable that several techniques were developed for the exterior skin, and more modern variants run the line from tarred canvas to vinyl. Traditionally shaped "Indian" canoes use wood and canvas, grp (glass-reinforced plastic, or fibreglass) and grp-balsa sandwich, and aluminum for construction.

Quite apart from the use of a canoe for collecting food and waging war, primitive man almost certainly used his boats for having fun. (After all, most recreation is a modified sort of war game—why win, otherwise?) From the European experience, this is deducible. The kayak was known in Europe circa 900 A.D. and the Hungarians had developed their own canoe by approximately 1100. Indeed, boating had become an acceptable form of recreation there by 1600.

Still, canoeing as a sport (kayaking can be said to be canoeing even though there's a difference between the two; these days it amounts to kneeling and using a single paddle—canoeing—or sitting and using a double paddle—kayaking) did not amount to much until one John "Rob Roy" McGregor astonished Victorian England with adventures in his modified canoe. He redesigned the Greenland kayak to his own specifications and explored the waterways of Europe. His endeavors were later to be matched here by J. Henry Rushton of Canton, New York, one of the world's less recognized craftsmen of small boats, whose canoes and whose influence on the development of the sport of canoeing and kayaking were considerable.

We have been brought up to believe that the great pioneers were those who rode horseback or traveled in prairie wagons. History has forgotten the men and women who adventured into the interiors of the continent by boat. And before these, there were the first newcomers, a loose-knit band of men, a waterborne group of artisans not unlike the Italian woods people called Carbonari ("the charcoal-burners"), but more interested in trade than in politics. The *voyageurs* were also loose-knit, being French, English, and Scots for the most part, who settled along the St. Lawrence River. The hippies of their time, they adopted Indian clothing and beads; their unofficial equivalent to the blue jeans of today was a red woolen cap, a beaded shoulder bag (containing a sewing kit similar to that used in the British navy today and known as a "huz'if"—housewife—plus toiletry articles), plus a brightly colored sash.

They were enthusiastic about the Indians, unlike the more uptight persons who followed them and who regarded the Indians as fair game for shooting. They were so enthusiastic about the Indian lifestyle that they went so far as to copy their mode of transport——but, being typically European in outlook, they concluded that bigger was better. Their transport canoes were blown-up versions of the light birchbark canoe, ran about thirty feet in length with ornate bowsprits (sometimes carved, copying European tradition), and were powered by bright red paddles. With a crew of twelve, these big-bellied craft could handle a load of 3 tons or so.

The more cynical among us might be persuaded that they adopted the Indian style the better to trade with those ignorant savages, since there was considerable demand in those days for items developed by Western civilization as there is today in South America. Clothing and ornament figured more prominently then than now, though the demand for mirrors seems to be as great today. Hunting weapons—hand axes, guns, and so forth—were greatly appreciated, much as they are today; plus machetes.

Like the Carbonari and the Masons, the *voyageurs* held initiatory ceremonies for new members. Blood-curdling oaths were invoked by the new member that he would not pass on those secrets discovered while in the interior, and tradition has it that several became initiates of the esoteric rites of the free Indians. New crew members were baptized with water dripped from "the topmost of . . . young twigs" of a Leganon cedar (Ezekiel 17:3) before making their first trip inland. The ceremony ended in a fusillade as the hoodwink (blindfold) was torn away from their eyes and they found themselves in a strange part of the river. (The *voyageurs*, like the Indians, learned to paddle silently.) On their return from their first adventure, the initiates were thenceforth permitted to wear a cockade of turkey feathers in their caps.

Those clubs who still remember this tradition might like to know whence it derives. The cedars are very important.

Despite the incredible desolation we have laid on our land, it is still possible for canoeists to enjoy some happiness upon these waters. If you don't mind being like a *voyageur* yourself, Canada's recreation grounds are still unspoiled. It is a chance to contribute a little something to making our

America better. Because the more we use these waterways, the cleaner we can make them. Cruising and camping canoeists actually pack far more clout than they know—because they have become citizens connected with their land.

Canoeing finally made international status in the 1920s, and by the 1930s, the railroad companies were running canoeing weekend specials. Somehow all that got lost during World War II—except for the Cockleshell Hero group—and subsequently, apart from being used for more obvious entertainment, the kayaks slipped into the hands of the military, chiefly for loading and unloading people into others' territory.

The Europeans, meanwhile, decided that it was an okay sport. The French, representing the West, and the Czechs, representing the East, fought fast and furious to win the honors. During all this we sat glumly on, watching the Europeans turn our discoveries into highly skillful play. But the status of the sport is improving. While we still tend to rely on brute strength rather than on physically inspired mechanics, we are getting better. We should be fairly solid gold-medal status soon. But it will mean all of us taking our share of work. And this means getting the water clean. We have the waterways to learn on. We merely need to clean them up and give them back to the people.

Too, unless we give opportunities to everyone, we shall pollute ourselves to death. And apart from its affording back-to-nature enjoyment (more in keeping with our increasing awareness of the importance of ecology), canoeing's the sport for the cheap date—for the one who really can't afford to put out money.

CANOE OR KAYAK?

The choice is difficult, since there is no all-purpose boat. You'll have to decide your main purpose: River, lake, estuary, ocean? White or wild water? Competition or cruising or camping? Racing, even? Or just a family boat to mess around in?

Regular canoes offer more carrying capacity than kayaks, and, from a family point of view, may make more sense. They can also be fitted with a half- or full-spray deck for rough passages. In terms of touring with a modern decked competition canoe, the biggest advantage is that you need only spray covers to enable you to roll out of trouble. The older-styled canoe can be slept in. A simple, tentlike structure can be rigged to provide covering for the night.

Single-hole kayaks have their own appeal, especially for those who enjoy exploring strange territory. There are also a number of folding-type touring kayaks which offer plenty of space for crew and gear, and with which you can trek in or out of wilderness areas from a bush-strip or lake. A light airplane takes you to your starting point, for your folding canoe can be packed in the rear. Klepper's Aerius II and Folbot's Super are examples of such kayaks.

Safety is another consideration. If you find kneeling is difficult for long periods of time—even with kneepads—you may prefer to think of sitting down. Canoes are best controlled from a kneeling position, using either both knees or one. With a kayak, on the other hand, you sit, but for anything advanced you'll have your knees braced out against the hull, this puts your weight on the lower back—and you'll have to get used to that.

There's a further point. Most family canoeists in America don't use spray covers or decking; without such devices, wind resistance is greater, and the dunking of freight in a capsize is inevitable. Obviously, in some regions it just is too hot to use a spray cover. But if you should capsize with one, in a kayak you can simply roll it back upright—usually without anything getting soaked.

Another consideration occurs—competition. Are you sure you won't want to try your hand in a race or regatta some day? What will you want then? Kayaks are faster and more seaworthy than canoes, but canoes are easier to paddle and are relatively more stable. This is something you'll really have to decide for yourself. Meanwhile, some thoughts on the subject:

Selecting a kayak. Your first consideration is going to be whether you opt for a folding or a rigid kayak. Folding boats are convenient for traveling with or for hiking into difficult areas. They are ideal for weekending in new places, and they take about fifteen to twenty minutes to put together.

The disadvantage of folding boats is that they must be properly dried out (they can be packed damp, but you should dry them out when you get home.) They also flex somewhat, so that, in these days of rigid canoes, they have slightly more drag through the water.

Folding kayaks consist of a frame over which a skin, usually of a rubberized vinyl fabric, is slipped. The frame is then expanded so that it stretches the skin tight. When not in use, the frame can be dismantled and stowed in one bag. The skin goes in the other. A typical 15-foot, single-seat folding kayak will weigh about 60 pounds in its bag, while a two-to-three-place one will weigh about 20 pounds more.

As against this, a rigid kayak, which does not come apart for convenient stowage and which you will have to carry on the roof of your car, is usually less expensive than an equivalent folding one. Because of its rigidity in the

water, it will be slightly faster. Rigid kayaks are mostly made of grp these days, and superior lightweight glass mats are used in their construction to lighten them. (More about grp and building in Chapter 10.) Cold (or hot) molded veneer is also used, and has found favor with racing kayaks. Grp's big advantage is that it offers strength with light weight and relative ease of repair.

The next question will be size of cockpit: One place or more? This is a crucial decision. If marriages are made in heaven, so are happy kayak teams. If you have never worked a kayak before, join a club, make a friend, amd learn in a single-seater. The most loving of married couples will find learning in a two-place kayak nearly impossible, since the cockpit can easily turn into the most abrasive place you've ever been—twenty times worse than the car you're attempting to teach your husband or wife or lover how to drive. And the cause of the difficulty is, quite simply, those double paddles.

Once you both know how to propel your craft, two-place vehicles are undoubtedly lots of fun, particularly if you enjoy doing things together. For those who prefer a smidgin of independence, two one-place kayaks are the answer. And you can play games with those too.

Two-place kayaks are slightly quicker than singles, and with their additional length are much better for sea work. Their extra length makes them more tricky in white water, and a canoe is much better for two people. And while two hearts may beat as one, in a two-place kayak someone's got to be in charge.

Two-place kayaks are much better than one-place kayaks on lakes, or slow-moving waters, and can even have a sail added to them. For sailing you are going to need dagger boards or leeboards, and sailing conversion kits are obtainable. Your kayak won't do as well as a regular sailing boat, but it will reach and run very nicely. Against the wind it will be tippy, and the sail should be used only in relatively light airs.

In terms of measurements, you might as well get the international regulation sizes since, should you ever want to compete, you'll be able to. This is 13 feet, 1½ inches long (slalom and white water), 24 inches maximum width, with a depth ranging from 11 to 13 inches at the deepest point. For downriver and wild-water racing, you go slightly longer in length to 14 feet, 8 inches.

For a two-place kayak (not competition), reckon on length being nearer 17 feet, and, depending on type, the beam will be about three feet or even a little more. In terms of supporting a load, the shorter a boat's length, the wider its beam must be. And the deeper a beamy boat has to

float—in terms of weight carried—the more effort required to get it to move through the water. So don't be worried about narrow beam. It works in your favor by making kayaking relatively light work.

Kayaks may be divided into three groups: slalom (and/or white or wild water), racing, and cruising (or touring.) Racing kayaks have a straight keel and a rudder and tend to be longer and thinner than kayaks of other designs. They're designed to travel fast in a straight line, for the most part; and they are steered with the feet by a rudder so that the paddler(s) can concentrate on power. Kayaks used for coastal cruising or big-lake cruising are also fitted with a rudder, either directly aft, or, in some instances, suspended beneath the stern. The latter works better in terms of steering, while the former has a tip-up device which permits going into shallow waters without grounding the rudder.

Slalom kayaks, which are built with a variable-depth keel, are intended to be highly maneuverable by paddle alone. Indeed, it is quite difficult to keep a slalom kayak going in a straight line, since with each succeeding stroke you have to compensate for its predecessor. And eventually you land off course again. Still, in competition, the course is going every which way with and against the current, so that what at first appears to be a highly aberrant system suddenly becomes a plus. Very fine corrections to direction can be made, and precision can be applied through the gates which mark the course.

Similar to the slalom is the recreational white-water kayak, which is excellent for learning white-water technique and can be raced with others in its class. While not as responsive as a regular slalom kayak, it is useful for learning such techniques as the ferry glide, for example.

Next you have the all-purpose- (or touring-) type kayak, which is a compromise vehicle which can be raced—though not very quickly; but in which you can tour—quite comfortably, thank you very much. There are several very good touring kayaks on the market, some of which make excellent support systems for camping.

Finally, there's the surfing kayak, which is specifically designed to plane on the smokers. The first people to try surfing used regular slalom kayaks (these still can be used), but more recently a specially designed kayak has appeared which is not too dissimilar from a surfboard in shape. These are a little over 10 feet long, with a width of 2 feet, and are gently tapered from bow to stern.

And Eskimo kayaks? Actually, there's an English firm which markets an Eskimo-type replica, and some have been sold in this country. The *Nanuk* (after *Nanook of the North*) makes an excellent touring vessel, is lightweight—about 35 pounds—almost 17 feet long, and rather narrow. It sells (at time of writing) for under $300.

The genuine article is rather longer (19 feet or so) and narrower (20 inches.) Its seaworthiness is admirably attested by the fact that, on one or two different occasions in recent years, Eskimos from east Greenland managed to survive the 1,600-mile trip to England, having been blown on their way by gale-force winds.

In addition to length, of which some more will be said later, hull shape is important too. In much the same way that an aircraft designer shapes the wing for the task his airplane must perform, so, too, do hull designers alter the shape of their hull.

Hull design is discussed more extensively in Chapter 10, "Maintenance & Building," but a few words won't be out of place here. The keel line in a racing boat is kept straight with respect to the horizontal axis. In a slalom boat it is rockered, that is to say, from a deep centerpoint it rises toward the bow and stern and will rock on its centerpoint. A touring kayak has less rocker than a slalom boat, but more than a racing boat. The long, straight keel keeps the racing boat going in a straight line, which is why it uses a rudder to assist in turning.

Hull shape is also important, but that need not concern us here. What happens when you lean is discussed in the next chapter, but, briefly, you are moving the centers of gravity and buoyancy from their normal, stable position. For this reason, you have to correct the incipient imbalance by hauling on your paddle (or pushing on it.)

Actually, too much stability is not helpful, since the usefulness of the craft may be affected. A kayak is thus better able to serve its master if it is not too stable, since at sea it might have a tendency to follow the profile of any wave approaching it beam-on. What then happens is that the kayak develops a heavy list as the wave passes, and you have to lean over heavily to prevent it tipping, maybe using your paddle as an assist. If the center of gravity falls outside the kayak's center of buoyancy when it tips, the kayak will tip over and capsize. Thus, a less stable kayak is actually safer, and it doesn't make you work so hard.

Hull design is also important, and three types are to be found: Swedishform; fishform; and symmetrical, sometimes also known as "modified" shape.

Fishform, in which the shape is rather like a fish, being slightly wider ahead of the cockpit and narrowing toward the tail or stern, was first adopted for Western kayaks. Then the Swedes decided that being slightly beamier behind the stern might be better, particularly for such techniques as the ferry glide, in which the kayak is back-paddled and the current moves the canoe across the stream. So the Swedishform is fishform in reverse. Then came the symmetrical, or modified, shape, which is where the beamiest portion of the kayak falls exactly at dead center. This is mostly found in downriver and wild-water racers, though some slalom persons like it too.

Perhaps the most important point in choosing your kayak is that you get one in which you feel really comfortable, and which you can be said to wear like a glove. The kayak becomes, as it were, an extension of yourself. Seats, hip boards or pads, footrest, kneegrips, and even the spray skirt all aid you in utilizing your body's flexibility to work harmoniously with the machine. Kneegrips and spray skirt are essential if you are going to master the Eskimo roll. And if you're going to be anything better than halfway good with a kayak, it must be mastered.

Lastly, if you are new to the sport, talk with people who are already into it. You'll not only meet some uncommonly nice people, you'll also make some very good friends—and you'll pick up a lot of tips which can save you time and money. The canoe world is a very nice place to be.

CHOOSING A CANOE

Fortunately for us, when they were butchering the Indians, our ancestors had enough sense to save the Indian canoe. Thus, American Indian-styled canoes were being produced commercially in the Chicago area nearly a hundred years ago. Old Town, Maine, still has a canoe company turning out replicas of these old-time favorites today. But canoe-making has become a business, and there are today more than sixty makers producing several different varieties of canoe from several different types of material.

Canoe length and shape depend to a degree on the number of persons to be carried, the use to which the canoe will be put, and the degree of skill involved by those who will use it. Most single canoes are from 12 to 16 feet, though an experienced paddled may be quite at home in a canoe of up to 18 feet. If you're just starting, or if you're returning to canoeing after an absence of time, a canoe of 15 to 17 feet should be fine, and also provide room for some company. The smaller lengths will be slower, but for ease of maneuverability they must be rated high. A 16-foot canoe is still light and can be used by one or two; under safe conditions, it can even be used to carry an additional friend. A 17-footer gives you just a bit more room for extra gear, and can be more easily portaged when a third is carried.

Longer canoes are usually used as workboats or in recreational programs. But 17- and 18-foot canoes are often used for extended cruising. As a general rule, if you want

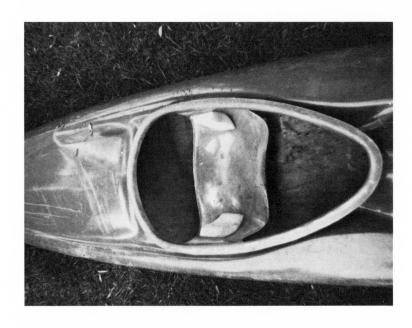

Non-adjustable seat, but provided with thigh braces. The knee braces are not visible in the photograph.

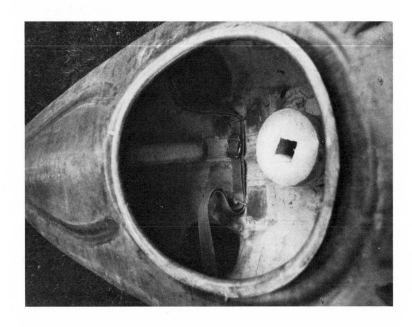

Interior of C-1 canoe, showing thigh straps and knee supports. The "seat" is added to the styrofoam piller, fitting on top of it.

Neoprene spray skirt, as used with closed canoes (C-1, C-2) snf kayaks. The bottom edging fits around the raised lips of the cockpit, forming a watertight seal.

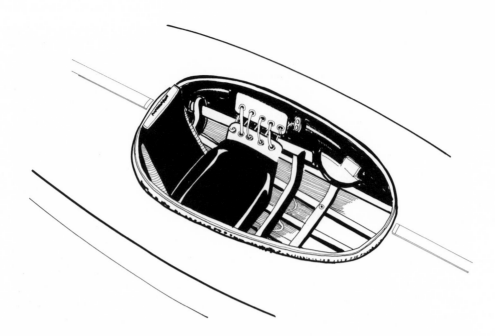

*Interior of cockpit of kayak, customized to provide both thigh
and knee braces. The leather lacing provides for a perfect
support. The knee braces are fixed.*

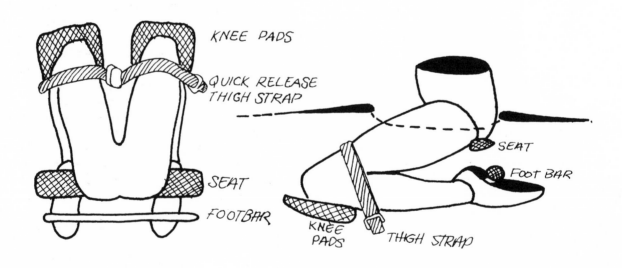

KNEE PADS

QUICK RELEASE
THIGH STRAP

SEAT

FOOTBAR

SEAT

FOOT BAR

KNEE
PADS

THIGH STRAP

*Two-view of canoeist's (closed canoe)body. Item marked
seat is actually a thwart or support and not a regular seat.*

maneuverability, look to a shorter canoe. But a longer waterline length is better for more open water and where speed will be coming from your paddle blade. Longer canoes—fitted with semispray covers—are also good for white-water use.

In addition to length, there's also shape to be considered. A wide, flat-bottomed canoe is relatively stable as a platform, but a round-bottomed canoe, usually narrower and less stable, is generally faster and easier to paddle from a center position. Long canoes are faster than short canoes, and a canoe without a keel is more maneuverable than one with a keel or keels. Additionally, a keelless canoe in white water is also less likely to ground in shallows. As against this, a flat or shoe keel gives better protection than a fin keel. A stubby-ended canoe will tend to ride waves and ship less water than a sharp-ended canoe, while a canoe that has much freeboard—and high ends—will make you work harder when there's any wind blowing. It's better to go for a low-profile boat. Lastly, underwater shape is important in that canoes with "rocker," where it is deepest at the center and rises to bow and stern, will be more maneuverable than ones that are simply flat. As far as the interior is concerned, experts prefer paddling thwarts, which give support to your seat, rather than seats on which you sit.

But we'll return to this in a moment. Meanwhile, the next question which must be dealt with is: What material?

The weight of a canoe depends on the material it is made from, which explains the increasing popularity of aluminum and grp, (glass reinforced plastic, or fiberglass) both of which are strong and light in weight. A 17-foot aluminum canoe will weigh about 80 pounds with a standard hull of .051 inches thick, whereas a lightweight hull will weigh in at just over 60 pounds with a thickness of .032 inches. Reckon a typical grp canoe of the same length to be about the same as the lightweight aluminum one.

A wooden, or wood-frame-canvas canoe will tend to be heavier, though some canvas-covered canoes are light. The problem is water absorption; on a long trip the canoe may absorb as much as 15 pounds of water.

In terms of price, canoes are only slightly more expensive than an equivalent kayak of the rigid type. It's worth shopping around. If you buy from a maker directly, you'll have to add shipping and freight to the bill.

All wood construction is still popular, and several different ways of making canoes from wood have been developed. The most popular—*longitudinal strip*—produces a solid, strong canoe. Construction requires care since the canoe is made up of an exterior of seasoned cedar strips, attached to closely placed frames. The strips are matched very carefully so that the outside of the canoe is smooth, and they are secured to the frames by copper nails. A stem and a keel of oak are then added.

Clinker-built construction, where the hull is built up of a series of overlapping planks, is also found, though this method is more often used in making dinghies. This method was used in constructing the original Rob Roy-type kayaks. While Canadian canoes made this way are heavy, they will stand up to considerable wear and tear.

Rib-and-batten construction is a method similar to longitudinal-strip construction, but here the strips—or planks—are much wider in section. This is quite a good way to make a lighter weight all-wood canoe, but the end product is not too strong.

Molded-veneer construction has been a popular way of making canoes in Europe. Here the builder takes strips of wood veneer and lays them diagonally over a mold. The strips are about 4 inches wide and very thin. Alternate layers are laid down in opposite directions, each being bonded to its neighbor by one of the new waterproof glues. There is a considerable saving in weight with this method of construction, and the hull is actually quite strong. International competition canoes are occasionally made by use of this method, though the veneers are laid in such a way that the exterior is an unbroken surface of veneer rather than a series of strips.

Finally we come to the planked-and-canvas-type canoe, which is similar in its design to the canoe thought to be its ancestor, the birchbark canoe. The original model for this historic boat had a short keel to which a framework of ribs was attached. Made of white cedar, these frames were first roughly trimmed to size and then steamed to the required shape. These were then secured at the top by long strips of wood to which the gunwales would eventually be fitted, and covered with a thin sheath of either animal skin—where the frames were spaced closely together—or with thin strips of spruce. The exterior was then covered with birchbark and caulked throughout with spruce resin for waterproofing.

The modern wood-frame canoes were developed toward the end of the nineteenth century, and their design has been slowly improved over the years. Because of the shortage of birchbark, canvas was adopted as an exterior covering, but today's wood framers still use the cedar frame of yore. A thin outer wooden planking, usually of red cedar—materials vary from builder to builder, and other types of wood may be found, depending on what's locally available—is secured to the framework, and then a canvas exterior is applied. This is then treated to take a waterproof paint. Several European firms have been using fiberglass fabric in place of canvas with reportedly good results, since fiberglass does not absorb water. It seems likely that U.S. canoe-makers will soon adopt this technique, since a number of excellent lightweight fiberglass fabrics have been developed for use by the aviation industry.

The trouble with the canvas covering is that it tends to absorb water, even when painted. Secondly, it will bruise easily on rocks, which means that maintenance becomes an important factor of ownership. Finally, canvas does not take too well to sunlight. Consequently, care of a wood-framed canvas-covered canoe is an ongoing process, which includes careful winter storage, regular painting and touching up, and occasional recanvasing. Against this you have a canoe with a flavor of history about it and one which will usually have those traditional qualities of good workmanship in its construction.

Before leaving the subject of wood-based canoes, it's worth mentioning that there are a number of canoe kits available, and several magazines feature canoe designs for do-it-yourself fans. Most of the kits are for marine-ply or the wood-frame fabric-type just described. If you are reasonably skilled and have the mental discipline to undertake a project like this, it might be an inexpensive way to get yourself afloat. But most people who build their own canoes usually know quite a bit about the subject of design and build their own solely because they cannot find a manufacturer who will produce something that suits their design purpose.

You should know something about hull design before you start, and be reasonably familiar with what's what. Homebuilding by the tyro too often leads to grief—and you wouldn't want to feel that way about canoeing, would you?

Grp seems to be the coming material in the making of canoes, not least on account of its strength-weight ratio mentioned earlier. It is also inexpensive. From the point of view of the handy person who has a small workshop, building a canoe is not too difficult and is discussed later in this book. What homebuilding offers the canoeist is a chance to get to know boats from their beginning and to design those features which experience has shown to be important. Briefly, you'll need to have the ability to construct a mold, which means you must have some knowledge of design before you begin.

Basically, a grp canoe is made up of layers of glass cloth and glass mat, over which resin and catalyst have been poured, or brushed. The catalyst causes the resin to combine with the glass at a molecular level, forming a very hard surface which is then worked over. Color can be added to the resin to produce a permanent color scheme.

In a practical sense, the grp canoe—because of its inherent strength—does not require ribs for internal bracing, which permits a flat floor. Similarly, thwarts for lateral bracing are sometimes omitted, which leaves more room for people and gear. Foam flotation units are usually fitted at bow and stern—and they should be there and not under the seats—since grp has no natural buoyancy. Several canoes have been made which have the appearance of the genuine birchbark canoe; others are in bright colors.

At the present, most canoe-makers tend to overdesign grp canoes, with the result that they are somewhat heavier than aluminum, unless you get the thinner hull. They are occasionally more expensive, but this is changing as firms become more experienced in using the material.

With the decline in aircraft production following World War II, aluminum became available for all sorts of new things, from beer cans to car wheels to canoes. Aluminum is a lightweight, silver-colored metal which is extremely corrosion resistant and easy to work. It is thus ideal for making boats, since it can be treated to resist saltwater corrosion.

The aluminum canoe is a tough machine, and apart from the noise—which may drive you mad—as you swish through shallow rapids, bump, bump, bumping downstream—represents a solid piece of equipment. Grumman-American, which produces light aircraft in addition to military machines, uses much the same technique in building aluminum canoes as in making airplanes. A sheet of the metal is die-formed, that is, stretched over a mold, and a press is then applied which shapes the sheet over the mold. When the press releases the material, you've got one half of a canoe. Both sides are trimmed and drilled and, following a special heat treatment, are then bolted together. Bracing and other features are added next before the canoe is tank tested to ensure it doesn't leak.

With buoyancy bags both fore and aft, the aluminum canoe won't sink. Some are even designed to right themselves in the event of a capsize. The principal drawback of aluminum is that it can become rather hot if left in the sun for a long time, and in cool waters the bottom gets very chilly. As against that—and the noise—it is relatively maintenance free, and you don't really need to even paint it.

What about secondhand canoes? While a secondhand canoe can save you a lot of money, you can easily end up spending almost as much money putting one into shape as you would have spent on a new one. Similarly, you'll come across several designs with which you'll be unfamiliar and which may have been built for a specific purpose not your own. These should be shunned until you've built up your own expertise. Therefore, it's advisable to have a friend who really knows canoes to help you out in making your purchase.

Lastly, you can rent, which frequently solves the problem of having to transport and care for your canoe. For the person who is uncertain whether canoeing is for him, a few outings in a rented canoe will help at decision-making time. Costs are still relatively expensive—usually not more than about $5 a day—and frequently cheaper during the week. You can be reasonably sure that the canoes are well maintained: except for some rowboat concessions which overhaul only once a year, most decent canoe agencies run a progressive maintenance scheme. The canoes will also tend to be of decent design for their waters.

Very often the rental outfit will offer a pickup toward the end of the day for a minimal charge, which means you've got more time to explore. Details of where to find out about canoe rental are listed in the end papers.

As far as hull design is concerned, most canoes come with a fin keel. These are nice for working lakes, but make it difficult to move sideways—an important maneuver if you're running white water. A shoe-keeled boat is better, and if you can find one with some rocker, this is better yet. If you intend to use your canoe in competition on a regular basis, get one without seats. You can't handle a canoe in rapid water from a seated position, since you have to use your body to balance the boat. The only way to achieve this in reasonable comfort is to kneel, which means wearing knee-pads.

Spray decks (or half-decks) are a very worthwhile addition to all canoes and are to be found fairly widely in Europe, where most white-water experts favor them. They're also found on those bilge-keeled canoes used in estuaries and under sail. In addition to keeping water out of the canoe, a spray deck gives considerable help in smoothing the shape of the canoe to the wind—that is, it reduces the effect of the wind when it catches the canoe. If you don't like the idea of a full spray deck, consider the half-deck. It's a practical addition. The diagram shows what this looks like, and you can make up your own using a medium-weight ripstop waterproof nylon or a 10-ounce proofed canvas for material. To attach it to your canoe, use press-studs with a simple frame to hold it taut. Another possibility might be to use heavy-duty velcro fastener.

PADDLES

Choosing the right size paddle to use is important to both the canoeist and kayakist. It will save unnecessary fatigue and consequently add to your enjoyment.

In choosing the right length paddle, the canoeist should follow this rule of thumb: stern persons, while standing on the ground with the paddle blade tip at their feet, should have the top of the grip level with their eyes; bow persons require a slightly shorter paddle, and the grip should be about level with the mouth. It's a bit like choosing the right length skis, in that it gives you somewhere to start from. Obviously, you'll eventually select the length that seems right for you, since some people have longer arms than others in relation to height.

Wood is still the most popular material for paddles. Aluminum, which is strong and light, tends to get your hands very dirty. Being hard and relatively light, with a certain amount of natural spring to it, wood is a well-suited material. Sitka spruce, which has a good strength-lightness ratio, is much used. Its drawback is that it tends to split or crack under rugged use. Maple, slightly heavier than spruce, is much favored; and ash, which is heavier still, is sometimes used, since it has considerably more resilience, or spring, which helps in easing the shock of inertia at the beginning of a stroke. Ash is also used in laminates of wood for paddle-making.

The laminates try to offer a little bit of everything, and some have even been designed to use an alloy shaft with a wooden blade—strengthened in this arrangement where the blade meets the shaft with a rib of ash—and a carved wooden handle. It's really a question of choosing what suits you best, unless you are going to go the competition route, in which case you'd better study what the top contenders use. In terms of blade shape, most racing people favor the square-tipped blade. For cruising, you can use either the spoon-shaped blade or the modified—or beaver-tail blade—which has rounded corners. The latter is also used for the slalom.

The width of the blade depends very much on the individual's shoulder power and overall stamina, which means that you should experiment to find which size is most convenient for you to handle. Too small a blade and you'll feel tired since you are not getting hold of enough water on each stroke and you're wasting energy. Too large a blade and you'll also become tired because you're trying to pull too much water for your strength. Balance is needed. Also, with too large a blade you'll find the paddle has a tendency to snake through the water as you bring it out. So don't hurry about the selection of your paddle, and if you can't find the one that looks and feels right for you the first time, shop around.

Lastly, there are some solo canoeists who prefer to use the double paddle of the kayak. Because of the width of a canoe, this means getting a longer pair than you'd normally use in a kayak. If you want to go for the double paddle, you'll have to learn to feather your blade as the kayakist does.

The ordinary kayak paddle is a double-bladed implement some 7 to 8 feet in length and usually made from spruce. To prevent splitting, the blade ends are usually tipped with copper, aluminum, grp, or even wood. If your blades aren't tipped, then either do them yourself, or get help. Do remember that the balance may be altered if you don't take the additional weights into consideration. It is customary to varnish and wax kayak paddles.

The racing paddle is expensive but quite a work of art. It is very light in weight, and its overall structure is spruce. However, to prevent its breaking in the heat of competition, it is strengthened where the handle joins the blade, usually with an insert of ash, while the carefully shaped spoon blade has laminations of mahogany slid into it to increase its strength.

White-water kayakists prefer a flat blade to the spoon, since when you back-paddle with a spoon you get a somewhat different effect than when you're paddling forward. This can be very confusing in the negotiation of a tricky run.

As a general rule, once you've found the length of paddle and the shape that suits you, buy the best you can afford—and buy a spare. Since paddle development is an ongoing subject of improvement at this time, the thing to remember is that when you reverse sharply while going forward, or use the blade to change direction, you put immense strain on the blade and shaft. Get the strongest and lightest you can afford.

As far as feather of the blade is concerned—that is, the angle at which the out-of-water blade meets the air—an angle of 60° or 90° is preferred. You may want to adjust the angle, depending on wind conditions.

Chapter 2
Basic Technique

Before taking your canoe to the water, there are one or two matters for your consideration. First, how are you going to carry it to the water's edge? Next, how do you put it on the water? Finally, how do you get on board without tipping it over?

If yours is a new canoe that you've just bought, there's one little item that requires attention before you answer any of these questions. It concerns hull registration. All manufacturers are supposed to have on record the details of the owners of the hulls they produced. This little bit of bureaucracy is supposed to help you in the event that someone walks off with your boat.

There is also one further consideration—perhaps the most important of all. You should never omit it. This is the prelaunch inspection. No matter that the canoe floated last time you used it. Unless you are sure before you put it on the water that it's going to float, you are being foolhardy. Sure, there are those who'll tell you an aluminum canoe doesn't hole. Most of the time they're right. There's always an occasion that turns up to prove them wrong—usually in midstream. And that makes accidents happen.

So, before launching, always make a thorough visual inspection of your craft for any signs that may signal something being not quite right. Then, when you're sure she's shipshape, go ahead and launch.

Depending on the length and weight of your canoe, and the numbers of people around to give a hand, there are a variety of ways to carry it. Competition canoes, which are super-lightweight, can be carried quite easily by one person. The more ordinary American canoe can be carried solo a short way by taking the nearside gunwale at its center, and lifting it onto the hip. It is also possible to launch from this position, by letting down one end of the canoe to the water, and then pushing the rest of it over your thigh. Regular-sized American canoes should not, as a rule, be carried overhead without the use of a yoke. They're very often heavier than they seem, and you could damage yourself lifting one.

If there are two persons available, you have a choice of carrying at the center, or carrying at bow and stern. The former is just right for launching, since you just drop the front end into the water and feed the rest of it in hand by hand. For longer distances, bow-and-stern carry is recommended.

If three persons are available, the strongest should go to the stern, while the other two carry from the bow. Four persons can carry bow and stern, or inverted.

To get underneath for the overhead carry, have someone hold up one end as you walk underneath. Once you reach the point of balance, get your shoulders under the yoke so that you will have a triangular support base where shoulders and each arm form the sides. Keep the end of the canoe slightly higher ahead of you so you can see where you're going.

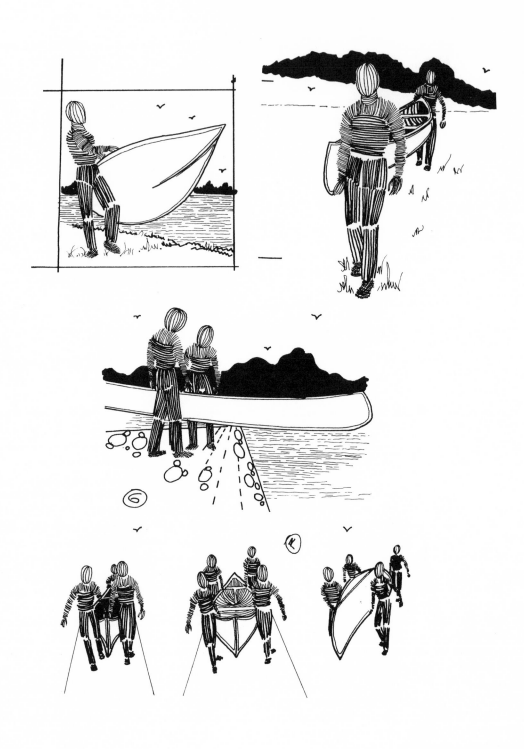

LAUNCHING (Beach or Bank)

While it isn't especially difficult to launch your canoe, there is a right and wrong way. The latter is to drag the poor craft across the ground, over rocks at the water's edge, and so on. This can easily damage the bottom. So do it properly, which means carrying it to the water and then feeding it stage by stage onto the water, avoiding any of the rocks at the bankside.

Canoes can be launched bow or stern first, and be sure that you have a line attached or you'll have to swim after it. Most people launch stern first, and the procedure is simple. Launch the stern gently onto the water and then feed out the rest of the canoe until it lies at right angles to the shore. On lakes and gently shoaling rivers, the bow will just be touching the bottom.

BOARDING

If you are alone, you put one foot in the center of the bottom of the canoe and, grasping both sides and keeping your body low, move to the center. The effect of your weight should have lifted the bow by this time, so you now take up your position and get ready to paddle.

If there are two of you, the stern person boards first and, once more, goes to the stern using a crouch. Meanwhile, the bow person is securing the canoe by holding the gunwale, and steadying the bow between the knees. Once the stern person is comfortable, the bow person lifts the bow slightly and, with a little push, boards and goes to the bow position. Next comes a delicate turn, and the bow person is ready. If the canoe is stuck on the bottom, the bow person goes amidships to free the bow, returning to the forward position once the canoe is afloat.

LAUNCHING (Jetty, High Bank, Dock)

This is a much easier way of launching and boarding, and it is worth looking out for. Here the canoe can be fed in from the two-person gunwale carry, also, two persons can hold the gunwale from the same side and lower it into the water. Provided there's not too steep a drop, the latter method is preferred.

In the former case, the canoe is brought alongside the jetty, while in the latter it is already there. The procedure for boarding from a jetty is the reverse of the procedure used for boarding from a bank. Here the bow person boards first while the stern person steadies the canoe. The boarding is done from the amidships point, and the first step should be with gradual downward pressure, rather than at an angle which might tend to push the canoe away from the jetty and

tumble the person into the water. Once the weight is secure, the other foot is brought into the canoe and a crouch is adopted. The bow person moves forward just short of the standard position until the stern person boards.

When a third person is carried, that person boards first amidships. The bow and stern persons board close to the centerpoint and make their way to their respective places while the visitor holds the canoe to the dock.

Always board carefully.

COMING ASHORE

The procedures for coming ashore are the mirror image of boarding. When you are using a low bank or beach, approach at right angles. The bow person steps ashore, and pulls the canoe in just a little--too far up and stability is lost, as well as possibly damaging the hull. The stern person then comes forward and jumps off. The canoe is then lifted out of the water. (For closed canoes, treat as for kayaks.)

At the dock, come alongside. Bow and stern persons exit from amidships. Where three are carried, you can either let the third person off first, or you can gather into a huddle amidships and let the bow person off first. He then secures the canoe from the dock with a painter and the others get off.

SAFETY MEASURE: Capsize

Normally you won't capsize a canoe, but it sometimes happens that you get knocked down by a wave and you're too slow and . . . over she goes. So that you know what to do in the event of a capsize, it is good sense to actually go and do it. First of all, you'll learn how stable your canoe and how far you can push it. Next, if a capsize should happen unexpectedly, you're not going to be in a panic, since you will already have practiced the procedure to be outlined below.

First consideration: There has to be a Coast-Guard approved personal safety device for each person aboard. This, by the way, is also the law for any boat. And while you are not required to wear the device, it must be there. In fact, it makes good sense to wear a lifejacket, since the extra buoyancy it gives you is useful if you're in a capsize.

Still, don't go out and buy just any life jacket. For canoeing, you must have one that is designed for the job, since many life jackets don't provide sufficient freespace for arm movement. This can be quite uncomfortable, causing you not to wear the life jacket. So get one that has been specifically designed for canoeists. Most catalog houses offer these specialty life jackets--check that they're approved--and a number of houses carry excellent life jackets of European design.

The British kayakist's jacket, which has reduced buoyancy so that it won't interfere with rolling the kayak, is a good buy. There are also two very good French jackets.

Buoyancy for your canoe is another important factor. Most modern canoes have buoyancy built in, but when you buy one, check this question with the salesman. If necessary, provide additional buoyancy by means of air bags secured—so they won't come adrift in a capsize—securely at bow and stern.

Now—you and your canoe provided with buoyancy—you're ready for the capsize drill.

The cardinal rule is to stay with the canoe. It will float and will still support the people who were in it. All you have to do is to hold on and, if in a lake and there is some wind, let the wind blow you shorewards. If you want to move it, go aft and push the stern along as you swim. DO NOT BE IN A HURRY. Take your time and rest as you need to.

Righting a capsized canoe that is upside down is described in the next chapter, but if you want to reboard a canoe which is right side up and which has shipped only a little water, there's a way to get back in. Swim to the midship position and, with one hand, take the nearside gunwale. Now reach with your other hand for the opposite gunwale, and with your legs straight, make a strong crawl flutter with your feet as you bring your hips to the nearside gunwale. You should end up draped across the canoe, from which position you can roll yourself in. Bail out the water.

The exceptions to this rule are mostly in whitewater, when it is obvious that you will have to let the canoe fend for itself since you are in danger. The other occasion is when the water is so cold that you must attend to yourself in a hurry. (If this does occur, you should have been wearing a wetsuit.)

In a closed canoe the procedure is slightly different, since you have to exit yourself. Before experimenting, just hold your breath for about thirty seconds. Can do it? It's easy. Everyone can.

When you capsize a closed canoe, you will find yourself hanging upside down beneath the water. For the first few times it makes sense to use a snorkel mask so that you can see what's going on. While it is perfectly possible for you to roll the canoe--discussed later--it is worth while learning how to leave it. The technique here is to use the quick release device on your spray skirt, and the quick release device on the thigh straps--if fitted. You should be able to do this in less than 10 seconds (about four when you've practiced.) Holding the sides of the canoe, just prise yourself out gently, clearing your feet carefully out, and swim up.

The key to dealing with a capsize successfully is to take your time—and don't panic. After all, the water isn't going to hurt you, and it will support you just as long as you keep calm and relax.

STABILITY AND WEIGHT DISTRIBUTION

Shallow-draft vessels, especially lightweight ones like canoes, are extremely sensitive to weight distribution, not only as a result of loading—though that is very important—but also from the movement of people inside them.

Don't be in a hurry. This is a good point to remember when you are on board and want to change your position. Do everything gently and easily.

The scientific reason for the need to move carefully has to do with the center of gravity of the canoe. The term *center of gravity* describes the spot where the total weight of the craft and everything in it could be placed and yet produce on the hull an effect identical with that produced under normal loading. What happens in a capsize is that the center of gravity has been moved outside the limits of balance.

Let's take a closer look.

The stability of any craft is related to the shape of its hull and to the distribution of its own weight and of the things inside it. The water provides a force acting upward on the hull equal to the downward force of the weight of the hull and what is in it. This is called displacement of the craft and refers to the amount of water which is being displaced.

The craft's buoyancy—what makes it float—can also be put at one point, but this center of buoyancy can also move like the center of gravity. The diagrams show how the center of buoyancy and the center of gravity are both in a vertical plane with respect to each other. The center of buoyancy moves as the hull shape presented to the water changes in shape, and the center of gravity moves when the trim of the canoe is changed.

Trim is of vital importance, and to ensure stability a canoeist keeps the center of gravity as low as possible within the boat. The reason for doing this is to maintain the natural righting force of the center of buoyancy. If the center of gravity is at a high point, it becomes much easier for the center of buoyancy to move beyond limits and force a capsize.

Take a look at the diagrams. The first shows the position of the center of buoyancy, and in the next the center of gravity is shown in vertical and above it. The third diagram shows what takes place when the trim is changed. To repeat, the center of buoyancy moves as the hull shape

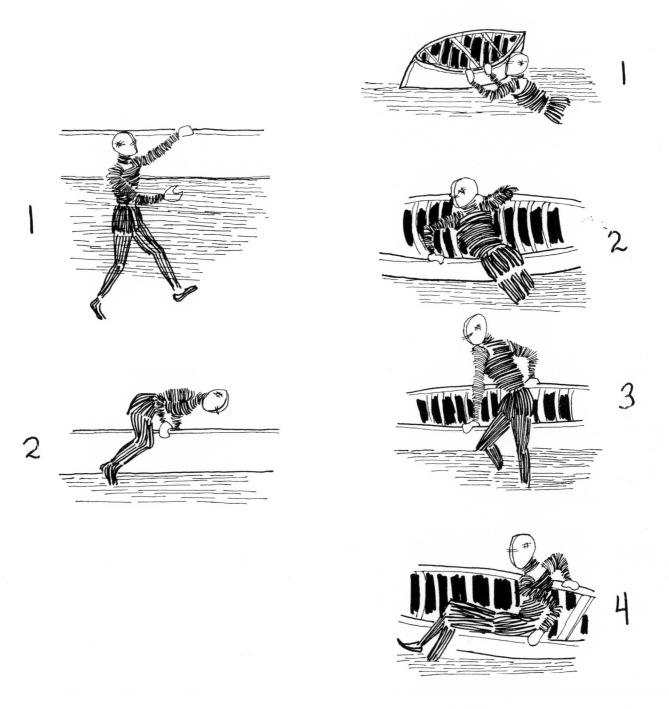

Getting into a canoe from the water. Left is good, but right is better.

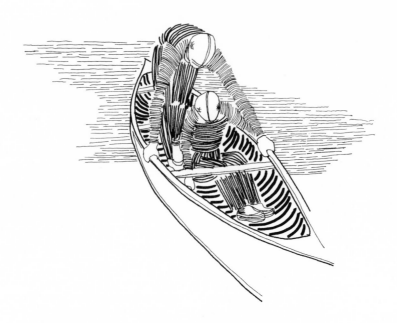

Changing position in an open canoe is a delicate matter. Stern person moves forward while bow person--who has shifted aft a little, keeps low down in the boat.

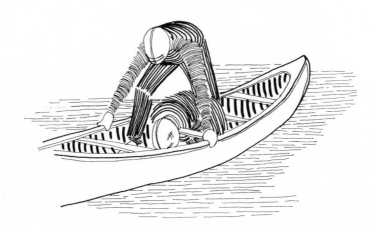

Another solution to the problem of changing position. Here the stern person straddles the bow person on the way forward.

presented to the water is changed. The center of gravity moves when the trim is changed.

In the next diagram you can see what happens when the center of gravity is too high, as it would be if you were standing up in the canoe instead of crouching. Move the trim—you're standing up, and you move your foot off the centerline—and you put the center of gravity outside, buoyancy has gone, and the boat twists itself into a capsize. Note that, had you kept the center of gravity low, you would not have capsized.

In the interests of providing additional stability, some manufacturers fit a keel to the hull. The keel provides a counteracting force to any tilt. This is all very well if you just want to paddle on a lake, but for river work it makes it nearly impossible to move the canoe sideways, which is one of the more important maneuvers for white-water work. In shallows a keel will also tend to get caught on rocks in the riverbed and can cause you to spill.

What we look for, then, is a boat with a fair amount of lift at bow and stern, with bulging flanks, which helps to resist the water, and which, when balanced by the paddler(s), can tackle almost anything. Special white-water canoes are now available which have an extreme tumble home—they look a bit like a sausage with a prow at each end—and which enables them to shrug off almost anything. And spray decks are fitted to keep the water out.

PADDLING POSITIONS

Although you may see people paddling from a seated position, you now understand why this isn't the best position—the center of gravity is much higher than with kneeling position. Kneeling not only increases the stability of the canoe but also lets you use your leg muscles and your lower back to help coordinate stability from the motion of the water.

But since, unlike our rear ends, our knees are not protected with layers of muscle and fat, we need kneepads if we're to remain comfortable on a trip. And, to provide additional support, we rest our rear end against a thwart.

Now try this out. Find a comfortable position on your knees, with your knees apart and your buttocks resting on the thwart. Now move your body from your waist slightly to the right, then to the left. You begin to appreciate now how you can contribute to the canoe's own righting moment.

In order to relax a leg on long distances, you can go to the relief position. To do this unwind one leg and stretch it forward, bracing the forward leg on a rib—if there is one. If there isn't, the easiest thing to do is to brace it where the deck starts to curve upward so that you extend your power

base. When the leg is rested, change over and give the other leg a rest.

Upright kneeling, facing slightly to the side on which you're paddling, is useful for moving about in the canoe. It is from this position that you go to the racing, or high-kneeling, stance, which you will see much used in competition. Here you are on one knee, the lower leg of which is placed diagonally across the canoe, and usually braced beneath a thwart. The other leg is placed forward with a slight bend at the knee. This position is used by more experienced canoeists for long-distance work with a minimum of effort.

Kneeling is the only stance to be used in the safe paddling of a canoe. Some sort of pads for the knees are essential. There are two ways of dealing with this. You can attach one of those long sponges for mops to the deck of the canoe, or you can make up kneeling pads, either from sponge rubber or foam. In rural areas it is still possible to find kneeling pads for gardeners, which do quite well. About an inch thick is best.

BASIC STROKES

Expert canoeists use a variety of strokes which are harmonized to produce the result they require, and it is often quite difficult to sort out what they're up to. The reason for this is the expert knows how to read and anticipate the water ahead. Since harmony of strokes is made up of such intelligent anticipation, there's usually little more need than to make half a stroke.

In learning strokes, there are two ways to go. The traditional method is to learn the bow stroke, the backwater and the j-stroke. A more modern method, adopted by Ed Bliss (Canoe & Kayak Club of New York) for one, is to start with the idea of turning. Here, the first strokes learned are the draw stroke, the pryaway (or pushover), the forward and reverse quarter sweep strokes. These are learned with two persons in the canoe, the beginner working from the bow position. Next, the diagonal draw and J-strokes are learned, and backpaddling is developed further. Finally, as a solo study, quarter sweeps are developed into half sweeps, sculling is developed, and the C-stroke (a modification of the J-stroke) is learned.

While the bow rudder and the outside pivot are listed here, these should be studied with an instructor, since both are unstabling strokes in terms of the overall balance of the canoe.

Marathon paddlers—events in excess of 15 miles—do adopt the seated position. Sawyer Canoes, whose products are favored for this area of the sport, provide specially moulded seats for this reason.

If you are paddling from the left side of the canoe, the top of the paddle—the grip—is held in your right hand, while your left holds the shaft. If paddling on the right side, the positions are reversed. Remember, while it may look good to be dipping your blade one side and then the other as you go along, this actually shows you don't know how to steer a canoe from one side alone.

Bow stroke. The basic propelling stroke in the canoeists repertoire, the bow stroke, is used to make the canoe go forward when two persons are on board (paddling, that is), or, when used by a solo paddler, to turn the canoe away from the paddling side while maintaining forward motion.

We'll assume that you are in the bow position, kneeling, and paddling on the right hand (starboard) side. In this stroke, you should be leaning slightly forward with your right arm extended and your right hand several inches above the blade, about level with your hip. A common error in this stroke is to hold the blade at an angle of 45-degrees to the boat rather than in the vertical plane. Your left hand holds the grip of the paddle somewhere close to your left shoulder.

The stroke is made by dipping the blade into the water fairly close to the bow, at a point where it can be drawn straight back without interruption. It is important to realize that this stroke is made in a straight line and does not follow the curve of the boat.

As your right arm draws back, the left arm is punched smoothly forward from the shoulder. The two actions should make a smooth and continuous whole so that the strength of the shoulders is applied evenly to the blade via the shaft. Once the blade has passed your right hip, it is taken from the water and feathered. The flat of the blade is placed parallel to the surface of the water to reduce windage while the blade is brought forward for the next stroke.

POINTS TO NOTE:

1. Power is applied smoothly through both arms.
2. The stroke is made relatively close to your canoe.
3. The paddle shaft moves through an almost vertical plane.
4. The punching forward of the left arm is made across the body, with the left hand being over the water and with the arm fully extended at the end of the stroke.

No power is applied once the blade has passed your hip, and the left hand drops down to near gunwale level to bring the blade to the surface. As the blade is swept forward in its feathered position, the leading edge should be kept slightly up so that if it touches a wave it will slice through or bounce off it.

The bow or forward stroke is a simple paddle stroke with a natural action. It doesn't require much comment. It is essential to create a steady rhythmic sequence of dip, punch-pull, and recover, using the feathered portion of the stroke to relax. The bow person is responsible for setting and keeping the rhythm. To begin with, keep your strokes short rather than long.

Backwater stroke. This is the opposite of the bow stroke and is used either to move the canoe backward or to slow or stop the canoe. As with the bow stroke, if this stroke is used solo the canoe will turn toward the paddling side. If you are moving with any speed, it's important to hold the paddle firmly and brake the forward motion of the canoe.

The paddle is held in the normal manner and placed in a position somewhat close to that in which the paddle finds itself at the end of the bow stroke, just before coming out of the water. The right hand is close to the hip, the left hand close to the shoulder, the blade behind the paddler. You now dip the blade into the water opposite your hip where it can be moved forward in a straight line parallel to the keel. The blade should be just shy of perpendicular to the centerline of the canoe.

Since this is the reverse of the bow stroke, the right hand will push firmly forward until the blade is vertical, while the grip is pulled backward. When you have pushed forward as far as you can, the paddle is withdrawn, feathered, and swung back for the next stroke.

The J or steering stroke. This is the stroke used to drive the canoe forward while correcting the veering tendency caused by the bow stroke. It is used by the solo paddler and by the stern paddler in a two-person crew when the bow person is stroking hard. The objective is to provide a balancing force.

The stroke is called the J stroke from the path of the blade through the water. Actually, if you watch experts using this stroke, it looks remarkably little like a J. To master the stroke, concentrate on its steering qualities to begin with, rather than on using it to push the boat through the water.

The J stroke is begun in exactly the same manner as the bow stroke. Paddle is held normally and is entered into the water in exactly the same way. As the blade comes up to the paddler its inner edge is turned sternward by turning the upper hand counterclockwise, so that the blade is at an angle of about 45 degrees to the keel line.

As the stroke ends, a slight outward pressure—depending on how much is needed to maintain a straight course—can be given by pushing the lower hand away from you. The blade is sliced out of the water by dropping the left arm and lifting the right. As with the other strokes, it is then feathered and carried forward.

The more experienced canoeist does most steering with this stroke, since, by varying the direction and thrust at the tail end of the stroke, it is possible to make easy turns without spoiling the stroking rhythm. How much the J stroke should be modified is something you will have to pick up for yourself. But it is an easy stroke to learn, though it will vary according to the shape of the canoe you are paddling.

Draw stroke. The draw stroke is used to move the canoe sideways toward the paddling side. It has the ability to make a sharper turn than other strokes. Once again, we'll consider this stroke being made over the right-hand side. And to make it easier, slide your right hand about 6 inches up from the paddle throat.

We'll assume you are amidships (at the center of the canoe.) You toss the blade out over the water at right angles to the keel line of the canoe, with the blade lined up fore and aft. The right arm is fully extended, while the left arm is bent with the left hand in front of your face. The blade is dipped into the water, and, while you pull in with the right hand, the left pushes out until the blade is about six inches from the canoe. At this point the left hand is moved toward the bow, downward, to lift the blade from the water.

With two persons aboard, both stern and bow persons may make the stroke on the same side to move the canoe toward the side they paddle. If they make the stroke on opposite sides, the canoe will pivot about its center. A keel attached to the bottom of the canoe makes it much more difficult to do the draw stroke. Since the draw stroke is one of the most important and powerful of canoe control strokes, many experts prefer not to have such a keel.

To save time, the more expert paddler will use an underwater recovery for this stroke. At the end of the stroke, he will feather the blade under water so that, instead of being parallel, it moves through 90 degrees, and he then pushes it out to the start position for the beginning of a new stroke. As you get more skilled, you will find that you can lean the canoe and, by reaching out over the gunwale and using a near-vertical paddle position, increase the power of the draw.

The pryaway or pushover stroke is the in-draw in reverse. It is used to move the canoe sideways away from the paddling side. When you practice this stroke, do it from a nonmoving canoe to begin with.

The edge of the blade is slid into the water behind you and brought to the vertical, and alongside you. Push out with the lower hand while pulling in with the upper. If you've a strong paddle, you can get extra leverage by resting it against the gunwale. An underwater feathered return is made.

While this stroke is not as powerful as the in-draw stroke, it is used when it might be inconvenient to use the in-draw, as, for example, when you need immediate action and there isn't really time to switch. Draw and pushover can be executed on opposites sides of the canoe for sideways movement when the water is too shallow on the riverbed at one end of the canoe.

Sweep strokes. The sweep strokes are used for making pivotal or partial turns without losing too much way. The paddle is used like an oar. The stroke may be broken up into three sections, the first pushing the bow over, the second driving the canoe forward, and the third drawing the stern up to the paddle. This will appear most obvious if you are kneeling amidships.

The more experienced paddler is aware of this and, by varying the relationship between the three parts, is able to provide good control over his craft without giving up much in forward speed when negotiating a moderately tricky section. It is well worth spending some time practicing the stroke, breaking it up into its three parts, and varying them—and noting the effect.

The forward sweep is executed as follows: the paddle blade is held forward (starboard side, again) in a horizontal position with the blade vertical to the water. Now dip the paddle into the water and sweep around through 180 degrees, with the right arm held straight while the left provides additional power at the end of the stroke. For solo paddling, a half-sweep is often used, bringing the paddle around from the bow to the amidships position (90 degrees.)

The reverse sweep is performed in reverse. The paddle is held normally, as if at the end of the forward sweep with the right hand aft and the left fully forward and down so that the blade lies vertical to the water. It is sliced in and swept out and around toward the bow through 180 degrees. For more power, lean into the stroke with the right shoulder, rather than relying on the forearms alone.

The reverse sweep can be used for slowing the canoe's forward movement if taken to the amidships position only.

The jam stroke. This one is used for braking. If you're moving with much weight, brace yourself to take the shock.

The technique is to knife the paddle downward so that the blade faces forward and let it be pushed to a vertical position alongside the hull. To avoid capsizing when two are on board, bow and stern should jam together on opposite sides.

In summary, it might be said that basic skills cover paddling forward and backward. Sweep strokes—bow and stern—slap support or recovery strokes, and sculling for support and sculling draw. For the beginner, this is probably

Executing the draw stroke.

Executing the sweep stroke.

the best way to learn since the most difficult strokes are learned last.

The secret of successfully using a kayak is to understand some simple physics. Because it is a finely tuned craft, a kayak must always be in the control of its paddler, not only in terms of forward motion, but at all times. In some respects a kayak is like a bicycle, in that it becomes easier to balance and to steer when there is some way on it—when it's moving.

In order to successfully balance a kayak, you'll use three parts of your body as support. These are: (1) your feet (heels and all); (2) your knees and thighs; (3) your seat and hips. You can think of them as being part of a moving pyramid, the upper part of which is your body above the hips and which also must play its part.

In customizing the cockpit, you should fit—if one is not already fitted—a strong, lightweight footrest, so that with your legs bent and knees apart, your feet have something to push on. Similarly, you can fit simple kneegrips under the deck where your knees press outward. Finally, some sort of support for your back is important—although you won't be pressing this so hard—since the lower lumbar region takes a while to get used to the work. Your hips are held snug by supports, and many kayakists like to use thigh grips or supports for greater stability.

Now, take the paddle. Hold it with both arms stretched out straight in front of you and then move your hands outward a little so that they are slightly wider apart than the width of your shoulders. Try this grip and see whether it feels comfortable. If you wish to move your hands outward a little more, do so. But do not separate your hands by a distance less than the width of your shoulders, since this will mean you are not working your body as efficiently as possible, and you will tire more easily.

It has been said that the best way for a would-be kayakist to learn to paddle is to learn in a Canadian canoe. While it is true that canoe paddling broadens the mind in terms of the scope needed to control it efficiently, there seems no harm in learning directly in a kayak, as long as it is understood that there's plenty to learn beyond the basic strokes. So let's deal with the basic stroke.

The first thing to notice is that there are left- and right-handed paddles for kayakists. If you are using a two-piece paddle, the rule is that the blade on the side you are using always comes out of the water with the hollow side nearest you. The blades are set at right angles to one another—feathered—to cut down wind resistance and to allow for power flow from your body. You'll see what is meant as you discover the rhythm for yourself.

Power is transmitted to the blade through both arms, and to operate efficiently you will have to limber up your wrists. This comes with practice.

The basic forward stroke is made as follows:

1. Reach forward as far as is comfortable with one hand, leaning your body slightly forward and dip the blade into the water with the blade facing you.

2. The stroke is completed by simultaneously (a) pulling back with the forward hand, and (b) pushing forward with the other hand *at eye level,* straight out from the body until the other arm is fully extended. It's like a slow-motion punch, and the arm provides additional energy along the shaft of the paddle.

3. You are now ready for the stroke on the opposite side as you lean forward again and dip the other blade ahead.

The beauty of using the double paddle is that the process becomes very automatic, and you can quickly settle into a rhythm. There should be no pause between strokes, and you'll find that if you swing your shoulders just a little with each stroke you can use the muscles of your back to help it all along. In addition, you'll be adding to the stability of the boat.

As far as breathing is concerned, work out what seems to be comfortable. There's a tendency among learners to let the lungs develop their own rhythm, but in fact you can borrow a tip from long-distance runners. Breathe in to a count of 2, 3, or 4, and then breathe out to a count of 2, 3, or 4—you decide which makes you most comfortable. This regulating of the breathing process is much the same as the rhythm you establish with your arms and is especially useful in competition, where you want to go all out.

A point to watch for is not to put the blade too deeply in the water and don't place it too shallowly, either. If you've got it right, the paddle blade will just be completely covered: no more, no less. If it's in too deep, you'll be using additional energy with no extra return. If too shallow, you won't be using the paddle as efficiently as it was designed to be used. Further, you'll be wasting energy. As you can see, paddling can be developed to a fine art.

Another point that some find difficult is to lean the body forward. It's all too easy when you are not used to the process to tend to use the back rest to help with your paddling efforts, but this will tire you very quickly. It can also strain your back unnecessarily. If you want to limber up at home, sit on the floor with your legs stretched straight out and the back of your knees on the floor. Now just let your body move easily forward—you don't have to touch your knees with your forehead. Do this just a few times in the

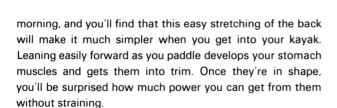

morning, and you'll find that this easy stretching of the back will make it much simpler when you get into your kayak. Leaning easily forward as you paddle develops your stomach muscles and gets them into trim. Once they're in shape, you'll be surprised how much power you can get from them without straining.

You now know how to go forward. What do you do when you want to stop? Well, basically, you back-paddle. This is not a difficult stroke to make if you imagine that you are putting your forward stroke into reverse. But you should practice it until you are proficient. For one thing, if you simply dig your blade into the water and hang on, you'll make a convincing imitation of the Victorian gentleman who was pulled off his punt which went away from his feet; if you've any forward motion, you must slow down methodically. A kayak is not like a car, and for braking you must apply forces opposite to the direction in which you're traveling.

The technique here is not to reverse the blade but to use its back. It's a simple technique and you'll remember that it is for this reason that white-water enthusiasts prefer the flat blade rather than the curved type. Since they must make a variety of strokes forward, sideways, and back, they need to know that there won't be a different result, as occurs when using the curved blade in this way.

When you are starting to learn there's one item you won't enjoy—blisters. There's not too much you can do to avoid them, though you can fine sand the shaft where you place your hands for extra smoothness. About the only way to make life easier is not to work too hard at the beginning. Make short trips and analyze what you do. As a preventive measure you could take a spade or a garden fork and do a little digging each day to harden your hands. Sweeping a carpet with a broom also works.

If you get blisters, don't burst them, either by paddling or with a pin. The fluid will drain away in its own good time if you leave it alone, and you can use a Band-aid to cover the area until it does.

If you haven't been exercising regularly, a few simple exercises each day can make you limber. Some kayakists use basic yoga exercises, and others use the Canadian Air Force system. Choose your own. You don't have to be an athlete to take up this sport, but being moderately fit will increase your enjoyment—apart from making you better able to cope with the stresses of our society. Both kayaking and canoeing ask your body to contribute with muscle and balancing power, and the muscles involved don't get used quite as much as they should in these sedentary days.

If you don't have time for all this, keep your first few

trips rather short and you'll avoid any discomfort. Once you get the knack of it all, you'll find that long trips won't tire you and that you have a pleasant glow of achievement at the end of the day. What's more, you'll have entered one of the easiest and most pleasurable exercise programs ever devised.

The essential difference between a canoe and a kayak is that in the canoe you kneel while making your strokes, whereas in the kayak you sit. The sitting position puts your center of gravity lower than it is in a canoe.

Modern kayak technique makes use of many of the strokes used in canoeing, as can be seen from a look at some of the Duffek strokes and the stroke developed by French and Czech enthusiasts. And as with the canoe, so with the kayak: you operate from a triangular base, or stability platform.

We'll assume that you have inspected and launched. Now comes the business of getting in.

You'll be boarding your kayak either from a bank or from shallow water. From a bank—assuming the bow of the kayak is facing forward on your right-hand side—you first crouch down with the cockpit on your right. Balance yourself with your left hand holding something reasonably secure, which you can still hold on to from the cockpit. It may be a lump of stone protruding from the ground, a clump of grass, or a small bough of a bush.

With your right hand grasp the front section of the cockpit, or, if it is a long cockpit, somewhere as near as is convenient on the farther side. Now put your right leg into the center of the kayak, leaving enough room for your other foot behind it. Next put your left leg in, behind the right, while your left hand is still holding on to the shore. The right hand now goes to the center of the cockpit while you slowly lower yourself into the seat, left hand still holding the shore.

Now get comfortable, but make sure that all movements are slow and balanced. If you need your hands to take your weight as you shuffle to a more comfortable position, put them one on each side behind you. Being comfortable in a kayak means being at one with it, and you should establish just what this means in terms of your own frame.

Now that you are seated, bend your legs and place your knees apart, one under each side of the decking, the feet comfortably settled on the floorboards. If your kayak has been customized to a modest degree, you'll find kneegrips where your knees should be. Your feet should find some sort of rest against which they can press, although a framer will do.

Your seat should preferably have hip supports, and for comfort should be of the hard-molded variety. Your stability platform is now made up of your seat, which is reinforced by your knees and your feet below the waist. The upper part of your body can be swayed as necessary to assist in the balance.

Before you push off onto the river, just move a little way from the shore (don't forget your paddle) and, with your hands above your head, rock the kayak from side to side by bending from the hips. You will be pleasantly surprised to discover that your stability platform works very well and that you don't need to be nervous when the water is sloshing up to the cockpit coaming.

Now try getting out. It's in reverse. First hold the coaming with your right hand and find something ashore to hold on to with your left. Feet in the boat, rise slowly into a crouch, and move your left foot out. (You may have to stand up if the bank is higher up.) If you haven't got someone else holding the painter, make sure you have this in your right hand when you start. Once the left foot is secure, move the right foot out and you're ashore.

The procedure is approximately the same when you have to board from a shallow river. The most important thing here is to get any mud or sand off your feet, as drying mud or sand will make you thoroughly uncomfortable.

Instead of holding on to the shore, here you hold on to the boat. First hold on to the far gunwale with your right hand. Now place your right foot into the kayak and bring your left hand up to the nearside gunwale; now you have a hand each side.

Carefully balancing, take up your weight on your arms and, with a quick twist, clean your left foot before bringing it into the boat. Now lower yourself into a comfortable position.

To get out of the canoe, merely reverse the procedure. Obviously, you won't do this in the middle of a fast-flowing stream, so find some shallows that run slow.

Getting out, the hands go behind the body first and, as you'll very soon discover once you have practices the maneuver, you more or less swing one leg out behind the other. You should practice both maneuvers until they're second nature and you don't have to think about them. Once you've done this, you're ready to take a closer look at paddling. But first of all you need to know about the paddle.

PADDLES AND PADDLING

The paddle is your engine. It takes the energy you direct through it and provides you with motive power to thrust your kayak—and steer and guide it—through the waves. Since you won't go very far without one, it is generally more economical to buy the best you can afford. First, of course,

you should decide what shape paddle you like best.

Choosing a double paddle is much like choosing a pair of skis—if you're opting for symmetrical blades—since all you do is stand the paddle on one end and see whether you can curve your fingers over the top of the other blade at the first joint. If you can, that's your size blade. If choosing asymmetrical blades, you go through the same procedure, except that you take a sideways step away from the blade, so that it is slanting slightly toward you at the top. Again, if the fingers curl over, that's just about your size. This is a very rough rule-of-thumb method, and as you get more experienced you'll be able to judge more accurately. But it is good enough to begin with.

Double paddle blades are normally set at 90 degrees to each other on fixed-shaft paddles, since this is the feathering position for the upper blade as it goes forward to ready for its next stroke. If you have a split shaft, make sure that the blades are set properly when you join it up. There's usually a space in the fastening grommet, so that it will set itself with a click. The point of feathering, of course, is to reduce needless friction from the air (called windage) if the blade were brought to it face first.

As you end one stroke and prepare for the other, a slight flick of your wrist sets up the incoming blade at the correct angle. Competition paddles are increasingly using an oval handhold, in which case you don't even need to look at the blade to make sure it's properly set. The flexing of the wrist muscles between each stroke actually helps relax the forearm and so prevent it from seizing up and aching.

Forward stroke. Hold the paddle shaft with your hands out in front of you, slightly farther apart than the width of your shoulders. This is the holding position. Now bend the elbows just a bit so they drop down, and push forward as far as you possibly can with your right hand, leaning forward slightly as you do to extend your reach—but not too much. Now dip the blade into the water with the blade flat, pulling back with the right hand and smoothly punching forward with the left. The right hand pulls back until your elbow comes abeam your hip. Meanwhile, with the left hand, you describe a slow left punch from the shoulder to eye level, and you lean your left shoulder in, much as you leaned your right when you made the first stroke.

You now make a stroke on the left, and your right arm punches forward to counterbalance the pulling of the left arm. There should be no pausing between strokes, and each should merge into the next without effort. Too, the strokes should be as long as possible. For smoothness, lean forward from the hips and let your shoulders assist, so that the movement resembles that of a boxer using a bag in slow motion.

The paddle should be just totally submerged beneath the water for optimum results.

Reverse paddling or back-paddling. There's no need to turn the blade around if you want to check your forward movement by back-paddling. Simply make the stroke with the back of the blade, but be sure it is presented flatly to the water.

POINTS TO NOTE:

1. Practice both forward and reverse paddling until they become second nature and you can paddle merrily along without getting tired.

2. Unless you are active in the garden, or use your hands a lot, you'll get blisters to begin with. Don't prick them. Let them disappear on their own. You can cover them with a Band-Aid until they go away. Preventive medicine—in the form of sanding the varnish on the paddle shaft—sometimes helps.

3. If you find that your forearms tighten up at the beginning, don't panic. Take a break, relax, and don't work quite so hard until you get used to the effort.

Chapter 3
ADVANCED TECHNIQUE: CANOE, KAYAK

It will be only a matter of a short time, if you practice the strokes outlined in the previous chapter, before you'll be ready to move on to the more advanced techniques.

The strokes which now follow require some experience in addition to strength, and you'd be best advised to try them out with someone more experienced than you. But first a word about who sits where in a canoe.

In Europe, the consensus is that bow and stern persons are just about equal in terms of responsibility to one another, and, as a rule, members of winning teams have total trust in each other. Among the less competition-minded, it is thought that both are equal, but that the stern person is just a little bit more equal. And here in the United States we have mostly the old school, which holds that the one who takes the stern position is the senior partner.

In fact, there's a little to be said for each point of view, and obviously, where the technical skill is the same, it matters little if two can work in fairly complete harmony together. This is the thing to aim for, but it does mean putting down one's own ego—transcending, if you like, the personality factor about yourself—in order to make a harmonious unit. A good paddler who is quite content to stay at the bow can be the cornerstone of a good team in much the same way that a good navigator is the cornerstone in international motor rally competition.

Quite often a strong, skilled, bow person will make all the difference in an event where changes are frequent and water conditions range between swift, deep currents and sharp chops of shallower waters. A good bow paddler has a better view and has just that much longer to assess the changing conditions ahead than the person at the stern. It is only tradition, after all, that insists that the most skilled person be at the stern. And as anyone who flies will know, all pilots learn from the command position—the left-hand seat—and it takes a little extra something to be able to fly from the right. So, too, does it take a little extra something—usually not worrying about people thinking you're the learner—to command from the bow.

The bow person in white water, for example, has a whole range of strokes to use for steering purposes and is frequently seen paddling on the "wrong" side of the canoe. One thing that occurs is that there isn't time to change hands, so the strokes have to be made with the hands the wrong way around—can you do that, yet, without it feeling strange?

There's one other consideration in two-person crews: the weight factor. In the more traditional straight-keeled American canoe it is generally accepted that a slightly stern-heavy aspect afford a more manageable canoe. But for some white-water events, a bow-heavy arrangement can work better. In Europe, the tendency is to have the stronger crew member foreward, with the canoe balanced about amidships in order to take advantage of the rockered keels which permit pivoting about the center.

Perhaps the concluding argument is that the stern person is responsible for the after half of the canoe, and since one views the total picture from the stern—hazards ahead created by one's companion's frenzied movement, the obstacles looming through the chop, the fragile hull seeking a friendly gap—the stern person has the last word. But it should be a last word that is in harmony with the bow, since argument will only take the team off course. Teamwork equals harmony: this is especially true in any form of canoeing for two persons.

STEERING AND STROKES

Bow Rudder

The bow rudder is used to turn the bow in the direction of the side on which the bow person is paddling. It is used to avoid last-minute obstacles which only the bow person can see. It is not a stroke per se, since the paddle is fixed—once in the water it is not moved. To begin with, try this out when the canoe is moving slowly so that you can learn what pressures will be involved when you are doing it in a swift-flowing stream.

To execute the stroke, you should lean forward with the right arm in front of you, with the left hand holding the grip close to your body near your right armpit. The paddle blade is turned so that it is vertical to the water, and the shaft should be angled about 30 degrees to 40 degrees to the theoretical keel line. There's going to be considerable water pressure as you turn the paddle into a rudder, so you should be ready to take the strain, with the right arm outside the gunwale, which can be used to brace with.

The stroke relies on the kinetic energy of the canoe, and if you are in shallows be careful that you don't hit some submerged obstruction as you knife the blade into the water. If you do, the blade will be driven sharply back—which is why you keep the grip at about your right armpit. The steering is accomplished by the trapped water between the bow and the paddle blade forcing the canoe in the direction of the blade. The forces involved are strong. You will usually need to brace, and you will lose some of your forward speed to accomplish the turn. If you have the time, and less urgency, you can achieve the same result by using a draw stroke plus a normal bow stroke.

CROSS-BOW RUDDER

This is virtually the same stroke except that it is made on the side opposite to the bow person's normal paddling side. Here there will be no time to change hands, and the body must be swiveled. Swing around to the opposite side (cross the bow) and knife the blade down. Bring your lower hand up the paddle shaft a few inches to keep it from getting trapped between the blade and the gunwale. Again, the grip is kept in the area of the left armpit, and the blade is knifed in at about 40 degrees. When not in a rush, you get the same thing done by using the sweep stroke through 90 degrees.

STERN RUDDER

This is similar to the bow rudder, but is used by the stern person on occasions when the J stroke can't be used, or when some reduction in forward movement is needed and a change of direction is required.

The stern person proceeds in exactly the same manner as for the bow rudder, though the stroke may be led into by a reverse sweep through 120 degrees.

THE C STROKE (Prystroke)

The C stroke is a development of the J stroke and is used in white water. Here the paddle blade swings under the canoe before swinging around to make a C. The C stroke is developed in slalom into what is called a prystroke, where the paddle shaft is braced hard against the gunwale. The prystroke takes advantage of the fact that most European canoes have rockered keels which permit them to pivot about the center. C stroke and prystrokes can be made from both bow and stern positions.

If you intend to take your canoeing seriously, it is worthwhile breaking down the methods by which your canoe can be turned. When there is a crew, there are several varieties that can serve, depending on the degree you want to change course. In competition it is very important that both partners are completely aware of what's required, and teamwork is best developed by training with a partner until almost every type of stroke has been tried against each other, from bow and stern. Only then will it be possible for the team to function as an intelligent unit—there's no room for guesswork.

For example, take a simple turn. The bow person can draw, and the stern person can simply make a forward stroke without a correcting J. To increase the stern movement, the stern person can angle the paddle blade to a drawing angle. Result: a turn with some forward way lost.

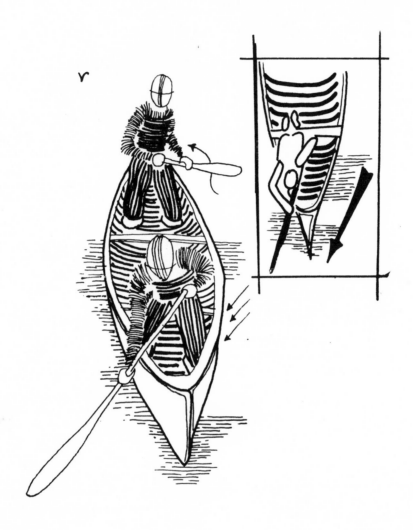

The bow rudder stroke which turns the bow towards the side on which the bow person is working. Don't put the left hand in front of the face. The stroke is used for an immediate turn--as for example, if you spotted a rock suddenly ahead. A draw stroke is better, but slower since the bow rudder causes you to lose some speed.

It is difficult to make pivot turns, which is why more and more canoeists are looking to the rockered-type canoes, which permit such changes. Here the pivot can be initiated by both bow and stern persons drawing on opposite sides.

BRACE STROKES

As their name describes, these strokes are used for bracing—most after where one crew member is leaning the hull while the other braces to keep it from tipping over. In such situations the paddle is kept in the water all the time, since it is possible to draw to, or push away from, the boat, depending on what is going on. The section on recovery strokes and braces for kayaks (Chapter 2) is useful to read in this respect, since unless you are in a regular Canadian canoe, the opportunity to execute a roll is denied you.

Bracing is used mainly in tricky waters, and the technique is to keep the blade submerged at the end of any stroke so that it is there to be used. It is quite practical to use the blade as an anchor and tug the canoe to it with your knees and thighs. But you will need to experiment a bit before you build up the confidence to do this. While you're learning, the main thing is not to be frightened of getting wet or of tipping over. It's much better to know the limits of the canoe and yourself in water where you don't have to worry about hazards such as rocks and tricky white water than to arrive on the scene and be faced with such problems.

SCULLING—FORWARD AND REVERSE

Sculling is particularly useful to the solo canoeist who needs to get the canoe moving sideways. The objective is to move the canoe toward the paddling side in the forward scull, and away from the paddling side in the reverse scull.

The method used is the same as used by old salts who row their dinghies from over the stern—sculling. The paddle blade is made to work a bit like a propeller blade in relation to the air in order to obtain thrust. The technique here is that the blade is put in the water about a foot from the side of the canoe, slightly in front of the paddler and with the upper arm and elbow at shoulder level. Keeping the blade angled about 45 degrees to the keel line, its inner edge points toward the bow while it is moved astern. At the end of the scull, the position is reversed, so that the outer edge now leads toward the bow.

One great advantage of sculling is that the canoe can be leaned if necessary, and quite a bit of weight can be placed on the paddle during the stroke.

The reverse scull functions in exactly the same way, except that the outer edge faces toward the bow while the blade is brought aft. At the end of the stroke, the position is reversed, and the inner edge is then moved toward the bow. The blade is angled at about 45 degrees to the keel line.

To perfect this stroke, remember that it is a continuous motion. There should be no more than an instant between the end of one stroke and the start of the next. Pressure is always applied to the outer face in the reverse scull, and to the inner of the regular scull. This is obvious from the diagram.

DOUBLE-BLADE PADDLING FOR CANOES

For solo canoeing, double-blade paddles make a lot of sense. For tyros they are useful since there are far fewer basic strokes involved, and a sitting position at the bottom of the canoe can be used. It is still preferable to kneel, however.

As with a kayak, the blades should be set at 90 degrees to one another so that the blade that is out of the water is feathered as it comes forward. Turns are simply made by paddling more on one side, or merely harder. Stopping is done by back-paddling, on either side. Speedier turns are executed by forward paddling on one side and back-paddling on the opposite side.

CAPSIZES

Capsizes do happen, but never have accidents that find their way into the newspapers need happened if the persons concerned had stayed with their canoe. It is folly to leave the boat, since the boat itself can provide support and can be headed toward the shore.

Open canoes can be righted from the water, but if it is cold it may make more sense to head for the shore and there simply tip it over. With a swamped canoe and reasonable water temperature in deep water, the procedure is as follows:

1. Secure any loose gear that might float away.

2. Next, swim around to one of the ends and, while pulling it lower by resting some of your weight on it, vigorously swim forward a few strokes. This will spill out some of the water on you, but that's all right—it is now floating a bit.

3. Swim amidships and start a gentle rocking motion. Very quickly a wave is set up, and, with some careful timing with your rocking, you can start emptying the canoe.

4. Once it is almost empty, you can reboard and finish bailing by hand. The technique for reboarding with two people is for one to steady the canoe amidships while the other boards from the farther side. The person then in the canoe balances it for the second person.

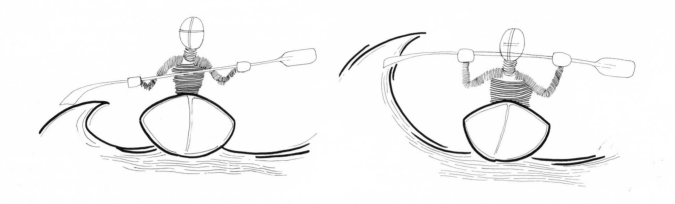

Top: low brace. Bottom: high brace.

Partial brace, but paddle is actually working as rudder too.

5. With one person only, you need to be a little more careful. The technique is again to use the amidships position. If you've a long enough arm to reach the other side, you start from here. If you haven't, put both hands on the nearside, and then making a crawl-stroke movement with your feet, climb up like a jumping trout, grabbing the farther gunwale with one hand, and dexterously slither your hips inboard. This will leave your legs below the knees dangling over the edge. Take a deep breath. Relax. Now swing them gently inboard. And finish the bailing. You'll find that, by keeping the elbow of the arm holding the farther gunwale rather high, you won't have any problem putting the nearside gunwale under water.

THE CANADIAN STEYR ROLL

The Canadian Steyr is actually preferred by many canoeists over the regular roll (discussed in Chapter 4.)

There are several reasons for its popularity, but perhaps the principal cause is that it is the roll for those occasions when, perhaps by the force of a strong body of water, the paddle blade has found its way to the rear deck. The force starts the capsize, and it's generally futile—and could be dangerous—to try to go to the forward position.

Such situations can occur in surf, or on fast rivers where rocks or the vagaries of the current create the circumstance. If it has snags, it is that the finishing position is rated poor. But it is a very powerful roll and it is a more difficult craft to roll than a kayak, this power is well suited. And it also needs a change of grip.

Instead of the thumb of the lower hand pointing up the shaft, it is reversed so that it is nearest the blade. The upper hand releases the handgrip and moves just beneath so that its thumb is pointing to the blade too. It's the first hand—the lower—that takes getting used to, and it's worth spending a bit of time practicing the change until it becomes mechanical. The upper hand won't take long.

The paddle is now brought to a position of about 30 degrees to the beam of the boat, across either the right or the left shoulder, depending on which side you started from.

The blade is moved forward and its leading edge is slightly turned up so that it functions as a moving point for you to start to pull yourself. At this point, your righting movement with your hips should have begun, and because the sweep is being made from back to front it is almost impossible to make a full return stroke. At the end as you right yourself, your hands will still be pushing down, and probably in the water. But it is a very strong roll, and the one stroke applied steadily is usually more than enough to get you up.

The point to watch is to make sure that the paddle blade is close enough to the surface when you begin. Don't forget, you're working back to front, as it were, so also watch the angle the blade is at.

The best part about this roll is that, with only one paddle blade to worry about, you don't have to take care of the other paddle, as you do in the kayak Steyr.

All rolls mentioned in this book should be done with an instructor. When learning roll techniques, it is frequently helpful to do the learning exercises wearing a scuba mask for the first few times. Once you get the hang of it, try it without the mask.

One important point in learning rolling technique is to understand that, even though you are upside down underneath the canoe, it is possible to get your head around to the side to breathe. This is also true of kayaks. You should have your instructor demonstrate this to you, as it is highly confidence-building.

KAYAK

You cannot consider yourself very serious as a player until you can roll your kayak. The easiest way to learn is to start on dry land.

All rolling techniques make use of two things: (1) the hydrodynamic action of the blade against the water, which allows you to convert the solidity of the medium into something against which you can exert a force to right yourself; and (2) the action of the muscles of the hip which provide a fillip at the last moment as you are ready to come up.

The clue to successful rolling is to develop this movement. If you want to start right, practice as follows in your living room. Lie down on your left or right side, whichever is most comfortable, in as close a position to that which you would be in if you were in your canoe. If you now move your upper leg down and your underneath leg up, you'll find that your hips have turned almost parallel to the ground while your shoulders are still sideways.

This is the movement that gets you out of the water. And while in the cockpit of your kayak, you obviously won't have quite so much room to shift your legs, you'll find that you have enough. First of all, try it out on the ground. Then get a friend to hold you with your ear in the water, and you'll see that you move the kayak upright by doing this. Now to rolling.

THE ESKIMO ROLL

The Eskimo roll was originally documented as early as 1767 when a missionary to the Greenland Eskimos, David

Position adopted for the Eskimo roll with two bladed paddle.

Position used for roll with single paddle. More hip movement is involved in the Canadian Roll (closed canoe, C-1) since it is beamier than a kayak.

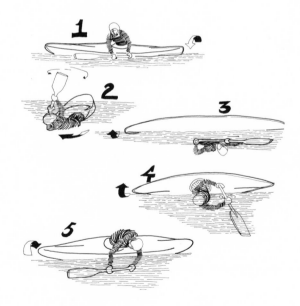

Sequence showing Eskimo roll in a closed canoe.

Crantz, published ten methods in the *History of Greenland*. But it was 1927 when Edi Pawlate learned the righting method, which was quickly taken up by others, known as the Pawlata roll. The British explorer Gino Watkins learned this particular roll, as he was planning to live with the Eskimos. The irony of it all was, as F. Spencer Chapman details in his biography of Watkins, that apparently it wasn't sufficient on the one occasion when Watkins lost his life.

But that was some time ago. Now there are several well-tested techniques for rolling, including rolling using only the hands—no paddle—and, once learned properly, by breaking each segment down and getting it right before putting it together, they'll work for you.

The only kayak in which not to learn is the pure flat-water sprint kayak. This type is not designed to be rolled and is too fragile.

In order to perfect a rolling technique you will need to have a secure footrest, kneepads to brace the knees against, and a seat that holds the hips and buttocks in such a way that you won't slide sideways or backward. There should be no back rest. (There should be no back rest anyway.) You are also going to need a properly designed spray skirt. the ones made from neoprene are the best, and you can make them up from kits for about half the price of the manufactured ones. (Once you've made one, you can make as many as you need since it is a very easy design to fix. This brings your cost down to about a quarter of the manufactured ones.)

You step into a spray skirt as if into a sheath dress so that it fits snugly around your lower abdomen up to your ribs. Once in your cockpit, the bottom part fits around and under the cockpit coaming. A quick-release device allows you to take it off in a hurry should you decide to exit that way—though there's no need.

Lastly—as with learning the canoe roll—it is helpful if a scuba mask is used at the beginning: it will keep water out of the nose and allow you to see what is going on down there. After you've mastered the technique, you can get rid of the mask, which actually makes it easier, since there's less weight around your head.

It is very important that you learn rolling techniques under proper supervision. This applies to all rolls listed in the book. Similarly, your kayak should have buoyancy bags or floatation blocks fitted, since at the beginning this will save you time in emptying out the water.

The first thing that you have to understand is that you are not suddenly helpless when you turn upside down. One good exercise with which you can start acquiring your technique is to lean the boat over and brace as hard as you can to right it. Also do this under supervision lest you fully capsize.

With your face mask on and your instructor nearby, make your capsize after having taken a good deep breath. Lean forward and learn the feeling of the knee and the foot pressures. When you've studied enough, tap the sides of the kayak and your instructor will haul you up.

Do this a few times more, until you know that you'll be pulled up. Now capsize again, and this time swim your head up to the side of the hull. Look—you can actually breathe if you want even though you may not be in the most comfortable position. Still, it's air, and you can always recharge your lungs if necessary this way.

On the next capsize, still with the mask in place, see how to leave the boat. Sanp the quick-release device off, and gently pry yourself down and swing your feet out and clear. Try this a few times until you can do it automatically.

Now for the roll proper.

As noted earlier, the Eskimo roll depends on two things—the action of your paddle on the water, and the coordination of hip movement added at the end to produce the final surfacing. Once you have mastered any one of the rolls outlined, make sure that you can roll either left or right with them, since it is the ability to be free to complete a roll on either side that makes a difference.

In competition—slalom—you have to get out of the water immediately if you bail yourself out. But if you right your craft by *esquimautage* (as Eskimo rolling is called by the French), no penalties are incurred. Indeed, until quite recently slalom courses used to include an artificial object which one was supposed to traverse in an upside down position to prove he could roll.

The person who aspires to advanced technique in kayaking will therefore be able to roll happily each way and, if need be, complete half-rolls—that is, capsize and recover from the same side.

The first thing you need to discover is how much force your paddle blade can resist when you are using it in a certain way. In the sculling exercise (Chapter 2), the paddle blade was brought in an arc from amidships to the bow in a sweeping movement, with the edge moving toward the bow, which was slightly up; as the end of the stroke was reached, the angle of incidence of the blade was changed so that what was the after edge of the blade became the upper edge as the blade was moved back toward the stern. It is this action that can support your weight, and from which you can hook yourself up.

Try the paddle movement first, and once you've made it smooth, see how much you can lean on it. You'll find that, provided you make the movement reasonably brisk, you can lean right over on your side and still recover, by pressing down as you go—since the blade would much rather come up.

The best way to accomplish this to begin with is to hold the shaft in your right hand, and the tip of the left blade in your left.

It is said that the blade wants to come up—and this is the whole point. As you move the blade through the water with its leading edge raised, you are using the same principle that applies to an aircraft wing when it moves through the air. The blade wants to come up, as does an aircraft wing if not properly balanced to bring the rest of the airplane up with it.

PAWLATA TECHNIQUE

To begin with, hold the left paddle blade in your left hand. The reason for this is to help you learn the movement more speedily, since you won't have to worry about fouling the blade against the hull. As you become familiar with the roll technique, you can go into a roll from the normal paddle position.

Lean forward on the left side with the forward blade in a horizontal position and parallel to the water, resting the forearm on the deck. Both hands should be clear of the deck, their backs facing away from you.

Capsize: count 3 and make sure you are still leaning forward. Now push the paddle with both hands up to the surface, keeping the wrists bent so that the edge of the blade moving away from you is slightly raised, that is, turned toward the surface. Through the mask, check that this is so.

You now have to combine several movements, which may be broken down as follows:

1. Simultaneously push with your left hand forward and upward while the right—which is straight—sweeps in an arc from the canoe. Since you are upside down, this brings the blade in a position from bow to amidships, and the leading-edge tilt will make it want to surface, so you'll be moved upward with it.

2. As the blade comes abeam of you, you will be on your beam ends. It is at this stage that you bring the hip movement into play while simultaneously dropping the wrists to reverse the tilt of the blade to make the reverse stroke forward. From this, you come upright.

THE GENUINE ESKIMO ROLL

The East Coast Greenland Eskimos—judging from film that has been shot—use a slightly different method of rolling. The forward lean is used, but the blade is angled slightly away from the kayak with its nearer edge (trailing edge) tilted up. Instead of tracing an arc in a horizontal plane, as in the roll described, the Greenland Eskimo moves through a vertical plane so that at the end of the roll—while still leaning forward—the blade comes up behind.

This is a very vigorous stroke indeed, and one possible reason for it may be to combat the chill of the waters in that part of the world, since considerable energy must be used to perform it.

HAND ROLLING

If you're unfortunate enough to lose your paddles, you'll be glad to know that you can roll without them, using one hand or two. It is vital that you have the hip movement worked out. You can lean either forward or back, and the hands dog-paddle you up. As you surface, the hip movement is employed, and you can give some more push by flinging the upper arm up and around the kayak.

ALL ROLLING TECHNIQUES SHOULD BE LEARNED WITH AN INSTRUCTOR.

SAFETY IS NO ACCIDENT

This is a slogan to be found on all pilot certificates issued by the Federal Aviation Administration, and it is a good slogan for anyone who indulges in adventurous activities.

Unlike the highs produced chemically on the body by the use of drugs—prescribed and proscribed—adventuresome activities which entail a degree of risk produce a state of well-being in the participant. This natural high is constructive and provides a good foundation upon which to build a contented and useful personality, because new areas of experience have been met and found good—if taxing to begin with.

Mountaineers always take good care that they have the appropriate skills and equipment before setting off on a difficult climb. They check their equipment carefully, paying particular attention to the rope which may have to support them in the event of a slip. Pilots of power and soaring aircraft make a careful visual inspection before even so much as getting into the cockpit prior to their flight.

So for anyone who wants to do just a little bit more than simply mess around in boats, the first thing is to be familiar with the water, to be able to use it to support the naturally buoyant body you call yours. And this means being able to swim.

Swimming is a slow means of getting around, especially without flippers. But you are going to have to be at home in the water, and this means that you should be untroubled if for some reason or other you are tipped overboard. Remember, the water couldn't care less about you—it is very busily doing its own thing, wearing away rock, hurrying down to the sea—or if in the sea, then allowing its surface to be played with by the winds and enjoying the rolling of its surface as waves.

Keeping this in mind, you know that it will support you if you use your body rightly. And with the aid of your life vest, it will support you even more with still less effort on your part.

If your swimming technique needs perfecting—or you're just plain out of practice—go down to the local pool for a week or two and put in a few laps every day until you get your swimming muscles working. You don't need to be a racer—though the butterfly stroke is very good for building up muscles for long-distance racing. The ordinary breast stroke is fine, and since the leg movement is convenient as the crawl leg movement when you have to push your canoe along, these are two areas to work on.

And don't be worried about fishes nibbling your toes. To them, the canoe looks like some big other fish—and even if you're behind the canoe, you make it look even bigger. They'll leave you well alone.

Swimming pool practice is always helpful when trying out new techniques, and most pools are happy to make arrangements for a small fee. Start your rolling technique here. Learn what it feels like to bail out when you're upside down. The clean water and the use of a mask will familiarize you with what you're doing. Once you've got it sorted out, go out onto a river or lake and practice in real running water—again with your instructor around. For small groups of people, instructors can get half the group to act as deputy instructors, while the other half do it, and then change around.

Even the deep-sea rescues can be practiced in a pool at first so that you don't have to worry about the bobbing and bouncing from the waves. But once you've got it right, go out into the real environment and learn it again there. Modify your technique as necessary to meet this changed environment. You're supposed to be having fun, but you won't be able to enjoy that fun if you are secretly calling your competence into question.

On the river, paddle as a group. The most experienced person should be last man—to see that no one gets left behind. The leader can be the next most experienced person, and leads from about thirty or forty yards ahead through rapids. If the leader gets stuck somewhere, the next person gets a chance to find a more useful route. And with any

rapids that look—and sound—interesting, do not be ashamed to get off the river and inspect them from shore before attempting them. This will take a little longer, but if you're not familiar with the rapids—and they don't appear on your map (they should if you've got a decent map)—a little inspection could save you a oroken canoe.

Remember, the minimum number in a canoeing group should be three boats. And parties should not be more than about eight. Anything larger, such as club outings, should be broken down into two or three groups, or more as required. Groups should stick fairly closely together and, if need be, pauses taken to wait until everyone regroups.

And as a general rule, if you should find yourself swung around backward at the beginning of a rapid, and you are unable to paddle back to calmer water to turn around, it is better to run it backward than to risk being swept down broadside. It looks inelegant, and you'll feel a bit stupid—but not half as stupid as you'd feel were you to smack a rock and bend or break your canoe.

Always paddle firmly when going through fast waters in order to keep steerage way on your boat; this is one of the exhilarations of fast waters. Water always goes fastest through its deepest point; for this reason, it is best to run around the outer edge of a curve in a stream. The fastest water in a rapid is your safest place and will keep you clear of most obstructions.

Lastly, you can always learn something new from the more experienced, so don't be shy about talking with them. Learning about canoeing is like learning about anything under the sun: the more you know, the less you discover you really know.

READING WATER

There are really only two forms of water—moving water and still water—and except for tidal areas, seas may be regarded as still waters, as may large lakes. Obviously there are exceptions, since there are places where the sea rushes along just like a mighty river. But here its behavior will be that of moving water.

Waves in the sea are the result of wind upon water. If you drop a pebble into a pool, you will create a wave effect which gradually moves out from the center. Now drop more pebbles, to the north, south, east, and west of your original throw, and you have roughly the appearance of almost any large body of water at almost any time.

In order for a wave formation to become manifest, something has to move. This displacement of water—created by pebbles or by wind sweeping across the

River

River
Bed

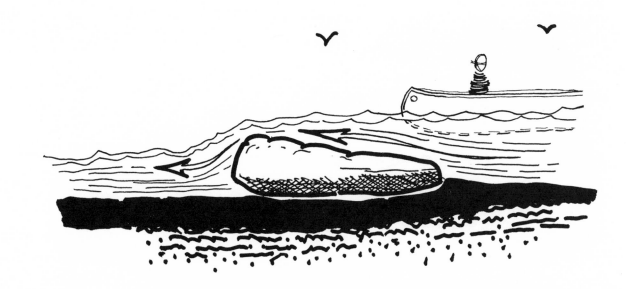

water—is the result of the movement, again in circular form, of water particles. Unlike the wave, which has an apparent movement, the water particles don't move very far in themselves, merely orbiting around a point through which the wave travels. This circular, orbital action explains why boats tend to broach in large seas, since the stern of the boat wants to go faster than the bow.

When the waves come up against the sloping floor of the ocean as it nears land, the seabed causes a frictional force which makes the wave unstable, since some particles are being held back. This point becomes crucial when the bed is approximately one and a half times deeper than the wave height. From here to the shore the wave is pushed up, slowed down, and finally overbalances itself, crashing upon the shore.

RIVERS

The same principle applies, but in rivers the water tends to do the moving while most of the waves may be stationary. Standing waves (those famous haystacks) are usually caused by too much water trying to flow through too narrow an area. The only place for the water to go is up.

Holes—or stoppers—are to be found where fast-moving water flows into and over relatively still water, and a strongly orbital force is set up in the horizontal. Some still water is removed by the force of the rapid, and must therefore be replaced. This sets up a reverse flow, which holds the canoeist.

Holes can also be caused by the water that has just flowed over a large submerged obstruction—usually a boulder. You should find a hole immediately downstream of it. This can be extremely helpful if you are working upstream, since you can pop in here, wait to regain your breath, and then spurt around to just ahead of this obstruction where there will also be a small area of nearly tranquil water just before it overflows the boulder. Coming downstream, again to take a break, you can telemark into the hole.

SOME THOUGHTS ON READING WATER

Downstream

1. Keep to the center of a stream or river where it is straight.

2. If the point of the V in white water is away from you, you will usually be able to make a clear passage. Where you have a choice of Vs, choose the farthest one away from you.

3. In curvy sections, keep to the outside of bends where the current will be strongest and you'll have the greatest depth of water.

4. If standing waves are pointed, colored greeny brown gold and only lightly flecked with foam, you're usually safe to go through.

5. If the standing wave is flat and white, it will usually be a hole and may be uncomfortable for you to get out of.

6. If the standing wave is smooth and round, it is most likely disguising a rock or boulder and should be avoided.

Upstream

1. Keep as close to the banks as is convenient on straight sections.

2. If the point of the V is away from you, the water nearest you will not be as fast flowing as the rest and you may be able to work up it. If it is nearest you, forget it.

3. In curvy sections, keep to the inside of bends where the current is weakest. You may even pick up return eddies to help you upstream.

4. Greeny gold standing waves lightly flecked may sometimes be surfed on when moving upstream. It won't help you advance much, but it may let you get from one side to the other without being sent back down again.

5. Flat, white standing waves can be used to hold you, but do not get drawn over the edge into the hole, as it may be impossible to get out of without having to capsize and leave your boat.

6. Standing waves that are smooth and round indicate that there may be a table of tranquil water immediately above them in which you can make some more progress upstream.

A good rule of thumb to measure the degree of difficulty you are likely to experience is to assess the rate of drop over the route. If the river falls 10 feet per mile you may expect 0 - 1 grade of difficulty; 20 feet p.m. - 1 - 2; 30 feet p.m. 2 - 3; 40 feet - 3 - 4 p.m.; 50 feet - 4 5 p.m.; 60 feet - 5 - 6 p.m.

Peter Dwight Whitney's book *White Water Sport* is required reading on the subject.

Chapter 4
SLALOM: WHITE WATER SURF

Slalom as a canoe sport was first recognized internationally in 1949. Since then it has provided competitors and watchers alike with some of the most exciting sport of our time: man against water against himself.

Slalom tests a canoeist's ability to handle his craft to the utmost of his ability in differing water conditions without letting the water take advantage of him. And most slalom runs 'pack two extremes into their 800-meter length: the highly agitated, turbulent, and awesome white water, from which white-water psort takes its name. Its opposite is the powerful, usually swift-flowing, deep black water. Almost sinister in appearance. these fast-running deeps have a driving power not to be dismissed.

Except for some wild-water events where gates are set up on a racing course, most regular slalom events can be completed in about five minutes. The internationally set distance is 800 meters, but clubs frequently set courses of lengths they set for themselves. Usually there are upwards of 15 gates (to 30 or so) which have to be dealt with. Gates mark the course that must be followed and provide problems for the competitor to solve. Solving these takes time—and this is what slalom is all about—time: measured in seconds.

If a competitor doesn't negotiate a gate properly, he acquires penalty points which are added to his time. In international competition, anyone touching a gate would be way down the list and out of the running. In this rarefied world it's native skill that counts.

The gates, as you might imagine, provide ingenious obstacles both upstream and down. Some are passed through bow forward downstream; some must be entered by going astern; others require the competitor to turn a complete circles around them before continuing. Then there's the yellow pole. This is a penalty pole which is usually slung across the river immediately below a tricky upstream gate, or it is one of those poles that must be circled. The penalty is 100 seconds if touched, but fortunately they'll only fine one—as a rule—on the course.

The poles are color coded to show whether they're to be passed left or right. Green stands for *leave to the paddler's right*, while red stands for *leave to the paddler's left*. The solid color indicates that this is a pole which must be encircled completely. A green-and-white pole also means leave to the paddler's right, and a red-and-white pole means leave to the paddler's left. If a green-white is placed on the right side and a red-white on the left, you proceed through this gate bow first. But if the colors are reversed—that is, red-white on the right and green-white on the left—the gate is either an upstream or a reverse gate. If it's a reverse gate, there will be a large "R" above it. This means it must be

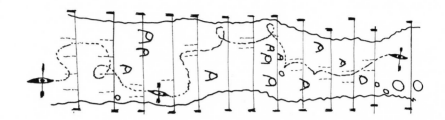

Diagram shows sketch of typical slalom course (copy editor--delete & wildwater shown at top of pic.)

Diagram shows detail of slalom gate layout.

taken in a downstream direction, but the paddler must first turn his boat and enter stern first.

If there's no R, it is simply an upstream gate and must be first passed and then entered from below, while paddling against the current.

Each competitor is timed from the start to the finish of his run. Timing is frequently carried out by radio these days.

Slalom is a ski term, and the sport has been borrowed from skiers. On snow the idea is to make the fastest run down a carefully selected obstacle course which forces the skier to demonstrate his ability. As in canoeing, the objective is to test the limits of the contestant's ability to maneuver with speed. The sport is truly international, popular in the United States, Canada, Eastern and Western Europe, Japan, Australia, and New Zealand. As a sport, it has been centered around the Alps in Europe, but with the building of an artificial site for the Munich Olympics in 1972, the feasibility of creating new sites will undoubtedly broaden its appeal.

Canoe slalom is considerably safer than ski slalom, and usually the worst that can happen is that a boat is wrecked. Obviously, *you* don't want that to happen, so you become very skilled. The person with the least number of mistakes as well as the fastest time wins.

To be a success, you must be able to "read" the water. That is, you must have developed your skills of observation from past experience, so you can apply them to the present eddies and waves that are in motion toward your boat. On top of this, you must have in your armory an extensive reservoir of strokes, each of which will assist you in getting the water to help rather than hinder your speedy progress down course. Obviously, if you're in control of the water, you'll get down faster.

It will be seen, then, that slalom is all about maneuverability and speed, and the person who is intending to take up its challenge goes about finding ways to improve efficiency in all areas. Of first importance is the canoe itself, for no matter how perfect you are in your understanding of strokes and in reading the water, you won't be able to run with the leaders in an inferior boat.

Hull shape is discussed more fully in Chapter 10, but, briefly, the choices are fishform, Swedishform, and symmetrical. Covered canoes and kayaks take part in slalom, and the essential differences are that the kayak uses double paddles (which must be carefully watched on some gates, since you lose points if you foul the gate with your paddle blade) and the competitor sits. In canoes, the competitor kneels and uses one paddle.

Fishform is fast, but not as maneuverable as Swedishform in the opinion of most experts. The symmetrical

design produces a boat that will move well either backward or forward and which behaves the same when moving faster than the current or when being overtaken by it. Generally speaking, the prime difference between a slalom kayak and a downriver racing one is that the racer is longer and is usually designed with a straight, frequently nearly V-shaped keel. The slalom craft is shorter, has considerable curve (rocker) along its keel line, shallowing to bow and stern, and a near V section at bow and stern, but widening to a very nearly flat midsection.

Experiment in design is still going on.

Since 1965, the folding-kayak singles class in world championships (F-1) has been replaced by the kayak singles class (K-1.) It is open to all types of single-place kayaks with a minimum length of 400 centimeters (13.12 feet) and a minimum beam of 60 centimeters (23.6 inches or just under 2 feet.) (This is something else you're just going to have to learn to get used to—the rest of the world is using the metric system these days.)

While folding boats maintain their popularity in a noncompetition environment, and especially for group expeditions into wilderness areas, rigid boats are almost de rigueur. The advantages are several, not least of which is that you can exercise greater control over hull design, and ensure that the hull does not flex but provides optimum performance at all times. Secondly, a folding boat needs to be dried out carefully before it is put away or, if packed wet, dried out when you get it home. You don't have to bother with grp.

To customize your kayak for slalom work, you'll obviously pay attention to each item which will be working for you. Paddles are obvious—and you should get the best you can afford—but considerable care must also be given to the power base you'll be operating from: your seating position. Get a seat molded to fit your rear end snugly and comfortably so you won't be slipping or sliding backward or forward. Site it as low down in the boat as you can. The lower it is, the better your overall stability. The ideal position is where your waist is about level with the cockpit coaming.

To improve your own lateral stability, and to let you use your hip muscles efficiently, you need to fit hip pads, so that there's no side-to-side movement. Some experts fit hip boards, which they then pad, but hip pads made of leather and which are laced have more flexibility. Try both and see which suits you best. In addition, consider whether you might not fit thigh supports, which a growing number of competitors swear by.

Next we come to the knees. Some form of kneegrip is essential if you are to master the Eskimo roll. Kneegrips are also necessary for the best control when the boat is leaned, as during the Duffek strokes, for example. Most people seem to prefer to have the knees about a foot apart, with no pressure on the actual kneecap, but with bracing available.

Finally there's the footrest. This must be adjusted properly so that you can exert pressure with the balls of your feet while paddling. An item often overlooked when tuning for competition, it can really add power to your strokes if set properly.

Clothing: two considerations apply—safety and practicality—keeping the water out, providing warmth, and allowing freedom of movement.

First and foremost is a crash hat. The head is highly vulnerable, and if you hit it hard with a rock you can get knocked out—if nothing worse. So crash hats are important. These days a number of good designs are making their appearance in lightweight plastic and fiberglass. Several have been designed specifically for slalom and wild-water work, and most do the job well. They're usually molded one-piece units, well padded for protection and with holes strategically arranged so that water drains out easily without falling all over your face. The crash hat covers the ears and sides of the head, the top and back and forehead, and most of them sit slightly high on the head so that they protect, but don't rub on your neck. This last factor is important. It is worse than unpleasant to wear a hat that rubs you up the wrong way when you're trying to make good time. Check the hat very carefully, and even wear it around the house for a few days in order to get used to it. The chin strap should be soft, but it shouldn't have too much give, so that even when you've got water in the hat—as in Eskimo rolling, for example—it won't pull off. Be sure that you can get strap replacements.

As a sensible person, you won't be going canoeing without a life jacket; and if you're going into competition you might as well get a regulation one and wear it during training. According to world rules, your life jacket should have a minimum of buoyancy of 6 kilograms (13.2 pounds) and, in addition, should not restrict paddling action, breathing, nor ride up your body if you fall in. But should you be unfortunate enough to have to swim down a rocky river, the jacket should be padded for shielding. If the amount of buoyancy provided seems rather small, the reason is that it won't interfere too much with Eskimo rolling.

There's still a certain amount of disagreement about the use of life jackets in the slalom event, but most of it is based on "macho-isms." It's unlikely you'll get any criticism except from the most uninformed, so don't let it worry you. If some people don't wish to be sensible, that's their prob-

lem—certainly not yours. So get a life jacket that you'll enjoy using.

Spray covers are absolutely essential for slalom work. The apron should fit snugly over the cockpit coaming, and be sufficiently secure so that several heavy dollops of water may crash on it without pulling it adrift. It should also be snug around your waist, with sufficient give to let you use your body fully for the swaying you'll do as you maneuver downstream. Finally, you want to have a quick-release device, so you can make a fast exit, if necessary.

For your own clothing, the same requirements predominate: keeping water out, as well as safety and convenience. Except in very cold weather, a lightweight, waterproof anorak shell over a flannel shirt is fine. If you don't like flannel, wool or cotton with a cotton tanktop is good. Whatever makes you feel comfortable is best, but it should have some ability to absorb sweat and not leave you feeling chill. A cheap spun cotton track suit is fine for warming up before and cooling down after taking part in a slalom event.

Now to paddles. The choice is highly personal, since what works for one person may not work for another. But buy the best you can afford if you intend to become a serious competitor. Rigidity is one key requirement, however, so split paddles are out. Most people prefer a rigid paddle with the blades set at right angles to one another.

What type of blade you'll use is also subject to discussion. Most people seem to opt for curved blades, which—since most of the slalom course is in forward motion—permits a more powerful stroke than other variants. Still, there are some conservatives who prefer to have their strokes mirrored when going backward, and these claim the superiority of the flat blade. Actual shape is covered in Chapter 10, p 000. More important is the paddle shaft, which has been subjected to much development, and which in Europe now sports an oval grip. One reason for this is that the paddler can feel at which angle the blade is set without having to take his eyes off the stream. Some mild flexibility is desirable to cushion the shock at the initial point of each stroke, but lightness and strength are also needed. These days, in international competition a paddle length of around 210 centimeters (about 6 feet 10 inches) is called for, with a weight of less than 3 pounds.

Good paddles are expensive, and you'll probably want to test cheaper ones before deciding to make a serious investment. Cheap paddles don't last that long, anyway.

It's assumed that you already possess basic kayak technique, including the Eskimo roll, and that you have acquired reasonable proficiency in the basic strokes.

Since slalom is a test of maneuverability, the strokes used are designed to provide highly accurate changes of position with minimum effort against the water. And slalom technique is a relative newcomer to the arcana of kayaking, mostly the work of Emile Duffek, a Czech refugee who is now a naturalized Swiss.

Duffek's genius was to adapt American Indian canoe-paddling techniques so they could be used by the kayakists with his double paddle. What this actually meant was including the paddle's driving force as an integral part of the stability platform the paddler uses. Duffek's success was to encourage a small group of followers who understood his reasoning, and they, in turn, have introduced these strokes to competitors around the world.

Before going on to these strokes, let's take another look at what they're designed to do. It may be worthwhile to break down the strokes into two groups: the plus, or positive strokes; and the minus, or negative strokes. The plus strokes are those designed by the paddler to achieve a certain course of action, which actually maintain the kayak on what—in the paddler's viewpoint—is its optimum and most efficient track through the water. The minus strokes are those designed to provide correction, to bring the kayak back to its selected route when it has veered either because of the paddler's error or because of an aberration caused by the water itself. Since time is of the essence for slalom, not only must corrective strokes be kept to a minimum, they must also be highly efficient.

For this reason, in much the same way as the slalom skiing expert goes about his run, the expert slalomist coordinates his strokes and his boat together so that they appear to merge one into the next while the course is traversed effortlessly. This apparent absence of effort on the part of the paddler is the hallmark of skill. Which brings us back to the point mentioned earlier: total command over reading the water; total command of one's repertoire of strokes. Once both have been mastered, you can select ahead of time the stroke that you'll need at any given point on the course.

Slalom is an obstacle course where the key obstacles are placed at their most inconvenient position in terms of the flow of the stream to test your skills. Maneuverability is what counts, plus careful anticipation through accurate observation. To maneuver effortlessly means having available a series of strokes to shift the kayak with the help of the water, even though the flow of the water may be apparently working against your objective.

The stroke most commonly used to effect a turn is the telemark—another term borrowed from skiers (who have since modified this maneuver somewhat.) As used on water,

the telemark permits a turn in the shortest period of time by using the kinetic energy of the fast-moving kayak while optimizing the slackening of speed as the boat conflicts with the current. The turn is made by leaning the kayak and supporting the paddler's weight on the paddle, which is why slalom paddle and shaft have to be so strong.

The telemark comes in two varieties, each designed for a specific objective. They're known as the high and low telemark, and you should be able to choose the correct stroke without thinking about it.

Let's deal with the low telemark first. The object of the stroke is to change direction in fast water. Go to your normal paddling position. Now, with elbows and shoulders raised and with the wrists dropped, present the *back* of the blade to the water, curved side down. The paddle is now pressed down and away from the kayak, and the effect is to push the boat away from the paddle (it sounds crazy as you read it, but it isn't, as you'll see.) The pressing action in turn provides a slight lift to the stern of the kayak, which also helps in the turning movement by providing less friction. The result is the fastest turn used in slalom. So, low telemark: lean kayak, present back of blade to water, and press down and away from boat.

The high telemark is designed to pull the kayak out from a fast-running current into slacker waters. Hold the paddle shaft as you would for normal forward paddling with the arms stretched out to the bow. Now raise the wrists and drop your elbows so that the paddle blades turn through 180 degrees, and the *face* of the blade is presented to the water. Your back must be kept straight, and you'll be leaning forward slightly.

Now angle the blade into the water—you can use anything from about 30 degrees to 70 degrees, and some faster people sometimes use even more than that—and hold the face of the blade toward the bow of the kayak. You now have a rudder around which the kayak can pivot. You can shorten the turn even more if, as you come out, you push the blade toward the bow. In the high telemark turn the kayak is leaned, and the paddle is almost vertically in the water.

A variation of the high telemark, the bow-rudder stroke, is used when the slalomist wants to make a slight change in direction without loss of speed. Here the blade is entered in the same way, but as far forward as possible so that the turn is not actually completed, but the boat is nudged, as it were, to the correct position. Experts favor following this nudge effect immediately with a normal forward stroke on the same side so that no momentum is lost, and the stroke is made from the nudge turn without the blade leaving the water.

A funny thing happened on the river today . . .

A

B

With kayaks you have an extra problem to deal with--just where do you put that other paddle blade? (A) & (B) show potential solutions to the problem.

The slalom kayak is a highly functional vessel, short, rather than long, and rockered for sensitive maneuverability.

Heading for the Gothic V--good paddling technique in white water.

A better place becomes apparent, and the kayak moves to make safe passage.

Two strokes that developed from the high and low telemark are, respectively, the hanging support and the slap support. Both slap support and hanging support are, as their names suggest, used to prevent an incipient capsize which can happen when a current slams down one side of the kayak, tending to capsize it upstream. The slap support, used promptly, can prevent this happening and is a variant of the low telemark in that the back of the blade is presented to the water, but here the water is actually slapped with the blade, forcing the kayak upright once more.

What happens if you don't get the slap support working in time is that you go to the hanging-support stroke. In the slap support—as in the low telemark—the forearms go to a near-vertical position before the stroke is applied. To develop the hanging support from this position, the paddler drops his elbows from their high position so that they are nearly parallel with the shoulders, and turns the blade through 180 degrees. The paddler now hangs from the paddle, which is still almost horizontal, and correction is made by pulling on the paddle to upright the kayak.

Both the slap support and the hanging support can be sustained by sculling backward and forward along the surface of the water, which is useful when a particularly strong tip is encountered.

Continuing on the theme of maneuverability and efficiency, perhaps the first technique that must be mastered by the would-be slalom expert is the ferry glide. Actually, although there doesn't appear to be much moving backward in a slalom event, a considerable amount is done by the kayak in its travels, which is what has led people back to the symmetrical hull in this event. You are not aware of it, since the stream is always moving downriver.

In the ferry glide you actually make use of the force of the current to work for you while you work against it. Your key to tapping into this phenomenon is a steady and strong backstroke on the side you don't want to move to. This has the effect of turning the kayak bow at an angle in the direction—once again—you don't want to move in.

Back-paddle once more on the side you don't want to go, and then take turns in back-paddling either side. The stream by now will have got the message and started to do your bidding, and you'll be gliding across in the direction you want. Keep on with your back-paddling until you can see a clear way ahead. In the slalom event you'll use this technique for cutting across from one side of the stream to the other to set yourself up properly for taking the gates, rather than just avoiding obstacles. The ferry glide is one of the most useful maneuvers for any white-water work and is worth practicing until it becomes second nature, even if you don't intend to compete very much.

The ferry glide can also be used while moving upstream, though naturally the technique is a bit different. Here, as soon as you see that you have to change direction, make one strong forward stroke on the side that you don't want to go. This will turn your bow in the direction you want to take—this, actually, is the essential difference between the two ferries, so remember it and make this also second nature.

Now give another forward stroke on the side you don't want to go, and then paddle on each side alternately. The technique works best, both backward and forward, when you are at only a relatively slight angle to the mainstream, for if you let the current catch much more of you, you can be swept broadside onto the very object you were trying to avoid. Slalom experts are as strong going forward as backward, and it is for this reason that the more conservative prefer flat-bladed paddles—you don't have to make allowances for the differences in behavior which occur when you back-paddle a curved blade.

Once you've achieved proficiency with the ferry glides, you may find yourself using them automatically to make slight adjustments to correct your course. But consider each problem as requiring the best possible answer, since with the ferry glide downstream you are losing a fraction of a second each time you back-paddle. Unless the terrain is such that makes the ferry glide the most obvious choice, course corrections may be more quickly made on forward strokes.

On the other hand, should you find yourself in some shallows, as occasionally you will, and through which you must thread your way, the ferry may well be your very best bet, since you'll be moving slightly slower than the stream itself and reducing your forward speed if you touch the riverbed.

One last thought about the ferry is that where there is a considerable current differential, always lean to the fastest part of the stream. This leaning inward helps stabilize the craft against the current's turning effect upon your kayak. This factor cannot be too strongly emphasized, since if you do not lean and brace decisively, fast currents will tip you out.

Before continuing with the strokes of most use, it may be well to review the point of slalom, which is, namely, to test a kayakist's ability to handle his craft to an optimum ability without letting the water take advantage of him. And it should be said that though it all sounds very simple on paper, it actually requires a high degree of motor skill in addition to experience.

Take, for example, the slalom gate. Commonly about 4 feet wide (47 inches is the minimum), they can very easily be thought to be 4 feet narrow, since even in slack water they would require some skill to traverse. Motor enthusiasts who have taken part in competition driving tests will understand the problems involved. They have to be taken precisely, since, if approached sloppily, you'll touch (with either the kayak or your paddle)—which will cost you points. So develop a technique to squeeze through them.

In Europe it is quite common to find gates set up where it is sometimes better to foul one, in order to take the others cleanly. But so far this diabolical approach hasn't caught on in the United States. Here, if you foul, you'll lose first place.

Strategy is another consideration. Do you make the best and fastest possible run in your first heat, or do you try to set a reasonably good time and go for broke the second time around? Actually, the experts favor the latter appraoch, arguing that a safe and reasonably fast time permits them to learn the course, while the second time they can really try it out. Practicing beforehand is, fortunately, not allowed. (Parenthetically, one of the reasons that motor rallying died out as an important sport was that in the European events factory teams would test out the special stages and prepare "course cards," giving instructions about the speed of every bend and how fast it could be taken.)

A final point on technique is that if you capsize you'll be disqualified unless you recover with an Eskimo roll, without leaving your boat.

Perhaps the most useful forward stroke for the slalomist is the forward sweep stroke, which allows for a change of direction while still moving the kayak forward. It is most useful when you need to start a change in direction, or to push the kayak out of the main current. And unlike the bow rudder, which tends to draw the entire craft sideways, the forward sweep allows the boat to pivot around the paddler's body.

Starting from the normal paddling position, bring the left hand up to your chest without changing your grip on the paddle, while keeping the right arm fairly straight. Now move the body anticlockwise to let the right hand reach farther forward; the right blade now enters the water with the right arm remaining straight. Make a semicircle while moving your body clockwise from the hips, and lean slightly into the turn. It is important to make as big a semicircular movement with the blade as possible, since you're relying on the blade to provide you with stability.

Now once more to the Eskimo roll. The version most useful for the slalomist is the screw roll, since much of the course is run in shallow water and no one wants to get bumped.

If you should tip over, it is important to get yourself back up again with the least amount of time lost, and without having to work against the current which toppled you in. The reason the screw roll works well is that there's no need to change your grip on the paddle—a very important consideration, since the current can snatch it from your hands while you are changing position. You have to lean forward, which minimizes the chances of injury to yourself from an uneven riverbed, and also protects your face. To make the screw roll work for you, you should be able to do it right or left.

A development of the Pawlata roll, invented by an Austrian canoeist of that name, the screw roll differs in that the paddle is held in the normal paddling position. (The Pawlata method is to put the paddle on the forward deck, and then sweep a large arc along the surface while the paddler rights himself.) Perhaps the most difficult point in learning the screw roll is that the rearward end of the paddle always seems to get caught up with the kayak.

This can be solved by taking the whole paddle over the coaming and—just put yourself in the cockpit for a moment—push downward using the rearward hand as a fulcrum while the forward hand acts as your lever in sweeping outward. The forward hand describes an arc across the surface of the water, and the leading edge of the blade is angled upward to provide support.

Modern exponents of the screw roll emphasize the importance of correct body movement in getting this maneuver accurate, and the chest should be facing the paddle as you capsize. Hip movement in this roll is even more important than in other rolls described elsewhere, since there is less support from the paddle.

A maneuver known as the storm roll has been developed for use in white water and is highly advanced. It is similar to the Pawlata across roll, except that the paddle is much deeper and is at right angles to the surface of the water. The storm roll is useful, since you can get to it from those strokes which use a perpendicularly placed paddle.

Becoming successful at slalom requires intensive practice. The slalomist is probably the best all-rounder in terms of river technique, and that ability depends on two things only: reading the water, and being at one with your craft.

CANOE SLALOM

While slalom seems faster and more exciting both in and out of kayaks, canoes can successfully take part in the sport. Perhaps the biggest problem encountered with the American canoe in slalom is that it has to be bailed out. Spray covers are the answer here.

The trick is not to touch the gate, say the experts, which is easier said than done. Sternman seen here setting up the canoe for gate negotiation.

With the advent of the C-1 and C-2 competition canoes—which are rather different from a regular canoe, being both lighter and differently shaped—it became obvious that some sort of rolling technique should be developed. And a well-fitting spray deck is essential.

Rather than deal with the strokes used for slalom technique in C-1 and C-2 categories, it is proposed here to focus on rolling techniques for this type of craft. There are probably several reasons why rolling has not been developed sooner, since capsizes are not infrequent. One of these, very likely, is a subconscious fear of being trapped under the boat, like a baby that cannot get born.

The other is that very few people who managed to "somehow roll" were able to analyze what it was that they had done so successfully. As with kayak rolling, so with canoe rolling: it must be practiced again and again, both when you are fresh as well as when you are tired. The need to roll may come up suddenly, and if you don't know how, you may not have an opportunity to try again.

The British Canoe Union first published details of a series of drills to be followed in developing the Canadian roll about ten years ago. They offered a version of the kayak screw roll, and a second, purely Canadian canoe roll.

The warm-up exercises in developing the screw roll are very simple and are designed to build confidence. As learning all rolls requires a degree of understanding, it may be helpful to run through this technique. We'll do it from the point of view of a C-1.

First stage: you are in the C-1 with the spray deck in place, but without your quick-release thigh strap fitted. Now lean over and completely capsize. Once underneath, release the spray deck, put a hand on each side of the boat behind your hips, and, pushing gently, release your feet and then swing your legs clear. Once clear, swim to the surface. This exercise should be practiced with an instructor until you are completely confident of your ability to clear the boat from underneath. You don't need to be able to hold your breath forever. It takes only a few seconds to get out and up once you've learned how to do it.

Second stage: this has already been developed in the section on Eskimo rolling in Chapter 3, but it's worth noting here, as it is a very big confidence-builder. Proceed as in stage one, but instead of releasing yourself from the boat, lean right back in the canoe and to one side. Now swim with your hands to bring your head to the surface. A couple of strokes are usually all that is necessary to break water in order to breathe. You'll discover that it is very simple to swim along while still in your canoe and be able to breathe properly. Taken a stage further, you can first get your breath

on one side, then swim under the boat, and surface on the other. As you master this technique, you'll find it perfectly practicable to swim along with your canoe for quite long distances, so that should you want to, you could make your way to the bank of the stream.

Third stage: your instructor will now get in the C-1 and ask you to stand on his right, immediately behind him in waist-high water. He will then get you to hold him under his arms while he leans into a capsize, at which point you are supporting his entire weight. Now he will do it leaning forward—you'll discover that it is very easy to get him back to the vertical. Now he leans back—this is much more difficult.

This time do it with yourself in the boat. The objective is to discover for yourself that if you lean forward you can pull yourself up fairly easily, but if you lean back it is much more difficult—if not impossible. So, to satisfactorily complete the screw roll, you've got to lean forward.

Fourth stage: back in the canoe again, lean as far forward as you can, and then capsize with your hands as far around the bow as they will go. The instructor will count up to 5 before righting you; meanwhile take a good look around. (If you find that water on your face upsets you, you may feel more comfortable learning with a face mask.) This stage is developed further by grasping the left side of your boat, with your right hand just in front, and the left just behind. Capsize again, but wait a bit longer under water before giving the instructor your right hand to pull you up with.

You are now ready to roll. The trick is to place the paddle blade on the surface of the water and haul yourself up by its shaft. How? As follows.

Take your paddle and run it through the water with the leading edge pointing slightly upward. Draw it around in an arc. Now, make what was the trailing edge point upward and make an arc in reverse. Note that the paddle blade wants to come to the surface as long as the leading edge is slanted slightly upward. (This is the same principle which supports airplanes in the skies.)

Now get into the canoe and practise moving the blade backward and forward. At the end of each stroke, change the angle by a movement of your wrists. As soon as you no longer need to pause for thought at the end of each stroke, try leaning toward the paddle. Incredible! Provided you keep up your rhythm, you can support yourself on the blade. This is an excellent way to support yourself if you've leaned too far. Rowboat enthusiasts use much the same technique when they propel their craft forward by sculling over the stern.

Having mastered the scull, it is now time to see whether you can do it from the upside down position. Remember: the leading edge of the blade must be tilted slightly toward the direction you want it to go. And to begin with, the blade should stay on top of the surface of the water.

The Canadian screw roll: kneel in your canoe with your paddle on the left deck, slightly in front of you. The grip should be held with your left hand by your left hip. Now lean forward, with the knuckles of both hands facing the deck.

As you capsize the boat, bend your wrists so that the outboard edge of the blade turns toward the surface of the water.

Stay upside down for a count of 3, still leaning forward. Now push the blade up to the surface with your left hand clear of the deck, keeping both wrists bent so that the leading edge of the blade is toward the surface. Check that you've got it right.

The next stage is very rapid, being a succession of strokes. The point to remember is that to complete your recovery properly, the body is the last thing to come up. Right the boat first is the rule, which means you must have good hips.

With the right arm straight, sweep out in an arc from the canoe while pulling very firmly down. As the paddle arrives just to your rear, drop the wrists so to reverse the tilt of the blade, and at the same time lean forward and push forward. The last thing that comes out is your body, and you slither it out as if you were a fish jumping. Keep sweeping until the roll is completed.

Key points to check each time while you are perfecting this maneuver: Did you lean far enough forward? It's the forward lean that makes this maneuver so much easier. Don't forget the exercise at the third stage of learning. Did you twist your trunk to the right on your way up? Did you remember the reverse stroke? And was the leading edge of the paddle blade pointed in the right direction for each stroke? Finally—since this can lead to muffed rolling—did you start your recovery before you completed your capsize?

Some paddlers find they can roll almost automatically, practically from the first time off, as if they had access to Eskimo-folk memory banks. Others have to work at it, first breaking it down into stages, and then putting it together. Whichever way you deal with it, make it a point of your own safe operating procedure to roll regularly, with a companion to right you. Really good aviation pilots always make a point of shooting two or three landings each time they fly. Really good canoeists maintain their rolling technique the same way, before setting off. It's also good to practice a roll or two

at the end of a hard day's run when you're feeling tired—that's when you'll be most likely to make an error, and you want to be sure that your technique is still good then.

Surf canoeing is for those who've mastered most of the advanced techniques, including rolling. If you've never experienced surfing conditions before, you'll be in for a pleasant surprise, since it is roughly akin to downhill skiing on the water—moving water, at that.

Slalom canoes are well suited to these conditions, but you can also try the new surfing kayaks that are being made these days. These taper toward the stern, their bow section being the widest part of the structure and giving the kayak the appearance of a surfboard you can sit in.

Make no mistake about it: surf can be dangerous. The waves that form the surf have traveled many hundrds of miles, and there is a great deal of energy packed within each one. Get into some tricky surf and you can lose your craft in milliseconds—snapped in two. It can pick you and your craft up and dump you down so hard you won't know what's happened to you, and it can drag your paddle out of your hand and break it as you might break a match with your thumbnail.

So, before you begin, make sure you've got a Coast Guard-approved life jacket—it could save some bruises if you get bounced—a good crash hat with a secure strap, and—to begin with—use the flat paddes. They're a bit cheaper, to start with, and once you get the hang of it, you can use your regular slalom paddle.

Obviously, you'll be taking along your spray skirt; and you should—before you start off gingerly experimenting with surf not more than about 3 feet high—try a few rolls in the seawater. You'll find the additional buoyancy helps, but it will feel a bit strange for the first couple of times.

If you're taking an ordinary slalom canoe along, you would do well to think about reinforcing in order to cope with the additional forces that will be experienced. Reinforcing down the centerline, with diagonally set ribs on both top and bottom, has been found to be helpful. Inside you'll want extra buoyancy: one way to accomplish this one is to use formed blocks of foam, which are shaped so they make a tight fit—this way they also provide additional beefing up of the structure. The area that lies immediately forward of the footrest must be packed in such a way that if the footrest breaks you won't slither into obscurity. And if you're going to do forward loops, you'd better check your footrest anyway.

An item which saves headaches is the use of a series of deck lines, which all intending to use canoes at sea should consider. The provide useful handholds, and they can be used to park a spare paddle. They must be secured tight.

For your first attempt, try to arrange to have a person on shore who can watch your progress and, if need be, come to your assistance. Also have someone seaward of you, so that if a rescue should become necessary, you have someone behind your back. Lastly, go and watch others before you start off yourself. The most important thing is to learn to use the paddle blade as a rudder—almost like a ferry glide but without the paddling.

Your first project is going to be to get through the surf, and the way to start is to position your kayak facing the breakers within the washing area, but so that as the water recedes it's on the sand. If you're too close to the water, you'll have to chase the kayak as the currents sweeps it away. Get in, fix the spray skirt, and then lift up everything and walk forward with your hands until you've got water deep enough to use a paddle in. Go straight out, even when the waves start breaking on you. If you paddle hard, keep leaning forward; you'll find that you can usually cut through a breaker—if your timing is right—about a foot and a half below its crest. The difficulty as you go through is to find some water to hang on to, so the best thing here is to brace and ride through it.

Some surfers recommend that beginners start by broadsiding the waves rather than running through them, but this is a matter for experts. Find someone who is doing it and ask his advice.

Surfing proper comes when you are riding the slope of the breaker. You can ride high up, or lower down on its frontal surface. Whichever you choose, you'll have to lean backward to prevent your bow from digging in, and your paddle will be working to keep your bow headed in the direction of the shore. You can also use bow-rudder strokes, but be careful you don't put your bow straight down.

When you've acquired some technique, you'll want to get onto the smokers. The bigger waves must be negotiated with some caution, not by plunging through them. If you are just plain unlucky and you see a big one about to smash down on you, the best thing to do is to grab as deep a breath as you can manage and capsize. The drag your body provides should prevent you being swept on in, but you'll be in for a roller-coaster ride underneath.

The procedure for getting through is to take it in easy stages, paddling hard when you've a lull, and waiting if you must. The big surf packs a big punch and shouldn't be trifled with.

Once you're through the line, select an incoming wave to ride on. As it moves up to you, start paddling faster so that as it moves in you're on the forward face. There are a number of games you can now play. The first technique is the zigzag, since with this maneuver you can play a whole wave backward and forward, along its front. See how many 90 degree changes of direction you can make, first paddling on one side, then on the other. Once you've got this in your rocker, try this just below the cresting part of the wave—since waves don't break all at once, they crumble along a line.

Loops and pirouettes are for skilled paddlers, but the techniques are quite simple and work well even with the snubber-nosed surf canoes.

The forward loop is really a somersault brought on by leaning forward with your body as the bow digs in. You'll probably happen into your first one by accident and wonder how you managed it. As you go up, be prepared to roll back up, so that your kayak is pointing out to sea.

The dry loop, which is the key to the pirouette, is done in the same way as the forward loop, except that while you are balanced on your bow, you bring the boat around with your hips so that it is right side up and facing seaward. You can assist in this maneuver by using your paddling to help you around. This requires some practice but, once mastered, leads you to the pirouette in which you describe a full circle, though 360 degrees. This last is very definitely an expert's number and takes considerable practice.

If you are going to be doing surf canoeing, please read Chapter 9, "Coastal Cruising," especially the section on rescue techniques. Anyone who wants to try this sport out owes it to himself (or herself) to be able to extricate himself from any problems.

Surf canoeists sometimes have to perform rescues of swimmers, and so this section should at least be read if not practiced. What you should practice are the deep-sea rescues. Apart from adding to your skills, it is good fun as well.

WILD WATER

Wild-water racing is a blend of downriver and slalom. You need skill, and you also need stamina. It is perhaps the best of all possible worlds for the serious competitor. If you're this serious, you'll already belong to a canoe club and will have started your competition work. You don't need further details here.

Surf canoeing provides moments for aerobatics, as seen here where the kayak makes a nose dive. Skilled surfers can make vertical 180 degree turns.

For most enjoyment keep just ahead of the breaking crest.

Whitewater is perhaps the most exciting challenge to all paddlers. But snow-fed northern waters can be chilly.

Much of the thrill of whitewater comes from the fact that you are traveling through surroundings that few others ever get to see as intimately as you do.

One person or two? Provided you enjoy company, it's nice to share the beauty of whitewater sport.

Chapter 5

RACING: Long Distance, Marathon, Flat Water

If practice makes a slalom expert, then training is one key to becoming a successful racer, since you must be physically fit before you begin.

Sprint racing became an Olympic event in the Berlin Games of 1936, and is run under three distances: 500, 1,000, and 10,000 meters. Long-distance racing is subdivided here into marathon flat water and wild water, which includes such events as the more-than-25-mile Arkansas River Race, the Danish Gudena 117-kilometer race, and the Spanish Sella River Race. Distances can range from 8 to 124 miles, this last being the distance of the British Devizes-to-Westminster Canoe Race, which first ran in 1949.

Wild water, as its name implies, includes white water, and here technical skill as well as brute strength pay off. But muscle power is important. While it is not very graceful to stick your paddle in and haul your canoe toward it with your knees, it can be done, and the ability to produce this sort of strength can make the difference between winning and losing national events.

In some events, certain sections of the river may require competitors to go ashore and portage their craft to a new point—in order to go around a dam, for example. For this reason a considerable amount of training is necessary, and, if there are two of you, the development of teamwork becomes an important factor in saving time.

Depending on the event, the boats used will range from sleek downriver racers to superbly gleaming open canoes. Length and weight are governed by the International Canoe Federation (a list of members is to be found in Appendix 2 and are as follows:

The materials from which these craft are made are either fiberglass or a similar product, or hot-molded veneer ply. The latter produces an astonishingly beautiful craft, which is also fast. Whether fiberglass or wood veneer, each is without any framework, being made up of a structure which is purely monocoque, where the sum contributes support to all its parts.

If you have ever done any running, you'll know that it is vital to train every day for at least a couple of hours. If you set yourself a similar training program—and stick to it—you can become either a sprint or a long-distance racer. Sprint racing requires more brute strength than does the longer-distance event. In both the 500 and 1,000-meter events, you use the optimum amount of energy you can extract from your frame all the way through the course. Obviously, you're going to be short of strength by the time you get to the end, and what you have to do is to build up a reserve of strength—in the form of stamina—from which you can draw fresh supplies.

The same is also true for longer events, except that

while you are driving yourself forward you are very canny about dispersing your strength, since squandering it early in the race means you'll have nothing left by the halfway mark. At the same time, you must want to win, and be prepared to work for winning. In sprint events it is usually the person who has done the most work in preparing for the event who claims the prize.

To get into the winning circle, you are going to need a K-1 in good condition (or a C-1 if you prefer canoe technique) with good paddles. And you need to develop a good technique for yourself which is well grounded in basic strokes. You must have a thorough grounding in such strokes as the telemarks, the draw, the reverse, the sweep, the slap support, and ferry glide. You should also be able to steer your kayak without using the rudder.

There's one more item required: a notebook in which you will keep details of your entire training program. This, you may say, is nonsense. But it isn't. As a reinforcer of self-discipline it is excellent, and the principle it uses is the same as that employed in teaching people to re-create their lives. It provides an instant record and should be quite an elaborate affair.

For example, your daily record sheet should show all the work you've done, including exercises, actual paddling work, how you felt when you got up—check your pulse rate on awakening, keep a daily register of your weight, list target times set for practice and whether you beat or missed them, and so on. The pulse rate is important, since, generally speaking, the lower the pulse, the better your condition. Weight, too, is helpful. A loss in weight might indicate that you are working too hard or that you ought to get your doctor to check you out. While there is a gradual loss in weight as you get yourself into trim, there's a point at which it stops: when you're free from excess fat, at what the experts call "racing weight."

In addition, read up about the muscles of the body and how they work. You'll be able to apply yourself much more usefully to your training if you know what each muscle is able to do, and which muscles need exercise in order to speed you on your way. Kayaking employs most of the muscles used by a boxer, except that instead of pushing out intending to hit, the arm goes out to grab the water.

The body itself is a fascinating structure. It is quite versatile and can be improved by doing certain types of work. Quite apart from getting you into winning form, all the training you do has an additional bonus in making you more healthy—and of laying down the groundwork for a healthy old age.

TRAINING SCHEDULE

The body provides us with a location from which to exercise our will. Interestingly enough, most of us don't use our bodies as much as we can, with the result that they become much less efficient. If you don't use certain muscles, they will become useless—which is what middle-age spread is all about. And people get fat because they underexercise and overeat.

Many of the exercises included in this training schedule can be used with advantage by readers of this book, since most people would like to exercise but don't know how to go about it. And as for signing up at a gymnasium, well, most of us either don't have the time or money or are a bit too self-conscious even to give it a try.

The first thing to understand is that the body is much like an internal-combustion engine. It requires fuel, and it can convert the fuel into energy by taking in oxygen. The old tag—you are what you eat—is very true. Most of us eat far too much meat, probably accounting for the high intolerance of heart disease.

The skeleton is a good place to start thinking about how a person is made up, for it is the framework upon which everything is dressed. But the clothing that we wear—our tissue and that symphony of organs which organize our habitat—requires feeding, and the blood is what we use to move it around to each and every part. Our skin and lungs bring oxygen required to burn our fuel. Our nervous system is a communications system of considerably greater importance than ITT, AT&T, RCA and Cable & Wireless combined. Our muscles respond to a series of commands, providing us, for example, with a variety of means of locomotion. Finally, microcosmic in size, yet macrocosmic in importance, is the lowly cell.

The first need of the body is air, and it is for this reason that the lungs provide the largest surface in our bodies. We can develop the efficiency of our lungs by breathing, for most of us breathe very inefficiently indeed. Every time we breathe in, we open up between seventeen and eighteen million cells to the air. Our lungs contain tissue which, if it were laid out on the ground, would cover an area of more than 140 square yards. Expert opinion suggests that even the best of us use only about a third of the available area, and most of us probably use only a sixth. Breathing exercises are therefore most important to the better functioning of our bodies.

Our body's second need is for water, since, for the most part, that is actually what we are made up of. The Greek philosopher Epicurus stated that "Water cures every illness," and the early fathers of the Christian church thought so highly of water that they insist to this day on its use as marking one's entry into their group.

Under the program outlined here, it is suggested that even when not in full training you make a practice of running through a series of basic exercises after you get up in the morning, to be followed by a shower. Daily showering, or bathing if you don't have a shower, is absolutely essential to good health. And a shower or bath before going to bed is also beneficial.

In order to tone up your skin, try using a slightly less hot shower each day, until you can get under and enjoy the cold water. You don't need to be a hero, and you can adjust it a little day by day until you end your shoer with just cold water. In addition, it won't hurt at all to make a practice of swimming at least a couple of times a week.

Instead of drinking coffee or tea or sodas, try drinking water. It's much better for your system, and thus better for your overall health. If the tap water in your area is impure—as it all too frequently is—see whether you can afford to buy spring waters, changing the brands around until you find one you like. If you're still smoking, maybe you can cut down—and use the cigarette money for spring water, instead.

Another fundamental need is sunshine. Here again is something we don't get properly. Too much sun too soon is bad for the skin, but an hour a day, worked-up to gradually, is beneficial.

The next requirement is food. Unfortunately, we have allowed our society to let food become a profit-making business, with the result that we are sold an awful amount of rubbish under the guise of nutrition. The food industry regulates itself, and there's not much to be done save to educate people so that eventually the manufacturers will be forced to provide food of better quality.

The body requires protein, and most of us look to meat to fulfill this need. Actually, most of the meat we get today is toxic, since meat manufacturers fatten their stock with chemicals harmful to humans in their march to bigger profits.

Fish is a good substitute for meat, and it is cheaper. But certain types of seafood must now be regarded as unfit to eat, since the pollution of our seas by industries such as oil and paper has made some species health hazardous. Any of the bottom-feeding fish caught near our shores become suspect, as do crustacea, such as oysters, lobsters, and clams. Good substitutes for these are cod and squid, the last being very easy to clean and tastes superb when marinated in red wine with fennel.

Other sources of protein are eggs, soybeans, cheese, and nuts.

Bread is another item which has been made into a tasteless, useless "food." Whole wheat breads are expensive, but you don't need to eat a lot. Alternatively, you can make your own—it's not difficult!

Instead of eating candies, add dates, figs, raisins, dried apricots, and other dried fruits to your diet. And instead of smothering your food with salt to make it taste better, try flavoring it with onion or garlic—either in powdered form or in its natural state. Celery, dill, and other herbs can be winners for flavoring. I, myself, use basil and marjoram as flavor enhancers. For salad dressing, use cold-pressed safflower oil or peanut oil, and instead of using vinegar, try lemon or lime juice, or even grapefruit juice instead.

For a sweetener, use honey; and, if your really enjoy your coffee and tea, try some of the health-food substitutes now available.

Try for a balanced diet, so that your meals include protein to build and repair body tissue, sufficient calories to provide heat and energy, trace minerals—such as calcium, phosphorus, to build and maintain the body and assist in regulating its own biodynamies. Vitamins are also needed.

You might also consider a year's subscription to *Prevention* magazine. Although it might be thought of as being for health-food "nuts," there's good sense and much truth running through all its pages.

However you go about it, keep a close track on your diet. * * *

Because the human body is made up of—very roughly— bone, muscle, and fat, one has to provide a regimen that is going to keep each of these items in good tone. You have some 640 different muscles, which account for nearly 45 percent of your weight, and each muscle has four distinct and measurable characteristics which concern our training schedule.

First, each muscle is capable of producing a force which can be measured as the strength of that muscle. Next, each muscle can store energy which lets it work for extended periods. This is called endurance. Next, it can contract at varying speeds. Finally, it can be stretched and will recoil. This is known as its elasticity. The sum of these qualities is known as muscular power, and it is to improve the quality of this muscular power—in order to perform efficiently in our sport—that the training is aimed.

If your muscles are to function well, they have to have access to fuel. Thus oxygen and nutrients are carried in the bloodstream to the muscle's headquarters, where it is distributed to independent cells according to their need.

Any form of racing requires a considerable usage of fuel if we are to stay out front. The actual thought processes are improved by our training, since we become used to the idea that our body *is* actually now capable of producing from the demands we make upon it. When we are paddling flat out, our thought processes are fairly quiet—except when we are working out ways to ensure we stay ahead. Indeed, it is not until the final stretch that our will power becomes a factor in keeping the system working when it's pleading to stop.

This sort of stamina has to be built up, by strengthening the muscles of the heart and lungs. As any cross-country runner will tell you, the thing that has to be stretched is the body's ability to know that it won't fall to pieces if you force it into work it's been prepared for. But in order to run a marathon—or compete in the Arkansas River Race—you've got to work up slowly from small items, letting your body puff and pant, until it can tackle larger items. And this is the essence of training for long distance. This requires constant practice and, the constant raising of one's personal target in terms of time and effort.

So the first part of the training schedule deals with getting fuel to the muscles that will do the work. This means exercise to help the heart and lung muscles function more efficiently. A strongly developed heart can pump fuel via the bloodstream to the muscles without tiring. Strongly developed lungs make for quicker enrichment of the blood with oxygen, so that the converstion process of fuel into energy can take place as you need it.

The second part of the program deals with building up strength. In most U.S. long-distance events, sheer strength rather than skill is required. Most of the international racers make use of weights in their training schedules. But before you go out and buy yourself a set of weights, a brief note of warning: the use of weights in training is a very serious business, since the misuse of a weight can quite easily cause a permanent injury. Before you start, therefore, be sensible—find a weight)training instructor who can put you on the right track. Explain that what you want to do is to build up strength for either sprint or long distance, that you have an exercise schedule, but that you'd like to know the right way to go about it.

EXERCISES—Daily, Before Breakfast

Trunk Turn with Forward Bend

If you can find some fresh air, do this and the other exercises in front of an open window. To begin with, do not force yourself, since these exercises are warm-up ones to get you moving. All exercise programs start at a low level of activity and work up in easy stages.

Feet parallel and apart. Slowly stretch the arms above your head as high as you can get them. Bring the arms down till they are stretched out on either side and are level with the shoulders. Make an easy movement, without moving your feet, as far around to the left as you can go. Now swing back as far around to the right as you can go. Now make a forward bend with the right hand to the left foot as far as you can go, with the left arm lifted up as high as it will go. Straighten up and repeat with the left fist to the right foot, the right arm lifted up as high as it will go. Relax. And do it again.

(Note: if you haven't been doing exercises on a regular basis until now, *take it easy*. You'll find that you'll very quickly be able to put some more oomph into this work, but that you must warm up to it gently.)

Suggested time for this exercise: 3 minutes. (As you progress, you can lengthen the time you use.)

Back and Leg Stretch

Lie down on your back with your feet about 6 inches apart. Raise your head slightly, so you can just see your heels, but keep your arms and hands beside the body. Now just raise your legs clear of the floor, and then slowly lower them. Repeat several times before you go on to the second part, where the legs stay on the ground while you raise your head and shoulders clear from the ground. The legs must stay straight.

Suggested time: 2 minutes.

Basic Leg Pull

Now sit up with your legs straight out, the feet together, and the backs of the knees touching the floor. Raise your arms out in front of you, so that your hands are at eye level. Now very slowly and gently stretch as far forward as is comfortable and grasp your legs at that point. Don't worry if you can't grab your toes—that'll come later. Again, very slowly, bend your elbows outward and pull yourself forward and down until you get to a point where you can't go any farther with comfort. Hold this position while you count to 10 slowly, and then slowly reverse the procedure. Relax.

Do this four times and never strain yourself. Try to let your movements flow, for the point of the exercise is to stretch the muscles easily.

Arm and Leg Stretch

Stand up relaxed, with your arms at your sides. Stiffen your left arm, and slowly raise it above your head and stretch up. Now ease your body weight onto your left foot and bend your right leg up behind you, holding the foot with your right hand. Slowly raise your left hand a few inches farther behind

you while raising your right leg upward. You'll feel a gentle stretching in your back. Now raise your head backward until you're looking straight up. Hold this position for 10 seconds, and then reverse the procedure. Do this twice for each leg.

Chest Expander

The objective of this exercise is to develop the lungs and stimulate the cells within. Stand relaxed with your arms at your side. Now bend your elbows and raise your arms slowly, bringing the back of your hands to your chest. Hold for a moment. Next, straighten the arms at chest level and bring them back slowly until you can hold your hands together behind your back. Straighten out the arms as far as they can go without discomfort while remaining standing straight. Don't bend just yet. Hold to a count of 5.

Still keeping your hands together behind your back and arms high, drop your head back a few inches, and look upward. Go only as far as you can comfortably. Again, hold to a count of 5. Now, slowly bending forward at your waist, bring the clasped hands and arms up stiffly over your back. Keep your knees straight and allow your neck muscles to relax as if you were going to touch your knees with your forehead. Hold for a count of 10. Very slowly straighten up. When you are upright, relax your hands for a few moments and go on to deep breathing.

Deep Breathing

Breathe out to a count of 4. Hold for a count of 4. Breathe in to a count of 4. Hold for a count of 4. Breathe normally and repeat the chest expander exercise. Each exercise should be done three times.

Stationary Run

Finish off your morning schedule with the stationary run. One step is each time your left foot touches the floor. Your feet should be lifted about 4 inches off the floor and each fifty steps you take put in six "scissor" jumps. The scissor jump is done as follows: stand with your left leg and right arm extended forward, right leg and left arm backward. Jump up, changing the position of the arms and legs before you land.

Suggested time: 5 minutes.

The exercises just given should be done every morning just after you get up. By the way, when you wake up in the morning don't bound out of bed straightaway. Give yourself time to get together, have a good stretch, and then greet the day.

As part of your regimen for getting better, make a point of walking at least one mile each day. If you don't live too far from your work, walk to it. If it's too far to walk, can you ride a bicycle? All these little things add up, and most of us get out of condition because it's so easy to jump in the car and drive.

For those who live in cities, bicycles are most economical, since they are mostly sturdy—you don't have to get the superest lightweight racing models, you know—and they provide you with exercise. Swimming a couple of times a week is also highly beneficial, and indoor pools allow you to swim in the winter.

Two training programs are outlined, one for intermediate-stage persons, the other for advanced. Each program is divided into three parts: October through December, January through March, and then the racing season. During cold weather, except when it really is cold, wetsuits can be used with advantage.

PROGRAM A

1. October through December
   Exercises: as above, plus two weekly sessions of Table A, working up to three sessions per week by December.

   Water training. At the beginning of this period, see whether your style cannot be improved. Break down each of your strokes and see if they can't be put together better. Next, test out what you've learned. Is it better?
   Distance work. Starting at 6 miles, build up runs to 15 to 20 miles. Aim for a brisk pace but don't let fatigue cause your style to become sloppy. Rest, and start again.

   A big problem at this time of the year is the deteriorating weather and increasing cold, and there's not too much that can be done about it.

   During the winter months, you've a chance to run a thorough maintenance check on your gear, and you should make up a timetable which includes what needs to be done—alterations to be made, and so on—and an actual time allocation when you'll do it.
   Additional Activities: if you can't get out on the water because of the weather, consider substituting a 6-mile run. Or set yourself an appropriate length to cover while swimming in an indoor pool.

2. January through March
   Exercises: as above, plus three weekly sessions of Table A, working up to four by the end of March.

   Because of the cold, northerners will have to spend their training time either running or swimming. For those in more moderate climes, water training should include the addition of some sprints. Such a schedule might include a

2-mile warmup, which will include ten sets of 20 sprint strokes followed by 20 light strokes; thru 1-mile sections, with the pace increasing to sprint at the end of each mile section; and a 1-mile warmdown. If possible, a mimimum of 6 miles should be paddled every other day, building up to a daily schedule by the end of March.

Watch your style.

3. April through September

As the weather improves, aim to start a complete weekly schedule of water training. For the first six weeks work up on speed. Do regular daily workouts of 6 miles or more, working with a stopwatch, setting high and higher objectives in terms of speed must be set. Style must be watched, and any sloppiness must be corrected.

This is a good time to get portage improved so it becomes second nature. Break up the work so that you have to leave the water, go a hundred yards downstream, and reboard.

Here is a suggested daily training schedule to follow at the end of the six-week period:

Monday: Two-mile warmup, including ten sets of 20 strokes fast sprint, 20 strokes easy. Two 1-mile sections concentrating on style, but with a sprint over the last third of a mile. One 1-mile section fast all through. A 1-mile warmdown.

Tuesday: Two-mile warmup, including ten 20/20 strokes. Ten 100-yard (meter) sprints, with a rest of 2 minutes between each one. You should be aiming to get the rest period between each sprint to about 1 minute after the first month, and to around 30 seconds as the season moves on. Take the time of each sprint. If you find your times are improving, start cutting down on your rest period. If they're getting worse, lengthen the rest period. During the rest period, just do some light paddling so that you won't get stiff. One mile smooth paddling, concentrating more on style than speed. Change the pace occasionally to check that style doesn't get sloppy.

Steady medium fast paddle for 3 miles with final third of mile at sprint. Warm down for half-mile.

Wednesday: Six-mile steady paddle with attention to style.

Thursday: Two-mile warmup, followed by sprints as for Tuesday; rest for 5 minutes, then do two half-mile sections medium fast. Steady paddle 3 miles, with sprint in last third of a mile. Warm down paddlelight half-mile.

Friday: Warmup 2 miles. Continue into a 6-mile workout broken down into two half-mile sections, each ending in a sprint; 2 miles medium fast ending with a sprint; two more half-mile sections each ending in a sprint; last 2-mile section fast. Warm down paddling easy a half-mile.

Saturday: If there's a race on Sunday, a light 2-mile warmup attending to style is all you do. This allows you to build up for the next day. If there's a race on the Saturday, then take the Friday easy, and move the schedule to start on Sunday.

Obviously, you will be flexible, but it is important to keep training hard. Running is very important, and it should be hard running, since this helps develop both heart and lungs. Don't just concentrate on running at a medium pace. Break it up with a 100-yard dash every half-mile or so. In the same way swimming is also excellent, provided it is hard swimming. While the breast stroke helps your legs and chest, the front-and back-crawl strokes and the butterfly trim those muscles most useful to the sport.

Fill out your record sheet each day, noting what you did, and if for some reason you left something out, note that, too—and why it got missed.

As far as the weights are concerned, you might like to note that endurance and stamina are best gained from using light weights, or the body's own weight, with a high number of repetitions. Strength and power come through using heavy weights with a low number of repetitions.

If you start using weights seriously, you'll most likely be advised to arrange your schedule to have a free day in between. When you begin, you can feel very stiff, and you'll need the break.

The other point to watch is that when you have established your training program, you'll probably want to change it around in order to add some variety to the work you do. This is fine, and, as far as basic exercises go, you can make up your own list. However, make sure that if you take, say, six exercises, each exercise deals with one group of muscles, so that you don't do two consecutive exercises which accomplish the same thing.

Another thought which may help: if you belong to a club, it can be useful if you all get together at exercise time. This can save expense, for example, in buying weights, since you can share them.

As far as winter training is concerned, the worst problem for water work is keeping your hands warm. British frostbiters rub the backs of their hands with grease, which helps, but it has a tendency to trickle onto your palms, which won't do.

PROGRAM B   Advanced

It is very probably that the more advanced competitor already has a schedule for training. What follows here is a synthesis of what is being used by advanced canoeists around the world.

1. October through January

   Water training will consist of long, medium-weight paddles with emphasis on style. Minimum distance is 8 miles, moving up to 15 miles (more if wanted). Should style deteriorate, take a break and start again.
   Gymnastics, weights, and running.

   Since the advanced canoeist will want to be in top condition throughout the winter, a full schedule should be adopted. A 4-mile run every other day is recommended broken into a half-mile warmup; 100-yard dash; a quarter-mile medium fast; a quarter-mile dash; a half-mile medium; 100-yard dash, and so on. Vary the distances to your own requirements. If you live near the sea, running along sand dunes is very good; running up hills is also recommended. The point about running is that it shouldn't be easy.

   On the days when you're not running, follow the schedule shown in Table B. In addition, try to fit in three swimming sessions per week. At least two days in the week should include work on the water.

2. January through March

   During this period—weather permitting—a slow change-over is made from land work to water training. Toward the end of this period, timed runs—particularly sprint distances—become important.

   Weight training is eased off slowly, but at least two sessions a week are required to maintain the strength buildup needed for the racing season. Running and swimming, should be too.

3. Racing Season

   Every effort is now needed to get water work as correct as it can be. One 6-mile run a week, broken down into sections as above, plus one day of weight training, are recommended.

   It is generally held by all advanced athletes that the best method to maintain form is to train to a high standard throughout the year, with special emphasis on training for two or three particular events. The point is that it is impossible to be in peak condition all the time.

   Three weeks before the special event(s), training is brought to perfection, ensuring the competitor that when the race arrives he or she is in top condition. In addition to the exercises suggested here, the work to be included during this polishing period should be extended running and extensive water work, with sprints of 500, 1,000, and 2,000 meters interspersed between medium and fast stretches.

   Always use a stopwatch, or a watch with a second hand, to keep a note of your progress. It is only by constant and honest monitoring of your performance that you can get to the top.

   And if you don't win?

   Here's a secret: it doesn't matter. Winning is important, but you win anyway, even though you may lose, provided you know that you did your utmost to reach perfection. You are the only person who can judge whether you did all you could—and if you did, well, is it really so important that someone's got that much more energy available? Maybe you need to make up for what you lack in brute strength in a different area—tactics. We will deal with tactics immediately following these tables.

TACTICS

It is always a useful thing to test the limits of one's body, and canoe racing over long or short distances is one excellent way to do this. Unfortunately, a great number of people all over the world have become very confused about the reasons for winning, and in places high and low, ethical considerations about the methods used in attaining victory have been nearly nonexistent.

It's worth remembering that any person who has an irrepressible urge to win is stating his insecurity. People who set out to become millionaires are saying they're scared of being poor, that they know only one thing about life—making money. People who feel they need to sabotage others for political ends are stating one thing—that they know their program isn't good enough to get them elected in a proper and honest way.

So it is not intended to discuss the ways and means you can gain a psychological edge over your competition. That is not what any game is about. What is discussed here are the legitimate ways in which you may use your mastery over the water to get yourself into the top listings.

Starts: An awful lot of very good long-distance people foul themselves up by not getting off quickly enough. As an integral part of your training, you must learn to be able to start promptly—but obviously don't jump the gun.

Whether you should attempt the lead from the beginning is a matter of much discussion. It is sometimes better to hang back half a length and let the other person pick the best route—you may be able to see more from behind and find a better line for yourself. In short events where the course is buoyed or flagged, it may be better to get out in front from the beginning.

Portage: portage becomes a factor in some long-distance events, and it is well worth going over the course ahead of time if you can in order to plan how you'll handle it. The word comes from the French *porter* (to carry), and it has to do with getting your craft out of the water and carrying it downstream to avoid some obstacle.

What is important about portage is that it gives you an opportunity to speed up. If the lead competitor takes 4 minutes to complete his portage and you can manage with 3, you've just gained a minute. So portage is worth the practice.

What you have to do is to develop a system by which you have everything stowed as you come to the shore. You can then pick up your craft, and, without anything falling out or coming adrift, you can get down to where you relaunch. This is especially true of two-person crews: in a twosome you must practice and practice portage until it is letter perfect, right down to knowing who is going to paddle which side first.

The key to good portaging is in knowing which position is most comfortable for carrying your boat, and not losing your paddle. You should memorize the course so that you know whether you will be landing at a portage on the left-or right-hand banks.

Wash-hanging: This is a technique in which you place your bow level with the cockpit of the craft ahead, so that you are riding on the other person's bow wave. Wash-hanging is allowed in the 10,000 meters up to the last 1,000 meters. It should be practiced in training, with a friend.

Unless you are racing within your own club, it is well worthwhile working as a team. Wash-hanging should be practiced so that two members of the same club can take turns in trying to catch the person ahead of them.

The placing of the bow in relation to the cockpit of the leading craft is crucial to using this technique, and a distance of about 3 feet is required. In the last 1,000 meters of the 10,000-meter event, boats are required to be 3 meters apart and with free water to paddle in.

Losing the Competition: While some paddlers are quite unscrupulous about losing an unwanted paddler by leading him astray, or onto a buoy or similar obstruction, it is quite fair to lose him in your wash.

This can be done by sprinting off at an angle and then returning to your normal course, which will leave him bobbing in your wake. This is quite legitimate, since it is your use of the water and the forces of the water which he has to solve.

If someone is wash-hanging on you, you are not being slowed down by his being there, even though you seem to be giving him a tow. The effect is mainly psychological from your point of view, and you should remember that on bends you may have an advantage even though your follower has an overlap.

In essence, tactics are decided before the race begins. You need to know who you are racing against, and what their strong and weak points are. If you have a game plan prepared, be sure to consider at what point it may need modifying in order to give you a better chance. You should always be able to judge when it is better to try to break away from the pack, and when to overtake.

Design is mentioned in detail elsewhere, but a few notes on the basic factors involved in the design of racing craft may be useful.

How fast a kayak will go is the product of its waterline length, its wetted surface area, and its hull shape. Its speed (velocity in knots) is directly proportional to the waterline length. This is true of any displacement hull. So, obviously, it would seem that waterline length ought to equal maximum permitted length overall.

But it's not quite so simple. If you have vertical bow and stern posts, how do you shake off weeds and other debris?

The wetted surface area is considered from the point of view of the crosssection. In crosssection, a semicircle gives the minimum surface area. However, such a hull shape might be very tippy indeed, so this has to be modified in some way.

Hull shape is determined in part by mathematics, in part by the rules governing design, and in part by instinct for what will or won't work. In addition, various other problems have to be solved, including the need to reduce the bow lifting when going fast, buoyancy, and maneuverability. In general, racing craft don't have to be as maneuverable as slalom kayaks, since in sprint events most things are in a nearly straight line, and a rudder is available for course correction. Racing boats tend to have a minimum of rocker—that is, the rise of the keel line from the center of the boat to the stern and bow— sufficient only to let the rudder do its work.

Downriver Races

This is long-distance racing American style in which the oldest and greatest event is still the Arkansas River Race at Salida, Colorado. The course, which is more than 25 miles long, has two difficult rapids and several other less difficult ones. The Cottonwood Creek rapid, which occurs toward the end of this event, is generally rated as the hardest rapid in the race.

Even the most beautiful streams sometimes have to be portaged. Fortunately the trend towards lighter materials in the construction of canoes helps solve this problem.

For the hunter or fisherman, lightweight canoes make the difference between a happy or harrowing day.

!arathon racers adopt the sitting position, since it's uncomfortable to stay on your knees for more than three hours at a time even with pads. This Sawyer Cruiser (nearly 18 feet long) has specially moulded seats, and is seen here on the Colorado River.

Frostbiters make plentyful use of wetsuits to keep warm. Note the coiled stern painter, ready for use if needed but kept tidily out of the way with tape.

76   CANOEING & KYAKING

Stamina is one of the keys to successful long distance racing. The other is the ability to read every ripple of water--and make it work for you.

Bowman waits momentarily for canoe to ease itself back into the water before taking the next bite with his blade.

Chapter 6

RACING: Sprints—500, 1000, & 10,000 Meters

A sprint event is like a magic drummer, beating his strange rhythmic melodies upon his drums. Each competing person employs his own range of drive to seek the winning point. In the sprint, the will to win is laid out more perfectly—in the sum of the training effort and the final suit—than in any other form of human affairs.

It was for this our Greek forebears played the Olympic Games rather than indulge in life-losing, economically busting wars. It was for this their sculptors hymned the Perfect Man, whom we remember today in that shabby wreck of *Venue de Milo*, a gorgeous, memorable work.

If this sounds contradictory in terms, well it is. Sprint racing is very much like that. You have to build up a producing power in your body so that you can sustain a high output of energy over a relatively long period of time, during which your muscles will cry: enough, enough. And yet you must go on. You will—hopefully—burst through the finishing line at a record speed, while those selfsame muscles are screaming: *halt!*

How do you go about achieving your objective?

Experience in field events over the past one hundred years indicates that dedicated training builds the winning will. The body can be developed almost endlessly, but the will to win must be trained (selfishly) alongside.

The training program sets up new habits for the body to learn. The training program also builds up basic, very basic, fitness, which is the starting point of winning technique. You cannot win unless your body is in pretty good shape and unless you can breathe freely, bringing oxygen to transform the glucose into fire within your muscular tissue. In brief, unless you are prepared to sacrifice some of your creature comforts to your winning abilities, you will not make much headway.

Depending on how much you want to win, you can make it easy or difficult for yourself. And if you feel you don't have too much natural ability, you may make it very difficult for yourself before you quit. This is something to ponder. After all, it just might be better to be a good class technician and enjoy yourself canoe camping.

Still, assuming that sprinting is where you belong, you've got to prepare an easily followed program. And the first thing you must consider is the amount of hours you are prepared to devote to this aspect of this sport. You will need to devote at least three hours a day to your new project, and very possibly more. It will depend on how high you want to go.

First, you should know something about the design of the craft you plan to race. Ultimately, you may want a boat designed especially for you in the type of international class in which you propose to sprint. You will find some hints on what is needed elsewhere in this book. And if you think you want to go into design and building, then take a look at some of the thoughts in Chapter 10, on "Maintenance & Building."

Racing vehicles are platforms for performance. Flat-water—that is, no white-water—vehicles are highly stylized vehicles. Yet despite this, they are the end result of careful design studies aimed at reducing drag and wetted area to the bare minimum. If these craft are unstable, that instability is something to be indulged in the interest of speed—and the would-be competitor takes this into his or her account.

The hull design is meant to keep the vessel moving in a nearly straight line, regardless of uneven energy distribution between left and right paddle. (We are usually more strongly balanced one way or the other—this is something we apply our technique learning to, to balance the outflow of energy more evenly. And with kayaks, in the racing class, add neat foot-driven rudders, so the paddler can spend most energy on pure propulsion.

The 500-meter event is nearly headed in the same direction as the men's 100-meter foot sprint is headed—slowly out the door. There isn't much skill involved in being able to dash 100 yards, especially if it is in a straight line. Still, it is the shortest official distance raced, and it takes world class competitors about 110 seconds (men) and 120 seconds (women) to complete. The starts are standing, and the course is properly buoyed and usually straight. Like swimmers in official events, the competitors are placed in lanes. There is also a limit of nine to a heat.

Since the depth of the water must not be less than six feet over the entire area of the course, it is easy to see that finding a place that meets this condition is difficult. This was true until the Munich Olympics, which set forth some new ideas—not least the creation of artificial courses, and moderately artificial courses. And with the impetus given to articial courses by the modification of existing streams in Europe—including two new centers now abuilding in Britain (if not completed)—it seems likely that most nations will settle for building at least a token aquasport center.

At the time of this writing, the situation is somewhat confused by the Olympic planners for the next games, who seem prepared to let the international slalom slide by in Canada in 1976.

The International Canoe Federation regulations listed in Appendix 25 gives the latest details on shape and weight and design for these international racing sprint vessels, but, briefly, they may be said to be K-1, K-2, and K-4 for kayaks, with the numbers referring to the persons on board, and C-1 and C-2 for canoes.

Many persons who think they would like to enter these sprint races frequently find that, although they have the stamina, they simply don't have the right body structure to produce the punching power needed to win on short hauls. Their bodies are capable of producing bursts of energy over a longer time span than others, but not with the intensity of those who win—and who are usually spent at the end of their distance.

This is an interesting physiological phenomenom, and may well have psychological ramifications which might be explored with interest. Still, in almost all field events, there are those who can sprint (and in track events distances up the mile might reasonably be considered sprints these days), and there are those who can outperform the sprinters over the long distance.

The key to producing maximum energy during the relatively short duration of a sprint event is to train the body to produce the necessary amount. One way which many sprinters work is—if the event for which they intend to compete is, say, 500 meters—the length they will train with for maximum performance is 600 meters. The additional 100 meters gives them a reserve of energy on which to call during the event. This extra length is mixed with a shorter length, say 300 meters to begin with, working up to 400 and eventually 450 meters, so that there is a balance worked out by the body.

This same technique can be worked out for the 1,000-meter event. Here the short distance might be 800 meters, and the longer 1,200 or even 1,500 meters. A mix is created, and during the day's training period the competitor trains more to one side than to the other. The next day's training, the emphasis is reversed. If the competitor is training full time)and full-time training is the only way to win Olympic medals against state-subsidized athletes—then the morning might be devoted to shorter sprints, with the afternoon devoted to the longer sprint. Every other day, a fast 6-to-10 mile paddle might be undertaken to help build up reserves of stamina, which while more important to the long-distance racer— who is actually using energy at a relatively high rate over the entire course—is also useful in building up the quantity of energy the sprint person can call on in need.

Some thoughts on diet are offered in the previous chapter, and may be read here too. Good, fresh food is vital; mass-produced convenience foods are out. Same goes for bread—the best is expensive, but you can always make your own.

While some trainers eschew the use of alcohol by athletes in working up training, experience over the years

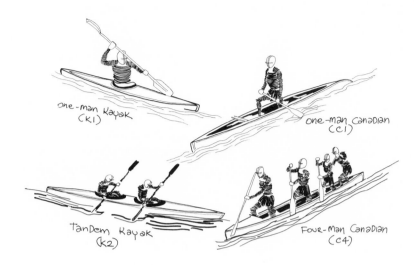

*Diagrams show racing versions of kayaks and canoes.
Clockwise from top left: K-1, C-1, C-4 and K-2.*

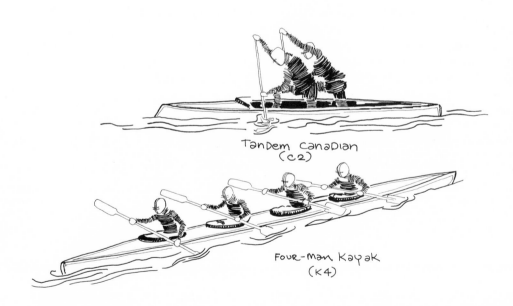

*Top, C-2; bottom K-4. This latter is sufficiently fast to tow a
water-skier.*

has shown that a glass of wine (red, preferably) with the evening meal, or a glass of a Guinness-type beer, has a useful effect in helping the digestive tract work more efficiently, as well as in helping to disperse tension at the end of the day.

Successful sprinting depends largely on the development of an efficient technique, since any energy that has to be wasted in correcting (and, of course, causing) a variation in the best possible line taken is not merely wasted of its own but represents a factor within the time problem of the event.

For persons racing kayacks, the first thing that has to be learned is that the knees are *not* braced against the hull: the legs are bent at the knees, which are held together or almost touching, with the feet holding the steering bar and the heels on the floor. In racing, you simply can't use your legs as efficiently, and a new movement has to be worked out.

This is done as follows: since the pushing hand must add to the power of the pulling stroke—and prepare for the next pulling stroke on the opposite side—the leg opposite is extended in rhythm with the push. That is, the leg on the side you are pulling is stretched forward against the footrest. A simple rhythm is set up, and you're in business.

The reason for this is that in sprinting, the stroke runs up from the hips over the chest and back to the shoulders, and the seat position is upright rather than forward, since too much forward lean will prevent the expansion of your diaphragm and thus limit your breathing. In the deep-breathing exercises you will be doing—a simple one is listed in the previous chapter—you need to aim at expension of the tissue deep down, which means that the diaphragm must learn to go down to suck the extra air in, and draw it into the upper reaches of your lungs.

These two areas are not normally used by most people, but are of exceptional importance to athletes—especially sprinters— who can make good use of this additional oxygen to spark the stored energy in their muscles.

Now let's take a closer look at a training program for sprinters.

TRAINING PROGRAM

While the schedule outlined for long-distance training in the previous chapter may be usefully followed, considerably more emphasis needs to be placed on the development of speed—and this means sustained speed, which in turn implies a relatively even flow of stored energy, especially in the 10,000-meter event. Long workouts, either running or in he gym, help, but variations are needed, not least to stop you from getting stale.

There's also the bookkeeping factor to be considered. What this means is that you should keep an accurate record of your progress, in terms of the workload you set yourself, and the increasing comfort you will feel with it. A daily check of your weight, morning pulse, and so on is up to you. But during workouts, you should aim to speed recovery from a burst of high output—say a sprint of 100 meters—to about half a minute, by which time your pulse rate should be down to about 120 beats per minute.

Another method of measuring output is to work on a system of 10, where 10 represents absolutely total maximum output. You will normally store up 10 for competition, and you will practice it rather discretely—not because you don't want to know what 10/10ths is about—but, once more, to keep you from getting stale.

Generally speaking, fairly high level workouts, at 7, 8, and 9 points, will assist in bringing you up to the 10 level. And the favored trick mentioned earlier is to work on longer distances than the event to be trained for, so that, for example, if you are training for the 1,000-meter event, you'll work on 1,500 meters at a level of say 8 or even 9. The point is that you will be building up a rather high quality of stamina which can be called on for the actual event—and, additionally, will permit you to develop a very much higher level of overall output.

Strength 10 has got to be viewed as your best possible effort. It must always, whether in training or for real, rank among one of your very best performances. It needs your will to bring it forth, since your body muscles will be screaming for a break— yet no break is possible. Finding the ability to tap into these hidden strengths in ourselves is possibly one reason why people take up athletic events.

Using the 10 system is an excellent way of measuring both effort and output, and should be used from the beginning of the warmup until you conclude the training session with a warmdown. A number of coaches have their own favorite methods of working, but if you can't afford a specialist coach at present, your warmup should work from about 1 through 5 on this scale over the first twenty minutes. A short two-minute pause then gets you working from 6 through 8. Another two-minute pause brings you from 7 through 9, and you can then decide if you want a burst of 10 before continuing with other items in your schedule.

Style is very important, and, as with distance racing, you should immediately correct when style goes awry. It means that you're either not paying sufficient attention to it, or you are overloading your "circuits," as it were. Stop, take a half-minute break, and start again. If it still isn't holding together, then take a longer break. You can usually resume working when your pulse gets down to 120 beats or less per minute (that is, 30 beats in 15 seconds.)

The importance of record-keeping cannot be stressed enough, since it is the written record which you use to keep yourself up to scratch. Obviously, you will know if you cheat and lie when you write it up, since the truth will be out in your real performance. And while you may kid others by saying, "Well, I really don't know what I'm doing wrong," you're not really fooling anyone but yourself. So be honest—it pays off in winning results—that is what you want.

A very easy way to organize your own training program is to prepare a set of file cards for a 31-day period. By working out your training ahead of time, you can easily set yourself interesting training tasks and avoid getting frustrated with too mechanical or frustrating a regimen. You can do three or four packs, depending on how much sprinting you're planning to do during the season, and how much leisure canoeing—such as inland cruising, or canoe camping—you plan to include. Obviously, if you're aiming at national and international events, you won't have quite so much time on your hands as those who are interested only in club or local events.

You can, however, lighten your task still further by preparing two or three wild cards. These you slot into the pack each month in a different place. Your wild cards might—if you're training for short sprints—give you permission to take a 10-mile training run on water, for example; a 3-mile run uphill (or through sand, if you've a beach nearby); plus a 3-mile stint on the water, practicing technique. The last might let you off with reduced training of only one hour, plus half an hour's reading about canoe design or technique, and a chance for the rest of the evening off. The point is to make it varied and interesting, not dull.

Swimming is an excellent aid to relaxing muscles and should be a part of your program at least one day a week. While it gives you the opportunity to relax those areas which might get too taut, it also allows you to exercise other muscles, so there is an overall balance to your training. Still, don't just putter around just soaking it all in—though that is good. Reckon to do some work in the water, too—it's good for developing your heart muscles. Depending on the length of the pool, include a couple of hundred yards of fast crawl—and work at it—and 100 yards of butterfly and breast stroke (each) at some pace. Also do the backstrokes, good for stretching those muscles; the back breast is also excellent for opening up the lungs. Finish it all off with a pleasantly warm shower and a brisk 30-second cold one (to

begin with) at the end. You should feel slightly but pleasantly used after a session like this.

Other varieties on the swimming theme are water games. If you've friends who enjoy water polo, this too can be used as part of your exercise program in the water. Since it requires spurts of energy to get to the ball first—and to intercept passes—it's useful for your sprint training.

Skiing in winter is also recommended as part of your fitness program. Many outdoor enthusiasts who are not interested in competition regularly ski in winter and paddle during summer months. Cross-country skiiing, which has only recently begun to become popular in this country, actually makes a lot more sense than the increasingly highly priced runs at various centers. Depending on how outdoors your own lifestyle is, you might like to consider ski camping, which is one of the most pleasurable of all sports if you kit up for it correctly. You don't have to be cold in the snow, and you can sleep very comfortably in a proper tent with the right equipment during the winter months. But proper equipping is vital.

The most important parts are knowing how to ski—though jogging through the snow is good exercise—and knowing how to camp outdoors in winter.

Still, even if winter camping does not appeal, consider cross-country skiing, which you can map out easily over a weekend. In the late afternoon you descend upon the hostelry of your choice, for food and company. Next day you set forth again. Don't forget to include a large-scale map of the area (at least 1 inch to the mile, and better more than an inch to the mile) plus a wrist compass. Land looks different when it is all covered with snow, and people who aren't used to it and who have lived by the numbers most of their days (88th Avenue, 51st Street, etc.) sometimes find it hard to work out nature's own geography.

From a training point of view, the reason cross-country skiing is so much better than just slithering down slopes is that it is an up-hill-down-dale sort of sport. You get variety and you get to use a lot of different muscles, especially uphill—which you wouldn't get if you just took a lift.

And if you are worried about falling down, cross-country skiing is best done—like canoeing—with a minimum of three persons. Actually, some of today's more modern bindings are almost foolproof in releasing you, should you do something that a few years ago might have cracked your leg. That's a further point for you to check out.

Soccer and basketball are both good games to play for training, as is squash. Unfortunately, it's difficult to find squash courts, which seem to have been preserved for the rich in this country. Handball and fives are also fairly good, though not as good as squash since they tend to over-develop your hands. Tennis is rather slow, by comparision, and you'll use more energy and build more stamina with the others.

As mentioned previously, weight training has become more and more important as part of training national and international athletes. Check with your local weight-training establishment and explain to the instructor why you want to do this type of work.

One of the best ways to train for immediate endurance, as is needed for high output over relatively short distances, is to do pressups (pushups) and hops. If your breathing is good but your arms are screaming *stop* toward the end of the sprint, these exercises are right for you. Still, group training has a number of advantages, not least in the element of competition that is involved. If you prefer to work alone, then time yourself as you do your exercises. For example, how many well-controlled pushups can you do in one minute—see whether you can better it by a factor of .5 to begin with.

Preparing for Competition

Many excellent would-be competitors lose their chances in events by not making a thorough preparation for an event. This goes for longer-distance events, too. For, to be able to win, you have to have the right vehicle; whether you are sprinting or running downriver work, you need the appropriate boat.

There are several points to be considered, the first of which is the depth of the water on which the event is to be held. The size of the river and its average flow rate for the time of the year are next. If there are curves, how many, whether there are any hazards within them, and how steeply they bend should also be included in mapping out the event. Are there many rapids? If so, how severe? And how much of the course do they make up? Any portaging required? (Portaging in an event can make or break you, depending on how well you've mastered it.)

If you have an opportunity to inspect the site other than from a map, you should note where and how many places will demand maneuverability on your part, and the overall size and pattern of the waves that will be encountered.

For several years now, European competitors in down-river events have usually had two (and sometimes three) different boats for competition. Usually one would be a rather deep V-profile-shaped hull for deeper water, and a semi-V or even flattish hull for shallower routes. Usually, it becomes a toss-up which will win, unless you are prepared to measure very carefully what is really there. Indeed, sometimes it is well worth walking the part of the route that poses queries, or paddling it a couple of times.

So, knowing the water and having the appropriate machine for the event are important. Likewise, careful preplanning so that on the day of the event you don't have to worry about where eerything is.

To save time, make up a checklist well in advance of what you're going to need. Boat and paddle(s) should be checked out ahead of time, and be in good shape. Always have something to use as backup in case of problems, or have some method of solving a potential problem. Nothing is worse than having to retire because of some sort of breakdown—steering went crazy, thigh supports broke. Keep spares so that if—an hour before you're due to go—something should come adrift, you have at least a sporting chance to put it right beforehand.

Warming up and resting the night before are both important. Change into your racing gear with time to spare, and start a warmup. There are two schools of thought. One is to warm up for about 20 minutes about two hours before the event, then do a 10/10ths version of the event to be raced plus 250 meters (except for the 10,000 meter where procedure is different), and then jog around in a track suit for a little before taking a short nap. The other is to warm up immediately prior to the event for about half an hour and then go straight to the line.

For longer events it makes more sense to modify the first version, omitting the 10/10th but substituting a reasonable sprint of, say 1,500 meters. Some exercises can be included in with a little jogging.

Don't forget to have spare clothes, warm towels, etc., at the finish.

The 10,000-meter sprint is an interesting event in that you may employ the technique of wash-hanging (described in Chapter 5. It may not be employed during the last 1,000 meters of an event. Tactically, how you should paddle such an event will depend on who is taking part and what the course is like. You may decide to stay with the leaders—or just behind—or you may decide to go for broke and try to lose your competition and stay out ahead. The danger of this latter course is that you can get too clever and find the race snatched from your grasp in the last 100 meters or so.

The best procedure is to work out for yourself what you can physically do. Can you keep up a constant-level speed all the way through, and then produce a burst of speed over the last 2,000 meters or so? The danger is that you may find yourself blocked if you do. Can you find additional energy to be the hare, and yet produce some more at the end of the event?

Chapter 7

INLAND CRUISING

Until the advent of World War II several railroad companies used to offer off-weekend specials to canoeists. Very often, canoeists could put in to an interesting stretch of water from the railroad's land in the wilderness, and make their way down to a selected village to overnight in peoples' homes. The next day, a similar stretch would be negotiated either downriver or upstream—with the help of the steamer.

That's almost all gone these days, but one wisp of hope was held in the air quite recently when a group of concerned East Coast canoeists banded together with a railroad company to produce a day on the water in the Lehigh Gorge. More than five hundred boats took part, and there was standing room only on the train.

The point of the exercise—in the words of Karl Brandt, who helped organize it—was to get together a group with different interests and to show how they could all work together to preserve a national resource. Consequently, the train carried backpackers, hikers, canoeists (and kayak fans), train buffs—the engine and stock were early 1900s—and some people from government agencies, who felt sufficiently at ease to find out what the people were doing.

As rivers go, and far too many of them have gone, the Lehigh is relatively clean. Only acid water seepage from the mines pollutes it, plus a limited amount of sewage from builders who don't know any better. The U.S. Army Corps of Engineers is working on the seepage problem, and the Commonwealth of Pennsylvania is attempting to get fishes to learn to survive the vaguely hostile environment.

With the turnaround in the way our economy works, there is going to be more and more leisure time. If the people are to enjoy that leisure, the outdoors is going to be turned to more and more. The clearing and cleaning of canoe routes and the setting up of decent campsites at put-in—pull-out points will be the work of several generations if the waterways of the nation are to be turned back to the people. We can have a complete water system encompassing the country if we're prepared to work for it.

And we all ought to aim at working for such a system since, if the present state of rivers and streams continues unchecked, there will be an ecological disaster in the near future. We permit factories, utilities, and towns to regard any moving body of water as a dumping ground for trash and effluence. This indiscriminate dumping effectively destroys the ecological balance of nature, setting off a chain reaction which destroys countless billions of organisms—and one day may kill us, too. Water is the lifeblood of the planet, and we, and all other creatures, depend on it.

One of the ways each person can help is by going and finding a river and learning about it. Most rivers in most states offer good recreation except those which have come to stink of death with fallout from industry. But the marginally affected—those which could be cleaned by community action—are easier to work with. The first thing that must be done is to learn the river itself. And, in the long term, it is this that inland cruising is all about.

For day touring, you may want to consider a less specialist vehicle than your slalom or racing canoe. The folding-boat people produce just the equipment, with relatively large cockpits—they do have spray decks for working rapids—and room for two or even three persons.

To work a section of river, one person is going to have to drive the car. In families, a routine can be worked out so that the person who drives the first leg gets to paddle the second. With two families, it's even easier, and with small groups of people, it's easier still.

Camping while touring is not essential, since hostelries can usually be found if one looks hard enough. In Europe, many rivers now have chains of canoe stations where people can overnight in comfort. And in Britain, one can rely on the village pub for a bed at night. Still, camping does bring a greater freedom to maneuver, and those interested should read Chapter 8, "Canoe Camping."

If you think you'd like to try your hand at touring, first contact the tourism department of your own state and any adjacent states that might be interesting. You can also try the Department of Conservation of even the Chamber of Commerce.

Other organizations which include canoeing in their programs are the Sierra Club; the Appalachian Mountain Club; the American Youth Hostels; the American Red Cross; the Prairie Club; and the Scouting organization, including Boy, Girl, and Explorer Scouts. American Whitewater Association affiliates—listed in Appendix 1—may also be able to help you by providing local information.

If you're not completely sure of your own abilities, another way to begin is to try out a day (or a week) with any of the several wilderness groups which run expeditions. Another way to get on the water—if you don't yet own your own canoe—is to check out a nearby rental agency. For the most part, these agencies provide a useful service and keep their equipment in reasonable condition. (If you should be gypped, report the firm to the local Better Business Bureau, local Chamber of Commerce, and at the state level: the only way we consumers can improve the ethics of shoddy business people is where it hurts—at their self-policing level, at the government regulatory level, and at the level of those who run for office. These people are our servants and not our masters, and we ought to remember that. If an elected official seems complacent about our needs and interested only in the requirements of the corporations that fund his campaign, he can be gotten off the ticket with the help of your not giving him the vote. Ideally, to make sure we get rid of corrupt representatives, we need to put on our slates people who care about people.)

Yet another way is to take a refresher course at one of the growing numbers of schools around the country. Most offer instruction at beginner, intermediate, and expert levels. And there are also training camps where you can train seriously with some of the best paddlers in the world. One such is the Madawaska Kanu Camp just outside Toronto, Canada.

The key to comfortable touring is to know what you're going to be doing ahead of time: where you'll put in and where you'll pull out; whether you'll have to portage any part of the route; whether there are any rapids you should check. If you want to enjoy yourself, *don't* get yourself on a river that's beyond your ability. And remember that a river you happily paddled down in the fall can become a raging demon when the snows melt off the peaks in spring.

To begin with, don't try to set any distance records. A 6-mile paddle is quite enough to break you in slowly. If you find you can hack that easily, make it 10 miles the next time. Long day trips of more than 20 miles are for experienced paddlers who've been on the water for a while.

Quite apart from the energy you'll use in guiding your craft downriver, you use energy keeping alert and reading the water, and if the sun is out, you'll tire from the dazzle off the water. Take and use a good sunscreen if you're not used to the rays, and you'll be fine.

Although several of the Great Lakes have been polluted, there are countless others scattered around the country where you can enjoy flat-water paddling. It is here that the open canoe comes into its own, such as Old Town's Carleton Voyageur--a deep-hulled 17-footer, designed for extended trips with heavy loads. The canoe itself is made of a reinforced fiberglass-balsa sandwich hull with no keel. There's positive foam flotation beneath the decks should you need it, but this canoe is very hard to tip. The same company—which has been making canoes for nearly one hundred years—also produces a useful white-water canoe with a loading hatch. The Berrigan, at 16 feet in length, conforms to ICF regulations for wild-water and slalom competition, yet makes an excellent touring canoe and has successfully cruised as far north as Ross River in Yukon Territory. The Voyageur is just short of 90 pounds, while the Berrigan weighs in at 65 pounds.

Which brings us to another point: How big a canoe

The Colorado is not all a hustly bustly river. Sometimes its quite placid.

*Kids dig canoeing too. These two lads seem not merely
proficient--note the correct bow stroke--but are correctly
fitted out with personal buoyancy aids.*

*This lady should be wearing a life-jacket, or maybe its inside
her kayak.*

Canoeing is for lovers--for almost anyone who can enjoy an outdoors environment.

The bow person takes a break while the stern person lets the river do most of the work.

Water is a living, moving thing . . .

Canoe jousting is just another way of having fun with canoes.

As long distance transport, canoes are hard to beat. Note the spray deck on this freight canoe.

The kayakist is just about to make a normal stroke on starboard side. The port blade is still "feathered" as it comes forward.

Two kayakists jockey for position for the path ahead.

should you buy? The standard answer is: the biggest you can lift gracefully. A portage trolley, therefore, makes a lot of sense. The collapsible ones weigh only a few pounds and stow conveniently, even under a covered deck. They may be difficult to find, since few stockists know about them, but keep trying.

If you're using a car to get to and from the water, you'll need to get a carrying rack for your canoe(s). The simplest carrier will cost around $20 and can carry two or three canoes, if an on-edge kayak rack is fitted. A better carrier, with longer cross arms, costs about $10 more, worth it since it is rather easier to load. Although most carriers come with straps, additional shock cord straps with metal hooks at each end should be bought for additional security. You can usually find these at better canoe stores, or at ship's chandlers.

You will also need a spare paddle (paddles for kayak) and life vests for you and the crew. The Coast Guard regulations stipulate that an approved personal safety device must be carried for each person on board. This can actually be a seat cushion, since the wearing of a device is not mandatory. Actually, you can get three flotation cushions for the price of the least expensive vest, but a racing vest makes sense if you're going to be serious about your canoeing and cruising. So spend some money on your safety.

If built-in flotation is not provided, flotation bags should also be added to your list. You can get specially shaped bags which are lightweight and which you just blow up. Flotation means that you don't need to worry about your craft going to the bottom with all your gear if you should have a spill. Waterproof cargo bags that can also double as flotation bags make additional sense. They're less than $20 for the biggest (60 x 28 inches) and weigh less than 2 pounds. They come with a patented mechanical and foolproof closure device.

Inland cruising includes things like picnic outings, which—depending on your personal taste—can range from the luxurious to the outrageous. Because you are out only for the day, you can afford to take things that a canoe camper could only dream about. Not least is a cold chest. You won't be portaging, or not very far, and you are only a few hours out of civilization, so be civilized.

You can create the French painter's dream—a picnic with champagne and linen on a river bank. Good food, and why not smoked salmon or pate de fois gras? Or *quiche lorraine*? Or cold roast beef with horseradish sauce? Trout in aspic? You can feast deliciously. And if you fear for rain, well, what is easier than to include a dining fly in your gear so that you can be comfortable?

And being comfortable in the great outdoors is one of the great things about inland cruising—going places, seeing new things and new scenery, and being comfortable with it all by not depriving yourself of creature comforts for too long. And learning too, that the outdoors is a habitable place that you can get to know and enjoy for its own sake. And being comfortable. Being without much pain.

There's a new music to the wind, not the dull, angry drone of a concrete corner. There's incense in the air—once you shake the soot out of your nostrils. And the birds sing with pleasure, instead of coughing into your consciousness. The colors are what you make of them—if you can.

The water itself provides a new sound as it works its way back in the cycle from sea to cloud to mountain peak to sea. You can share with waterrat and muskrat and beaver just why there's nothing quite like messing around in boats. The water itself will tell you why, whispering on rills, insisting through gorges, and shooting you down in all directions until you really understand in wild water. Haystacks—approach with caution. Though they may move with the tranquillity of a field of corn, wavering uncertainly under your very eye, they represent nature imitating nature.

Haystacks are a power trip: the irresistible force meeting the immovable object. The corn seed ripening and making new corn. The earth insisting that the water move out of its way, and slowly, slowly, suffering the result, the wearing away of itself, the total humbling of rooted earth, in rock. "There is no Rock," said the prophet a long time ago. The water helps you understand that. A cosmic yet earthly baptism, perhaps?

Help yourself to the wilderness and come back into civilization renewed and refreshed. Get in touch with your being again. You don't need to pack guns and snake boots. The only person out there who'll hurt you is yourself. Shed your fear when you get into your car at the start of the journey. Leave it behind. It'll keep until you return.

Here is a new dimension to which you belong. It is, after all, your heritage. It is your planet—little spaceship earth if you want to be romantic. But it is yours as it is ours. So use it and understand it and preserve it and—if need be—help in its upkeep. Because it seems like the only one we've got. Moon: no atmosphere, and it will take ages to create one even in domes. Mars: slight, atmosphere but essentially the same thing applies again. What's wrong with here apart from ourselves?

So this also tells you a little of what inland cruising can be about if you choose.

What type of craft?

You are going to be only for a day or so and want to be

mobile so you can go two ways. You can take a spacious canoe (or two) if you get the larger carrier. And take almost everything with you—bar the kitchen sink. The only work you have to do is to load and unload if you plan your route properly. The spacious canoe is ideal for lake canoeing, especially where there are islands.

The more "sportif" might opt for a gaggle of slalom kayaks. You can fit four on that big car rack with the vertical on-edge rack. A party of four to about a dozen is ideal, since everyone can be together yet enjoy what they want to do. A truly nice way to spend a day with friends.

And with slalom kayaks, you can enjoy fiestier waters, which is fun once you've perfected your Eskimo roll. And that's important if you're taking to kayaks. It makes you safe at all times. You can afford to shrug off a capsize, like an airplane pilot who knows what to do in a stall or a spin, how to get out of one, and how to avoid one. Obviously, you don't want to keep tipping over all the time, but it's nice to know that should you happen to do it, you can get out of it without harming yourself or your gear. So read it up. It's explained here in Chapter 3, "Advanced Technique"; learn to do it.

Inland cruising also means fishing, and even hunting. But don't fish or hunt unless you truly plan to eat what you kill. Don't be Cainlike, mounting your trophies on your living-room wall when the food should be cooked in the kitchen. There's no need for that. Don't abuse this other life; it isn't necessary. Fish and meat we can eat, but we don't have to. And if we elect to hunt it ourselves, we should respect the life we take. There simply is no other way. And—I suspect—it is because we do not understand this side of things that we give ourselves such items as heart disease and cancer. The one in recognition of going against another bit of life, the other, a desperate attempt at the cellular level to replace that which we have chosen for food.

If you are going to take life, give thanks for it, and kill it with your hands so that you can feel that fear. It will be your own fear when you too must die. And it may be the fear of fear that will kill you, not anything else. So, be bold, and see that what you kill is put to good use, since you will not be able to justify your action otherwise. Why else do you suppose the saying has it that a man is what he eats?

If you like fishing, why not harmonize your hobby with some eating? Did you ever try trout cooked Indian fashion over charcoal? The technique is to cook the fish in the old way. Cut from the back and remove the backbone so that the belly holds the sides together. Using skewers or sticks (one either side X three), provide support for your fish. Next take an extra long stick and thread it through the skewers—you may have to put the long stick in first, depending

on its width. It should extend at both ends from the fish since you are going to be cooking it over charcoal and you want the fish baked all over.

If you are cooking over an open fire, you can either cook near-vertically with one end of the stick in the center of the flames, or you can balance the fish from a stone grate. (If you are using a stove—which hopefully you will be—it can simply be placed on the grill and flipped over every so often until cooked.) The flame should be very low, and you can squeeze lemon over it to baste it. A touch of butter or oil on the surface before you start makes a real treat, and for a feast, sprinkle both sides with garlic powder and chopped fennel leaf. Delicious!

Before you do open-fire cooking, please check out the notes on fires in Chapter 8, "Canoe Camping." More wooded areas are burned down through ignorance of matches and fires generally than through any natural agent. Thoughtless, careless people cause fires. Almost no one else does. Also, take a small extinguisher with you. They don't cost much, and they weigh about a pound.

Musical instruments don't normally do too well near water, but with the advent of modern materials there are a number of things you can take with you to make music in a pastoral setting. For a start, forget guitars and violins. They warp.

But plastic recorders can provide accompaniment, as can modern autoharps which use a plastic base. Or simply use your voices. There are innumerable songs that fit into these surroundings. Better yet, make up your own. Start with a kazoo, graduate to a harmonica, and who knows what you'll achieve. But study closely the harmonies of the outdoors when you begin—and don't leave beer cans lying around, nor the debris of plinking specialists. It can be recycled.

Snakes?

Yes, there are snakes, but they'll give you warning. The North American continent's own snake—the rattler—gives you plenty of warning. Pretend you're crossing a street: stop, look, and listen. See where it is and what the rattler is complaining about. The message is: *don't come closer—I'm nervous—and when I'm nervous I don't know what I can do but I usually bite, and it's fatal (or so I like to believe.)*

If you can't tune in to snakes, take a snakebite kit and read the instructions. Come to think of it, take a snakebit kit anyway for the first few times. You don't need the karma.

There are no true water snakes. The water moccasin likes water but has to swim with his head out of water: he won't bother you if you're swimming where he is. You have to go to South America for those, and discover the *creeping vines,* as they call the anaconda water boas down there. And it is highly unusual for them to attack a canoe since it is almost their size. Except for whale sharks, most amphibians could care less about mankind. Whale sharks are the missionaries and the Moslems of the seas.

WATER AND SURVIVAL

It's highly unlikely that you'll get stuck in an unpleasant place when inland touring. Still, if you're nervous you could pack a small survival kit. You'll need a small plastic tent (for shelter overnight) and a space blanket. Plus something which contains water. Water you need, but food you can do without, certainly for the couple of days or so that it may take you to get out.

You might also pack some waterproof matches, and even some of those instant fire tablets that enable you to burn green wood for smoke signals.

But read the chapter on camping before you decide. You may just prefer to do the whole number, once you've put your foot into the water a few times. Because it is so great.

And is easily done.

But if you are really worried, check out the wilderness section of *The Whole Earth Catalogue.* There are some excellent listings there.

Inland cruising is the first step to learning the wilderness with a canoe. And it can be a delightful new experience. Listed in the appendices are canoe associations and so on that you may want to get in touch with for more information. Member canoe clubs who belong to the International Canoe Federation can also be found, so if you think you would like to do some canoeing abroad you have someone to write to. Like the earlier *voyageurs,* canoe people really do help each other out.

Most states are becoming quite responsive to tourist-type requests. The Army Corps of Engineers also can provide river and lake information. They make very good maps too, as does the Coast and Geodetic Survey, though prices have rocketed during recent years.

Chapter 8
CANOE CAMPING

Sport and recreation are among the great attractions that canoeing has to offer, but cruising is one of the greater appeals of this water sport. Having mastered your technique, the canoe or kayak can become an important part of your own personal plan to venture deep into the interiors of continents with friends or as part of a wilderness team.

The continental United States is still one of the lesser explored land masses of the world. And while Lewis and Clark guided their rough craft over the Missouri, to cross the Continental Divide and paddle merrily down the Columbia River to the Pacific Ocean, there are more modest adventures to be had. It is here, too, that the folding boat comes into its own, since it can be packed up on the back of a motorbike, carted along on a trailer behind a regular ten-speed, or even stowed neatly in the rear of a light airplane.

Folbots have been finding their ways deep into the South American bush for years now. The Hans Klepper Corporation's (founded in 1909 and still going strong) Aerius models venture deep into Africa, and Amerimpex's folding boats' ruggedness made them the choice for the Cherbourg raid during World War II.

Canoe camping, as this continent's Indian forebears discovered centuries ago, is highly practical living as well as fun. In a canoe you can carry all the equipment you'd normally take on a backpacking trip, plus the luxury items you'd prefer for an extended tour. By following waterways, you have a more direct route into the hinterland, a fact attested to in the history of our colonization of this great land. Until the advent of the locomotive (and, it should be admitted, the Colt .34 six-shooter), almost all advances were made by water.

Camping goes hand-in-glove with canoeing because you can reach places no one else can. And even allowing for portaging on the higher reaches of rivers, you can still carry an awful lot more gear than when hiking. Obviously, you'll draw the line somewhere, but unlike a backpacker, you don't need to limit your load to one-fifth, or at most one-quarter, of your own body weight. You can afford to be generous.

Where to begin? With your gear.

The years since World War II have seen a real development in camping equipment. New materials and a desire to cater to creature comforts have made camping a thoroughly pleasant undertaking. Much of the impetus has come from motorized camping, which has led to lightweight picnic tables and chairs, plus hibachi-style cooking. White hunters popularized by Hemingway long ago decided it was okay to be sybaritic in the bush, and, if wearing a tuxedo for

This Cessna floatplane will carry a canoe on one of its two floats, enabling wilderness people to make their way back to civilization on water. Lightplanes and canoes go well together. Even wheelplanes can carry folding canoes.

A loaf of bread, a jug of wine. . .and Thou beside me in the wilderness.

Awesome is perhaps the most useful word to describe the mystery of a highland canyon, where over the ages ice and water have driven away their passage through the rock.

A small clearing on a river's edge makes a fine place for putting in. Canoeists generally share their lore amongst each other.

The end of a long day and the club heads for home. Note the canoes have kept to the outside bend of the river.

dinner is no longer the fashion, you can still enjoy a hot bath or shower if you go on safari.

But more seriously, what are *you* going to need?

To begin with, you'll need some warm clothing, water and food, cooking gear, shelter and something to sleep on and in, and a few basic tools. Finally, you will need something to put all these things in. Depending on how long your trip is, you'll draw the line between necessity and luxury somewhere about the middle.

First of all, clothes. At least one complete change of clothes should be carried, preferably in a properly made waterproof bag so they can't get wet. Extra socks and underwear make sensible additions. A sweater, lightweight windproof jacket, shorts, and swimming gear complete the minimum. You may want to add a sweatsuit, which can double as pajamas at night in cooler areas.

Some sort of rain gear is also important, since the ability to stay dry in the rain is a key to enjoying the trip. The Bukflex rainwear developed by Peter Storm of Scotland some years back is still the best—but also the most expensive. This lightweight nylon gear is exceptionally close-ly woven, so that it is completely waterproof, but the weave also permits the garment to breathe, so there's no condensation inside. Waterproof suits used by cyclists are also quite good, though they're not as good as Bukflex. Camp Trails' two-piece parka solves the problem by fitting a breathable yoke piece which works quite well.

What to wear on your feet is a decision you'll have to make, but take an extra pair of dry sneakers if nothing else. While deck boots may seem somewhat inappropriate in a kayak or canoe, they're good for wandering around a wet environment; it can be wet on land, too. Or you could choose the waterproof version of the lightweight hunter's boot, of which several are made at reasonable prices. Most people develop their own favorites.

Some sort of headgear makes sense, and not just to keep the rain off your head. The sun comes beaming at you, and to begin with, until you develop your eyes and skin, may prove a little too warm. Most useful is one of those hats that can be bent into any shape, and will re-form, a soft and squashy hat. For rain, many use sou'westers, which serve well on more lordly yachts but still seem at home in small craft. Sou'westers keep the rain from trickling down your neck. (As an aside, a small hand or face towel, wrapped around the back of your neck in wet weather, keeps out most of the damp.)

Keeping your gear dry is the name of the game for enjoyable canoe camping. And this means having several properly made waterproof bags. The rule of thumb here is that anything which can be spoiled or damaged by water must be stowed in one of these bags. And this is especially so for your change of clothes, bedding, and so forth—not forgetting perishable food. If you are using a traditional-type canoe, smaller bags are easier to stow. Folding boats and molded canoes and kayaks are more easily stowed using only a few bags. If you can manage it, use only two—one fore and one aft of you. Also make sure that these can be kept secure, so they don't disappear in the event of a capsize. This is quite easy in a regular canoe, since you can tie bags to the thwarts. In monocoque structures you may have to make up a special fitting.

Waterproof bags can be bought, and you should see that they are about a foot longer (taller) than the gear they hold. If you are able to use a sewing machine, it is quite easy to make your own, and the advantage is obvious in that you can make them the correct size for your own gear. Canvas or poplin are obvious materials and can be waterproofed after they've been made if you can't find tent material already proofed. Canvas, thinly backed with rubber or vinyl, or backed nylon or acrylic can be made up. With all these materials, you will need to waterproof the seams on both sides with waterproof tape. See diagram for how to make a bag and how to fasten it.

Under the heading of clothes we might also include toiletry articles. Cleanliness, it is said, is the next thing to godliness, and this is particularly true when camping out. Being clean is pleasant and, after a warm day sets you up to relax in the evening, is a real comfort. A small canvas washbasin can be included, to be used with a second one for washing up pans. This is a lot more pleasant than using a kitchen pot. Hot water can be prepared—and males who shave don't need to martyr themselves with cold water, or by putting themselves through the itchy first few days of a beard. (If you want a beard for the trip, start about ten days before you leave.)

A sponge—or that washcloth for rainy weather—can provide the means for taking a stand-up bath, which is very pleasant in the open air. Soap can be a problem, even in a waterproof container. Some canoe campers therefore prefer that very stimulating liquid soap which can be used as shampoo, as toothpaste, and in about fourteen other different ways. It smells of peppermint, and leaves you feeling nice and cool. If you go for regular soap, pamper yourself a bit and buy something luxurious. The scent will be accentuated by the out-of-doors and by the fresh air in your nostrils.

Some sort of mirror—preferably metal, you don't need shards of glass around or seven years' bad luck—is handy, though the metal underside of a Hoffritz razor box works pretty well. Don't forget a toothbrush, and some toothpaste, if you can't get used to the taste of liquid soap.

You'll also want toilet paper—and keep it dry. In a pinch, you can use regular facial tissue, but why not spoil yourself? Only problem with regular soft rolls is that they take up space. Still, carefully packed, they can fill up odd spaces.

Before going on to food and cooking gear, let's take a look at what you'll be using for shelter.

It is totally false economy to skimp on camping gear. You should always try to buy the best you can afford, and you should shop around for stores that offer discounts. None of the tourist organizations ever talks about mosquitos, sand flies, or rain, yet bugs and rain occur throughout most of the world. Assume, then, that on a ten-day trip you'll have at least one day of nearly solid rain, during which time you stay in your tent. If you have more, I'm sorry. I didn't program it that way for you.

Now your tent. Get something that's sufficiently roomy to move around in. It needn't be large, but it ought to have at least decent sitting headroom. It should also have some sort of storm entrance so that cooking can be done out of the rain. Finally, it should have a sewn-in ground sheet.

If you are not too tall, you may be able to find a reasonably lightweight tent which can give you headroom. For people over about five ten, this could be a problem. But it needn't be. There are several pyramidically shaped tents that can give standing headroom of about six feet at their center. Usually this doesn't give you more than two or three paces back and forth to pace around, but it is a help. And there is nothing more frustrating than having to remain holed up in a low mountain tent on a rainy day. A secondary consideration is that if you have a tent with headroom and want to cook inside because of rain, it will allow you to prepare a banquet. But without much headroom, you'll have to cook on your stomach—which is rather difficult, to say the least.

A tent is a major investment, and considerable thought should be given to its selection. And before deciding on shape, you might just as well decide on the fabric it is made of. Your worst enemies are fire—so a fire-retardant fabric is useful—guy ropes that shrink in the rain and take a long time to erect; and, in the case of organic (canvas, cotton poplin, etc.) fabric tents, mildew.

Our word *canvas* comes from Late Latin *canabaceus*, meaning cloth woven from hemp, or cannabis. Modern canvas is made from cotton, and a good clue as to whether you are getting value for your money is to check how many

ounces of material per square yard are being used. This information will also give you a clue as to its weight. The second item to inspect is the thread count of the material, since the more closely it is woven, the better it will resist wind and rain and wear. At present, four types of cotton fabric predominate in the making of tents, ranging from Army duck, the heaviest weight, through drill, poplin, and "tent" or single-filled duck, the lightest. In terms of value for money, poplin—which is lighter in weight but has a high thread count—is usually the best buy. And of poplin, the combed poplin—which uses only the long fibers of cotton—is the best, though expensive. In the better tents of combed poplin, a 6½-ounce variety will normally have a thread count of better than 200 threads per square inch.

Perhaps cotton's biggest drawback is its price, since there is a world shortage, and the same material used in a modern tent can earn considerably more for a manufacturer if used for other products. One point to remember about cotton is that, in untreated form, it will shrink. Check that the tent has been treated with a water-repellent finish, and when you get your new one, set it up in the yard and spray it a number of times with water, letting it dry before you soak it again. Any leaks that occur can be treated with wax if they do not cure themselves as the fibers swell up.

Since nylon first made its appearance some thirty years ago it has found acceptance in almost everything from parachutes to rope. Lightweight and strong, it has found increasing acceptance with campers, not merely for tents, but for sleeping bags and clothing. The nylons used for tents are either ripstop or taffeta.

There are two drawbacks to using nylon. First, being a synthetic material, it won't absorb water. Consequently, it needs to be treated to make it waterproof. Depending on how it is treated, you can have a problem with condensation in bad weather. Or you may need to use a fly over the top of it. Secondly, sunlight tends to attack the molecular structure of nylon, and extended use ultimately weakens the fabric. This takes quite a long time to happen, but it is a point worth bearing in mind. Nylon's great advantage is the weight reduction you gain through using it.

Plastic tents which are inexpensive are quite useful for emergency use. If you decide to make a trip inland from a river, one of these may be useful for getting some sleep if you are delayed. But while they are light in weight and could make the difference between being able to sleep in some shelter rather than spending a miserable night, their big problem is that they puncture and tear rather easily. They are certainly useful if you need to put a visitor up overnight, but for long-term use, they are not so good, especially in view of their marginal headroom.

As far as size is concerned, if you are going solo, take a two-person tent; if two of you, a three-person tent. A minimum of 7 x 7 feet provides room for two, while 8 x 10 feet will provide comfort for three in a cabin-type tent. The Boy Scouts of America, which is considerably well informed on the realities of wilderness camping, suggests 30 square feet of floor space per Scout, and recommends standing headroom to let you get dressed and undressed. This means a minimum of 6 feet of headroom for most of us.

Don't forget the sewn-in waterproof floor. The bathtub type, where the floor section comes up a few inches around the sides, is best.

Your tent should be suitable for the area you are intending to visit. A good all-around roadside tent is the Thermos Poptent, which, while it doesn't meet the requirements of headroom, is very easily put up without ropes, poles, or guys. The two-person version is cheaper and lighter ab about 13 pounds. It is worth shopping around for, since prices vary from place to place.

If you're still affiliated with the Scouting movement, you will know that several excellent tents are made. These used to be obtainable with a sewn-in floor for an additional sum, but the practice seems to have been discontinued. This means using a sod cloth for a ground sheet.

The Stephenson Warmlite is a two-to-three person backpacking and mountain tent designed by an aerodynamicist. It is super-lightweight with sitting headroom and is well designed. Using tapered hoops, Jack Stephenson obtains considerably greater headroom than in conventional A-frame-type tents. The basic model costs around $150 and up.

Another excellent limited-production tent is produced by Bishop's Ultimate. This company produces tents for winter camping, and the four-person tent is truly excellent when used by two. Using an exterior frame with a pyramidical shape, there's more than enough room for a rainy day, or even a rainy week. The price is high—$200 plus.

Unfortunately, not nearly enough has been done in the design of modern tents, and the arena is open to anyone who can come up with an inexpensive and yet comfortable and lightweight creation.

In the meantime, several mail-order companies continue to offer good value. And the magazine CONSUMER GUIDE publishes a review of "Camping and Backpacking Equipment," which is a good place to get your thinking started.

Sleeping gear is the next item for you to consider, since getting a decent night's sleep sets you up to enjoy the day ahead. Several excellent imports are now available from Japan (including backpacks and tents) and, if not widely available at present, are worth looking out for. In sleeping bags, be sure to get a bag that will keep you warm enough. As with your tent, buy the best you can afford. And seriously consider the possibility of using an air mattress. This makes for real outdoors sleeping comfort and is much easier to stow than foam. Camp beds are a bit heavy to include, and an air mattress is possibly more comfortable.

An additional item to seriously consider including in your sleeping gear should be one of those Space Rescue blankets. It can be part of your survival kit, and is a wonderful lightweight means of keeping warm.

Sleeping bags keep you warm by retaining your own body heat—operating on the same principle as the Space blanket, by the way. The better the insulation, the warmer you will be. Down, an organic compound made from duck and goose feathers, is light in weight, and a near-perfect insulator—near-perfect, since it is expensive. Synthetics, which are cheaper, and which have made possible less expensive camping gear, are both heavier and more bulky. The great thing about down is that you can squeeze it into a small space for carrying and then shake it out to let it take up its loft. Most manufacturers today indicate the comfort range of their sleeping bags.

As far as shape is concerned, the rectangular bag is being produced in large numbers, and, when zipped with another, makes for an excellent and large double bed. However, if heat loss is going to be a problem, you might consider either the semimummy bags, which have a moderate taper toward the feet (and which can be zipped together), or a full mummy bag, of which only the more expensive models allow you to form a double bed.

It is well worthwhile shopping around for the sleeping bag that you will like, and while there are some very cheap bags on the market, a sleeping bag, like a tent, is an investment and it is always worth getting the best you can afford. Don't forget to stow the bag(s) in a waterproof outer. Some bags come with liners which add to the insulation and which you can take out and wash like sheets.

If you don't sleep in the raw and you still want to take some pajamas, consider that sweatsuit or even make up a nightshirt which is actually a lot more comfortable and keeps you much warmer.

COOKING GEAR AND FOOD AND WATER

While there is nothing to beat a camp fire, unfortunately an awful lot of people are wandering around who don't know a thing about fire safety. Actually, the traditional camp fire is not nearly as efficient as some of the small camping stoves available today. And since it is assumed that you are pretty serious about conservation, you will understand that you do much less damage to wilderness environment if you cook on a small stove than if your time is spent searching for deadwood.

The true wilderness person is known by the small fire he (she) uses, and since you're probably going to build one fire anyway, you may as well know how to go about it.

Safety with open fires begins in choosing a safe spot, in making a safe fire, and, when you're done, in making sure that the fire is out and that the area is covered over with sand or soil.

A safe place to put a fire is not less than 5 yards from any brush or shrub or tree. Take a centerpoint and then clear away any twigs, grass, and leaves, for a radius of 6 feet all around. If you're making a fire on a grassy area, you should put down a level of dirt and make a small pit with stones, so that the grass underneath can survive. An alternate is to dig up the turf and replace after use. And should the ground be wet, you will need to build your fire on a simple platform.

There are two ways of making fires. There's the old woodman's way (still taught by the Boy Scouts), which is to make a small pyramid of sticks and then to fill the underside with tinder and wood shavings. And there's the square fire, in which you build your pyramid by placing four fairly stout logs at the sides, filling the center with tinder, and then building up on each side, two at a time. The latter makes a smaller fire and is easier to control. It is also easier to cook over, since you can put a grill on top of it and cook directly over it.

The secret of a good fire is to gather all the materials you're going to need before you begin. Dry deadwood burns best, while leaves, twigs, and dead grass make good tinder. There should be sufficient tinder to create enough heat to let the deadwood catch alight. Don't use damp wood directly without letting it dry out. If it should light, you'll get a very smoky fire.

Once the fire is lighted, someone is going to have to supervise it. And you should have spare water available in case a spark pops out and is carried out of the cleared circle by the wind. When done, sprinkle water on the embers and, by touch, make sure that all are dead. The ashes can be buried and the turf replaced if you dug it up. Any stones can also be deposited.

One of the drawbacks of using a wood fire is that utensils are difficult to clean. And while you can put a coat of liquid washing up on them beforehand—on the outside, of course—you can eliminate a lot of work by sticking with a small camp stove.

Now to fuel. Three types are in general use: alcohol, white gas, and propane (or butane.) But kerosene stoves are also found. White gas (and Coleman fuel) has not apparently been affected by the fuel shortage, but stoves using this fuel have to be pumped to build and maintain air pressure during use. Some people prefer white gas because it can be used in a pinch to set fire to green wood for signaling purposes. But actually it is annoying to have an inflammable liquid around, and for this reason many outdoors people prefer to use propane or butane.

The disadvantage with propane and butane is that it is more expensive, and the small cylinders are—incredibly—not rechargeable. This is simply inefficiency on the part of the manufacturers, who obviously have a team of cost accountants confirming the probability of "disposable" cylinders. The bigger cylinders are quite heavy, but smaller sizes are now being marketed which would make sense for canoe camping. Butane and propane are fairly similar, except that butane will not vaporize below 32 degrees F (the freezing point.) But propane will (down to 44 degrees below zero.)

Alcohol stoves are lighter, fuel is usually obtained easily, and although the flame is not as hot, the whole stove is a lot safer, since you can put out the flames with water.

In choosing your stove, you should decide what type of cooking you are going to be doing and what you're needs are. Good cooks can make do with a simple one-burner stove. Gourmet cooks prefer two burners. And eating good food in the wilderness is a pleasure indeed.

GOOD FOOD

Cooking good food means having the proper equipment in which to cook it, and it is well worthwhile putting together kitchen gear for camping. There are quite a number of excellent items on the market which are specifically designed for camping, and which pack together neatly to form a small package. One very neat package is Gloy's Compact Storm Kitchen, which comes with an alcohol stove, a frying pan, two kettles, a tea kettle, and a pot lifter. The entire kit nests together in a neat package of 4 x 8 inches and weighs about 2½ pounds.

Another good package is the Palco 420 series, but it is rather larger, taking up about 1 cubic foot of space. This may be felt to be unacceptably big. Also, that doesn't include a stove. Their 505 kit, which costs about $5, on the other hand, weighs only 14 ounces and includes a frying pan, a saucepan that you can use as the frying pan's lid, a pot with handle and cover, and a drinking-measuring cup.

You are also going to need utensils and plates. While many campers favor paper plates—which can be disposed of by burning later—there's a lot to be said for solid plates. Ship's chandlers usually have a good line of "unbreakables," or you may find them in the picnic section of your favorite department store. Since they don't weigh much—having a plastic base—you can afford to be quite lavish, and get a general-food plate, a bowl and side plate, plus a mug for liquids.

If you enjoy wine, consider packing a gallon jug into your kit so that you can enjoy a glass of wine at your evening meal. If you are going to be near civilization and want to save weight, pack a corkscrew—the French ones that hide themselves within the handle are good—and get a bottle for that special occasion.

Given careful preparation, one can dine as elegantly in the wilderness as one wants, and the food tastes better. So it is worthwhile taking along the wherewithal to make it happen. The best rule is to keep it simple. And really, aren't the best dishes always also the simplest?

Convenience foods are quite popular these days, and some of them work. They're more expensive than the raw materials would be, but they do help cut down on weight. If you're going to go that route, take some herbs—basil, marjoram—to perk their bland flavor. Garlic powder is also good. For soups, and for flavoring stews, there are a number of variously flavored cubes around—such as Knorr—offering bouillon, chicken or onion, to enhance the meal. Lipton—the tea people—do a Cup-of-Soup which, while expensive, is good value, and comes in several flavors. They also do a prepared salad dressing which comes in envelopes, so that you don't need to take anything made of glass.

A number of excellent mixes for home use—such as pancake mix—transfer easily to the open-air environment. All you have to do to make your pancake is to add to the mix water (or milk) and an egg. Mix it all up and then pour into a hot skillet. Many of the products designed for camping use come in sturdy plastic bags in which the mixing can be done—this saves on washing up, too. A number of other items come in bags in which you just place the article in boiling water and then open up after it has been heated.

If your favorite home brand doesn't come in such a container, you can prepack it at home into serving portions in plastic bags.

Canned goods are also excellent standbys, despite their weight. But if you are using cans, take the empty cans out with you and dispose of them properly. Also, don't forget to include a can opener in your kit.

Freeze-dried foods are also worthy of your consideration, since they are light in weight and easily prepared. But test them out at home before you decide on using them. Many are precooked, and all that's needed is some water and heat. You can even get some pseudo-gourmet items such as shrimp creole, boeuf stroganoff, and so on. This is another good time to put those herbs or garlic powder to use, since their taste is also somewhat bland for the most part.

The better camping-goods stores usually have an extensive line of such weight-saving foods, and, while expensive compared to the bulky, reak thing, they are worth looking at. For nourishing snacks for your morning and afternoon break, try health-food stores for candy bars that provide you with energy rather than just sweetness. Or you can make these at home before you set out: oatmeal, or nuts flavored with maple syrup and honey and coated lightly with flour is a typical recipe. A modern version. . . .

An important part of your equipment is aluminum foil in which food can be cooked. Not just baked potatoes, but fresh buttered fish tastes delicious when cooked in its own juices. Fruit can be baked, and you can even make shortcake using it. As with cans, take your used foil out with you.

Kebabs are an easy way of dealing with meals where you'll be using meat. Take some long skewers with you, which can also double for fondue sticks, and cut into 1-inch squares steak or lamb (which you can marinate in a cupful of that wine you brought), and put on skewer with sliced onion, mushroom, bacon, tomato, green pepper, or what you will. Alternate meat with vegetable, sprinkle on some herbs and garlic, and then cook it yourself. Delicious.

Stews are easy camp meals. The trick is to first cook sliced onions in a closed pan on low heat until they get mushy and gold colored. Take the pan off the heat at this point and add sliced vegetables to about an inch up. Favored are potatoes—sliced—carrots, mushroom, and so on. Then, if you're making a pot roast, put in your meat, and cover it up with more vegetables. Add herbs and garlic powder and a touch of wine if you like. Cover with water and cook on low heat.

A modern version of the milk-and-honey cookie for wilderness snack fare is:

2 cups wheat germ (or bran or oatmeal)
2 cups powdered milk
4 tablespoons (1/8th lb.) clarified butter
¼ lb. organic or wild honey
3 tablespoons of water

1 package of flavored gelatin (your choice of Jell-O)

1. Mix wheat germ and powdered milk. Add just a touch of ground nutmeg or cinnamon or mace for additional cookie flavor to taste. (Allspice can also be used, but very little.)

2. Clarify butter. Taking only sweet butter, melt under low heat until foam appears on surface. Scoop off foam (animal fats) until butter is clear. In a separate container, melt honey and water to which you add the butter. Slowly add the dried produce (you can throw in a few raisins to sweeten) to this mix and stir thoroughly. Finally add the gelatin—you don't need very much, and if you don't mind baking very, very, slowly you can dispense with it.

3. Pour into a rectangular cake tin (8 x 12, 9 x 13, depending on thickness you want) and bake in very low oven. On modern ovens you should leave the door ajar at about 200 degrees. The object is to drive out moisture so that you have a dehydrated cookie. Cook until reasonably solid, about five hours. Cut into small mouth-sized wedges and wrap individually in foil. The outers should be deep gold and crunchy, the inners still vaguely moist from honey. These keep without refrigeration and spoilage (unless water gets at them) for at least a year.

4. Two small wedges plus boiling water in the field make a meal. They are also delicious to nibble at.

The great part about this dish is that it can cook for ages and not spoil. The low heat is the secret.

Rice is an excellent standby for your carbohydrate needs. Many prefer it to potatoes for this source of food. Perhaps the only drawback is that it must be washed. If you don't mind taking the trouble to do this before you leave, you'll always be assured of good rice. A little oil with the rice when you're cooking it helps to avoid the problem of it sticking to the pan. Reckon two measures of water to one measure of rice.

Chicken is another easy dish to prepare. Parts can simply be fried, or you can spit a small whole chicken and roast it. Place some foil underneath to catch the drippings and use this to baste it from time to time.

Aim to have at least one good meal a day, and have a reasonable meal somewhere around noon. Milk or tea and a light meal is really all that's needed before starting out, so that you can work up an appetite for the midmorning break. If the sun is strong, it makes a lot of sense to be off the water when it is at its highest. A siesta can be enjoyed—rig a tarp to provide shade if there are no trees—and then set

off to complete the day's run after you've enjoyed a good relax.

Aim to be off the river not much later than six at most, since although you'll quickly pick up the routine of setting up camp and striking it, the longer you have to explore in daylight, the better your camp will be. Always leave your site cleaner than when you found it, even if it means cleaning up after other campers who don't know any better.

More thought on food: dutch oven cooking, standby of the pioneers of yesteryear, is practical since lightweight aluminum ovens are now available. The secret to successfully cooking with a dutch oven is to regulate the heat. Don't make it too hot—low and slow is best. You can oven-fry, pot-roast, and bake, and from a cook's point of view, it makes outdoor living very easy. Check it out.

If you are fairly close to civilization, it is sometimes nice to see whether there is a good restaurant to try out. It gives the cook a day off, and it breaks up the work. Similarly, if you have access to a place where food can be bought, this too helps cut down on the amount you need to take for yourself.

Water is an important commodity, since far too many of the natural streams have become polluted by industry and cheap builders, who use them to carry away effluence. Water can be sterilized by boiling, but it may not taste too good, so always have a supply with you. You can also buy sterilizing tablets which can be added to local water to purify it. But it's better to carry your own supply from a decent source.

In order to avoid carrying glass with you—which nearly always manages to get broken at an inconvenient time and can cause cuts—a plastic jug which can be folded when empty is one of the best ways of dealing with liquids. Plastic containers are inexpensive and almost indestructible and serve very well for keeping foods fresh. For a touch of class, you can use plastic glasses for drinking, but be careful, since they can crack. They also leave sharp edges.

A real time-saver is planning your menus ahead so that you know what you'll be cooking. This is also helpful when you do your shopping for the first part of the trip. Basic keys to all food buying should be nutrition, keeping quality, economy, weight, and bulk. For milk, use powdered milk except on special occasions when you can get it fresh. You can also get powdered eggs and various fishes which are dried. Oatmeal is an excellent standby and can be served with fruit. Be sure to include some fruit in your diet every day.

SETTING UP CAMP

You can actually sleep in your canoe, if necessary,

though it may not be quite as comfortable as your bed. But a properly set-up camp is useful, too, since you can enjoy the wilderness at your leisure. Most people take far too much junk with them when camping, and you should work out ahead of time those items that are necessary and those which may just come in handy. You'll have to be ruthless in cutting it down, but do it. You're the one who's going to be carrying the stuff when you have to portage.

There probably isn't an ideal campsite any more, but it is usually agreed that the best sites include a good view—especially of sunsets—some trees for protection from high winds, some sloping ground so that the water runs off, and so on. When you find a place, check whether you need to get permission. Many excellent campsites you'll come across are accessible only from the water, so here use your own discretion.

To decide on how you're going to set up your site, you'll need to take three things into consideration. First, where's the wind coming from: you need to know from which direction the wind'll be blowing so that you can set up your cooking area and your latrine. Then you can decide where you'll pitch your tent. If you carry a fly (tarp), you may want to set that up at the eating area, especially if it is at all damp. Eating in the rain can be fun—when you're sheltered.

Obviously, there'll be some places when you'll be able to use a regular campground, which may or may not have all the extras such as showers and restrooms. But when you are in the real wilderness, sanitation is important. Your latrine trench should be about 8 inches wide, about 1½ feet deep, and around 3 feet long. Try to preserve the section of turf from the top, so you can replace it later. The soil you dig out should be kept at one side and added slowly. Don't forget toilet paper.

The latrine site should be some way from your main site, and downwind of it. The cooking site will be nearer, and should also be downwind. While it's nice to smell outdoor cooking, it's better to avoid the chance of sparks flying into your tent area. Also. some foods can hang around on canvas for days.

The tent site should be checked carefully to see that there's nothing underfoot that could tear the floor of the tent. Also, you don't want to put the tent up on a clump of poison ivy, for obvious reasons. Twigs, rocks, stones, etc., should be cleared away. Choose somewhere flat—if possible—and if your site is not on a relatively high piece of ground, dig a small channel for water to run off into around the tent. Set your tent up with guylines properly sited so that it doesn't sag—it will keep the water out better that way. If the guys are nylon, you don't need to worry about their getting wet, but you may need to check that they don't slip. If organic fibers are used, slacken guys periodically during rain.

If you are using a regular fire, keep wood piled up, and take some inside your tent at night so that should it rain (or dew form) you'll have dry wood to start the day with.

Air matresses work best if you let just a little air out of them so that they will mold to your shape.

If you are planning to be at a particular site for a day or more, airing the sleeping bags is good practice. It makes them feel fresher at nights. And the river can be an excellent means of keeping food cool. You can make a little pool with rocks so that the stuff doesn't float away. Use properly sealed containers so that the food doesn't get spoiled by water leaking in.

MAPS AND KNOWING WHERE YOU ARE

It's foolhardy not to know where you are on a wilderness trip, so include in your baggage a map of the area you're going to, plus a good hand compass. There are a number of excellent maps available, and you should check out the ones which seems most useful to you. Inch to the mile is a good scale to work by, but there are bigger (and smaller) scales which can work.

In a pinch, and if the sun is shining, you can discover the north-south of where you are by pointing the hour hand of your watch to the sun, and then dividing the segment of the circle formed by the hour hand and where the minute hand would be at twelve o'clock. The southerly direction will be toward the sun.

STRIKING CAMP

A check list is always useful. You'll have used one when you were putting your gear together. Use it again as you stow things away.

Each carrying bag—and Duluth bags are excellent companions for canoe camping—should have its own items, and you should stay with it. This may seem a little compulsive, but it saves a lot of time and nervous energy involved in self-querying: "Where did I put?" And you don't really need the bother of not knowing, or forgetting.

Be sure to tidy up each area, especially the latrine area, and, again, leave the site in better condition than it was when you first saw it.

LIGHT

Here you can run the gamut from old-fashioned miners' lanterns to supermodern brilliant gas lamps. Actually, now that slow-burning nondrip candles are available, candles make a lot of sense. Perhaps their only drawback is that they create heat.

Candles should always be used with a proper candle lantern. Naked flame should not be allowed to get near tent or bedding or clothing. There are two types of lantern, one small and circular which opens up when you want to use it, and another, which looks like the Stonebridge folding lantern. Both are good, and run about $5.

Carbide lanterns have been popular for a long time and give a good light. The brilliance is regulated by controlling the flow of water on the carbide. Their only drawback is their smell. Otherwise, they are light in weight, don't take much room in stowage, and are cheap to run.

Each person should have a regular flashlight, preferably a rugged one somewhere in their gear. Kellite make a series which are extremely tough, and the Mallory compact is also pretty indestructible. There are a number of inexpensive battery lanterns which won't sink, and which are waterproof. Seek these out at a ship's chandlers, or a good sporting-goods store.

For a general light, gas lanterns using either propane or butane are useful. Trailblazer has a propane model PL-2200 which has one mantle and automatic ignition. It comes with a protective case. The Primus Explorer #2220 uses butane, as does the Garcia L-200. The Primus is a pound lighter in weight (it costs more), and its base also doubles as a protective carrying case.

MISCELLANEOUS

First-aid kits are something most outdoors people build up for themselves. Unless you are extemely careless, you're unlikely to be troubled by anything more serious than the odd bruise or occasional cut. Far more likely is sunburn, and a sun-filtering cream, oil, or gel should be on your list. You can also include some organic vitamins, such as C. And if you must use drugs, then aspirin is probably the safest. An antiseptic should be carried—and everything should be stowed in plastic bottles—not glass. A snakebite kit also makes sense, though most snakes are distinctly antisocial and won't bother you unless you bother them first. Be sure to read and understand the instructions in the kit before you set out, so that if you do happen to be unfortunate enough to argue with a snake, you know exactly what to do. An ounce of prevention, though, is worth a pound of cure.

If you can't be bothered to assemble your own first-aid kit, there are several on the market designed for campers and boaters. If by mischance something does occur which requires attention, don't be your own Marcus Welby. Get out and get proper help.

PICTURE TAKING

About the only thing you should really take out of the wilderness apart from what you took in is memories and pictures. The pictures act as a focal point for your memories, allowing you to recapture a moment lost in time.

Cameras and water don't go well together unless you have one of those special waterproof cameras designed for taking pictures in the sea. If you have one of those, then you won't need to read on. Otherwise, you should get a heavy-duty plastic bag which can be sealed at the top with a wire twist. Tupperware containers also are handy for carrying lenses and filters, and they will float, provided you don't overfill them. Use a couple of elastic bands to make sure the tops stay on tight.

You obviously don't want to be taking in lots of paper and cardboard, so get your film out of the boxes and carry it in their plastic containers. You can mark these with a felt pen to show you have unexposed film in them, then rub off the marking when it is used.

Film doesn't like either extreme heat or cold, so make sure that it is kept cool and out of the sun.

REPAIRS

As part of your original check list, you should have included a repair kit. Repairs to the canoe are essential, since this is your regular means of transport. What to include in the repair kit is covered in Chapter 10, ''Building & Maintenance.''

Other repairs will include material for the tent, and running repairs, which make use of a needle and thread. Similarly, you may want to include something for the air mattress, which may get accidentally punctured, or on which the valve may decide to expire. If you checked these items before you left, you should not ordinarily run into any trouble.

POCKETKNIVES, SAWS, AND AXES

As a general rule you shouldn't need this, but occasionally in wilderness areas a folding saw can be handy. Some sort of entrenching tool is more useful than an ax, and can be used for digging your latrine. As far as pocketknives are concerned, there's little point in buying anything expensive. What are you going to be using it for? If you fish, then a fisherman's knife makes sense for cleaning fish, but most so-called hunting knives are strictly for show. If you really had to use them for skinning an animal, you'd probably find you could do a better job and quicker with a regular kitchen knife.

FIRES

Unless you know what you are doing, stay away from making fires. Millions of trees are uselessly burned every year because careless people go into wilderness areas and toss around cigarette butts without making sure they're extinguished, by throwing hot matches—apparently out—and by making fires.

For lighting lanterns and stoves, you'll need matches. Kitchen matches of wood are the best, and you can waterproof them very easily with canning paraffin, or even with candle wax. All you do is let soft wax go over the head of the match and let it dry. When you want to use the match, the wax should be carefully scraped off. Boxes of matches can be stowed in different containers, and should be additionally waterproofed in plastic bags.

For those occasions when an ordinary match just won't do, there's a thing called a Metal Match which works well in lighting tinder. It lasts forever, too. Also handy are self-consuming fire cubes. These are excellent, but if you are going to carry them, keep them carefully stowed where they are not goint to go off accidentally.

Fire extinguishers. Baking soda is one of the best extinguishers around, and you may find room for it in your food box. As an alternate, you can get a lightweight refillable extinguisher which weighs in at one pound, rated as all-purpose, and which costs about $4. Sears Roebuck sells a nonrefillable extinguisher which is also quite good.

LOADING

The safe way to load your canoe for your trip is to watch its weight and balance. The easiest way to do this is to work out your problem logically. That is, load in first that which you will need last. Load in first that which you will pack first when you *strike* your camp. Anything you are going to need, or may possibly need during the actual traveling part of your trip, should be loaded last or next to last so that it is easily accessible.

This will include a bag containing change of gear, swimming gear, wet weather clothing, food (separately packed so it won't get muddled with the clothing), your

repair kit, and possibly a fly if you want some shade for your midday meal.

If you don't take a fly, consider packing your tent in a reasonably get-at-able position so that you can take a siesta if you want one, or if it's raining, pitch it promptly.

Those who have discovered the advantages of portage trolleys for canoe camping will already know that these should be stowed in an accessible place. If you are taking a heavy load, your trolley can be stowed on deck in a waterproof bag.

You can considerably simplify the loading before you start. Depending on your type of boat, and being the owner of bathroom scales, most of the loading equation can easily be done before you set out. Your main consideration should be that the boat should be balanced about its true center of gravity. If it is out of balance, it won't be stable. Take a little time to keep it seaworthy. Your aim should be that the canoe float level when you are in it. If you are two, you may need to modify your loading to take care of a discrepancy in weights.

If there is a prevailing wind and it is coming from the direction you're headed, trim slightly heavier to the bow. In a following wind, trim slightly heavy sternward. If there is no definite wind pattern, trim for a level boat.

SUMMARY

Planning a canoe-camping trip with care will bring you the greatest rewards. Ask yourself: Where will we go and for how long and why? What are we trying to achieve? What do we want to do?

Getting these questions honestly answered will help enormously in your decision-making. As more and more of our legislatures wake up to the idea that they're supposed to be of some use to us, more and more states publish water routes and set up accessible campsites for organized recreation. A list of those who can help is provided. Several states even mark portage trails on their charts and keep the water clear of debris, though most are too influenced by the polluters to do much more. There may be times when you will need a permit or permission to portage or set up camp.

If you should happen upon a piece of private land where the lessees are unfriendly and stroke their sidearms while speaking back to you, don't get uptight. Groups which find themselves becoming a minority find it very difficult to adapt and use hostility to disguise their discomfort. Also, remember that the Constitution protects minorities, so there is absolutely no need for you to be rude or ignorant.

So, when canoe camping, be polite and have respect for yourself and your canoe (or kayak)—and for others. And enjoy yourself. After all—why shouldn't you?

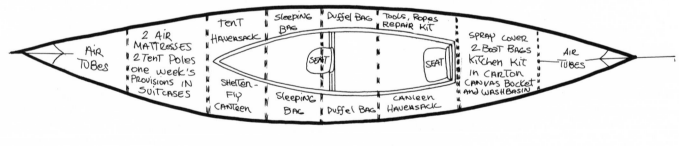

AIR
TUBES

2 AIR
MATTRESSES
2 TENT POLES
ONE WEEK'S
PROVISIONS IN
SUITCASES

TENT
HAVERSACK

SHELTER-
FLY
CANTEEN

SLEEPING
BAG

SLEEPING
BAG

DUFFEL BAG

DUFFEL BAG

TOOLS, ROPES
REPAIR KIT

CANTEEN
HAVERSACK

SEAT

SEAT

SPRAY COVER
2 BOOT BAGS
KITCHEN KIT
IN CARTON
CANVAS BUCKET
AND WASHBASIN

AIR
TUBES

"Loading Plan"

Loading plan suggested for twin kayak. Don't forget the air
tubes fore and aft for buoyancy.

Chapter 9

COASTAL CRUISING

Sooner or later the call of the sea is heard. Most of the canoeing fraternity heed it—once. After all, if inland waterways can provide so much interest and excitement, how much more the sea with its vast openness?

Coastal cruising represents the highest state of the art of small boating. Some cruising enthusiasts go even further and use their kayaks to cross oceans—most notably, Dr. Hans Lindemann, who in 1956, sailed the Atlantic in a standard, folding Klepper Aerius II kayak. But for most of us, coastal cruising is more limited.

As a general rule, the Canadian (American) canoe, even when fitted with a spray deck, is by no means the ideal sea boat. Although the American Indians used canoes for coastal work, most present-day North American products in this line are ot suitable for seaways. Bilge keels and spray covers add to seaworthiness, but the kayak—as the Greenlanders have proved successfully over the centuries—is the one to look for if coastal work is involved. *

The secret to successful cruising in any small boat—whether inland or coastal—is meticulous and careful preparation ahead of time. If you work out all the angles, you can

---

*The convenience of the Canadian canoe for inland cruising is covered in Chapter 7, "Inland Cruising." The enormous advantage it offers in bush country is that you can sleep in it on the water and avoid most mosquito bites—a very considerable advantage if you've ever camped in the bush.

be pretty sure you won't have an "emergency" on your hands. Use a check list as if you were flying an airplane, since it will ensure that you remember to take such items as spare paddles and navigational charts.

Finally, be prepared to follow, as it were, to the letter of the law, these three cardinal rules for coastal cruising:

1. Minimum number of boats is three—whether singles or doubles.

2. Each crew person must be able to swim—and to Eskimo roll with proficiency.

3. Each crew person *must* wear an appropriate life-saving device (preferably equipped with plastic whistle) at all times while at sea.

It probably seems unnecessary to emphasize that if you want to get to sea with your craft, you ought to practice ahead of time. But there are some folks around who think that everything will work out fine anyway—and then are surprised when things go wrong, and don't realize that the only ones to blame are themselves. Some points, therefore, do need to be considered.

If you want to go coastal cruising, be sure you have the stamina to handle the long flog it involves. This means a training program, unless you simply intend to putter around the shore and surf. Paddling any distance consumes energy, so building up stamina is an important part of preparing for coastal cruising. If you're still smoking, see if you can't stop, or at least limit your consumption of tobacco. Sound lungs are very much part of your equipment as a coastal cruiser.

Another item worth looking at if you are going to cruise long distance is sail. Several of the folding kayaks have a sail or sails as optional accessories, plus the all important dagger boards.

Dagger boards act in much the same way as a center board or keel, providing lateral stability and maintaining the upright position of the vessel. They are not exclusive to kayaks, being used—in larger form, of course—on such vessels as Dutch cargo barges. If you are getting a kayak which does not come with this option, it's not too difficult to make up a rig—but we will discuss this in the next chapter, "Maintenance & Building."

Although you can use a normal (small) mainsail and jib, or even a Chinese-style junk rig, the easiest type of sail to handle in a kayak is the lateen type. This sail was originally developed by the Arabs many centuries ago and was later adopted by Portuguese explorers. Its advantages include the use of a relatively short mast, the ability to spill wind fast in the event of a sudden squall, and ease of reefing. Reefing means shortening your sail and is done when the wind pipes up too much for comfort.

The next items which ought to be considered are the waves: How do they function, and how must you function with your kayak in order to stay upright and to get where you are going?

If you have never been on the sea before, it would be useful to take a short boat ride to investigate the surface of the sea. Large lakes are similar, but, being bounded by land, they do not offer quite the same sort of dynamics as the ocean itself. Your objective will be to study the water and see how wave formations work. Like the white-water expert, you must develop your ability to read wave patterns to avoid surprises, since from your kayak your visibility will be limited—you're sitting very close to the surface of the sea.

Waves

Waves are formed as the result of the reaction between the surface of the sea and the winds. They develop across vast ranges of the oceans and frequently travel immense distances before you meet with them. They have considerable momentum, and were it possible to harness their power we would never have an "energy" crisis again.

What all this means to you is that waves must be treated with respect since they have the capacity to smash you and your boat. Like a sailboat captain, you will soon discover that waves are at their fiercest when close to the shore. While this may mean good surfing, if that is what you want—it can also spell peril if you have a rocky coastline to your leeward. What happens is that the wind creates new waves near the shore which often become superimposed on older ones, creating considerable confusion. With the addition of rocks or underwater obstructions, you can find yourself in difficult surroundings. So use a chart and learn some lore. At the beach you'll sometimes notice a series of large waves followed by a series of smaller ones. What's happening is this superimposition effect, the larger waves being the older ones, the smaller the newer.

Most waves can be dealt with by the basic strokes, but for safe cruising you should expect to be proficient with all the regular strokes, including the high and low telemark, the slap recovery—important for balance on a sea—draw, and the scull for support. You will not go to sea without having previously practiced sea rescues, of course, including the Eskimo bow grab, the paddle grab, and the deep-sea H or rafted T.

It can't be emphasized sufficiently that it is vital that you and the members of your party are completely at home with all these methods in addition to the Eskimo roll. It is prudent, not to attempt any sea work until you can confidently perform these maneuvers. And they are not *that* difficult if only you'll work on them a bit.

The point is this: a kayak in the hands of one who knows what he is doing is one of the safest forms of water transport in existence. Its potential for safety is excellent *in the hands of one who knows what he is about.*
Indeed, some kayak person have actually ridden out near hurricanes—though one does question their wisdom for being there at the time. Still, your kayak is safe and will look after you as long as you're prepared to get your technique together.

In discussing wave technique, it will help if we think of them in terms of *bow waves, stern waves,* and *beam*—from the side—*waves.* Obviously, if you turn around, a bow wave becomes a stern wave and vice versa. And if you turn through 90°, a beam wave can become either bow or stern, depending on which way you're pointing. Finally—and fortunately rather rarely—there's the *combination wave,* which is usually only found around obstructions, though when wind and tide are working in opposite directions they're known to appear from time to time.

Bow waves are taken in relation to their size and will provide you with an acid test of whether your kayak is a reasonably good sea boat or not. You should be able to paddle straight through the smaller ones, the bow of your

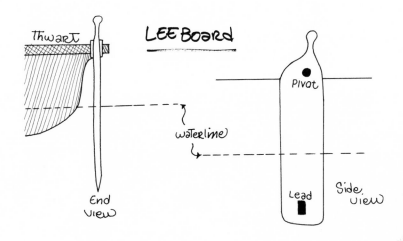

Detail of a leeboard.

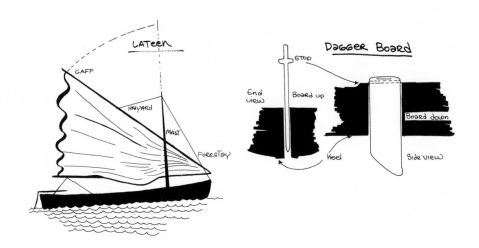

Detail of lateen sail, invented--and still used today--by the Arabs, it is thought. Dagger board is yet another solution to the stability problem for vessels which draw little water.

*Double paddle theme amply demonstrates that canoeing is
for all ages.*

kayak neatly slicing the water aside somewhere near the top. (Many kayak owners fit a small-wave deflecting device to the bow which looks and acts in much the same manner as those once popular bug-deflector devices made of plastic for cars some years back.) If you find that the wave should splurge up on your deck and even to the cockpit, it's very likely an indication that you have too flat a deck and too shallow a bow. Check this out early on. Apart from the frustration of having water flopping up at you—and it is frustrating—your vehicle is inefficient. Except in heavy waters your kayak should keep you reasonably dry around your shoulders, and you should not be expected to provide additional momentum to counteract the force of the water sloshing on your deck.

The best method for tackling the steeper waves is to lean well forward in making your stroke toward them, placing your paddle blade about one-third of the way down from the top of the wave. Pull yourself through the top and use your reverse paddle blade rather like a ski pole-rudder, to guide you down the other side. It's exciting the first few times, but you'll pick up the flow. With a little practice, you'll soon set up an easy rhythm which won't be tiring. However, as a safety measure, in this sort of water it's important for each member of the party to keep a good (constant) lookout for one another—especially if the water is at all heavy and you are all bobbing up and down, in and out of sight. Remember where your friends were last seen: keep a constant lookout and project your vision to where they ought to be. (It's with this in mind that coastal cruisers use international orange or scarlet to mark both life jackets and paddle blades—so they can be seen easily.)

Stern waves can be the kayak sailor's best friend if used properly, since their momentum can be utilized to advantage. Basically, you deal with the stern waves in much the same manner as the surfing enthusiast, using their impetus to thrust you forward as they lift you up and then roll on beneath you. Indeed, you can surf along with them if you want, though you'll work more efficiently if you get moving more modestly. The trick is to work by getting on the face of the wave, but carefully watch your boat for any tendency to slide off its 90° angle to the wave formation. This can cause considerable problems, not the least of which is being thrown on your side and even partially capsized. For this reason you must be accurate, since once the vessel takes the bit between its teeth, it is almost impossible to correct. So when dealing with stern waves, always remember to use the stern paddle to assist with steerage way.

If you've done any sailing, you'll know that one of the problems the boat must deal with in a following sea is the danger of being "pooped"—that is, having a stern wave breaking over the after end of the ship. Because of the pointed bow and stern of a kayak, this is most unlikely to happen to you—except in very shallow water. And if the reverse should happen—that is, you manage to run your bows into the water so that you start to loop—the cure is simple: stop paddling and, if necessary, reverse.

Beam waves can create problems for the less experienced, and the two telemark strokes should be practiced. Depending on their size, a beam wave that is relatively rounded is best dealt with by staying parallel to it until it is about to overtake you. At this point, you want to sweep-stroke the bow round to an angle of about 45° to the wave top. As it overtakes you and lifts you up, it will swing you around and carry you over. If the wave should be breaking, you'll have to brace-paddle—that is, stick your paddle into the wave beneath the breaking area and pull down. This turns into the high telemark stroke we mentioned earlier, as you pull into the wave. Then you can go over the top, skidding down the after side of the wave with your paddle for support. (See diagram.) For lower)breaking waves, use the low telemark position, leaning forward over the bow.

Combination waves, as mentioned earlier, are unlikely to be found except toward the shore or where you have a condition of wind against tide. Preplanning should help you avoid them in open waters, where you'll normally find them only under very trying conditions—when you should not be there, unless your some sort of expert proving a point. At sea they are mostly caused by storms, but just offshore they can occur over underwater obstructions—check your chart—such as rocks, sharp ledges beneath the surface where you get a deepening or shallowing in a limited space like a cliff edge, and so on. You'll sometimes find them around harbor entrances even in only a slight sea, around jetties, piers, and breakwaters. *Check your chart ahead of time so that you can avoid them.*

Depending which way one of these waves comes at you, you go up and come down, usually in the bow-wave position and using your paddle for support. The trouble with this type of wave is that your paddle really has to work hard—and could break. So much for technique: What about equipment?

Equipment

The best kayak for sea work and for traveling long distance is usually agreed to be the Eskimo kayak, which is specifically built with this in mind. A British firm, Gaybo Ltd., produces a replica of this type of boat called the Nanuk, and by all accounts it is excellent for touring. Good runers up in this field are the general-purpose or touring kayak, of which several good examples are now available. The K-1 Prijon Combi 435 is one of the better ones made in the United States. Or you can investigate folding kayaks: both Klepper and Folbot come to mind as seawovthy boats in need of little modification for coastal cruising.

Your check list—a real time-saver as well as being a reminder—will include the following items for cruising:

i.	Bailing	ix.	Kit, repair
ii.	Buoyancy	x.	Life jacket
iii.	Chart(s)	xi.	Paddles (include spare)
iv.	Clothing	xii.	Rudder
v.	Compass	xiii.	Sailing rig
vi.	Deck layout	xiv.	Spray cover
vii.	Flares	xv.	Stowage plan
viii.	Gear, camping (optional)	xvi.	Weather forecast

You should also have actually practiced your rescue techniques within the previous seven days, preferably the same day you set out. From your chart make notes of rides and rocks—where they'll be.

Bailing: if your kayak is rather full of gear, it may be more convenient to use a dinghy bailer for getting water out in a capsize. A bleach bottle with the upper part cut off works very well. If you're fussy, you can use a sponge to finish the mopping up.

Buoyancy: airsponsons or buoyancy bags are a really good idea and ensure that very little water will enter your boat in the event of a capsize. These should be placed both fore and aft, and should occupy those areas not being used by you and your gear. Don't—repeat, *don't*—use just one. If you capsize and have to get out, you'll find it highly difficult to recapture your boat.

Chart(s): these are a must. A road map is no substitute. If you're going to be at sea then you'll need a seaman's map, which is what a chart is. Prepare your route before you set out and check it every ten or fifteen minutes as you go along. A strong waterproof cover which can be attached to the deck is very handy, and even if water does splash onto it, you can simply wipe it off to read.

Clothing: keeping dry during coastal cruising can be a headache, especially if there's much wind. Most sailing gear is not suitable unless it is the porous type—what happens with the others is that you soak in your sweat. Wetsuits as used by scuba divers aren't the complete answer either, since they restrict your paddling. Chris Hare, the British

Canoe Union National coach, recommends wetsuit trousers, and either a wetsuit top with no sleeves, or sweaters plus an anorak of the type used by slalomists.

Compass: vital, to know where you are going. A small boat compass works very well, especially the gimbaled variety. Swing it before you set out so that you know it's pointing in the right direction. Be especially careful you don't stow any metallic gear around it. You can secure it to a mounting on the cockpit coaming, or if you prefer, secure it beneath the spray cover within the deck. It's more difficult to peek at, but it's out of the way if you have to be rescued.

Deck layout: this is important, and it's well worth thinking out what you want to stow on deck. Recommended are spare paddle—the joining type—well secured, your compass, and a freshwater bottle so that you can have something to drink when you get thirsty—as you will. The type used by bicycle racers works quite well. (See diagram.)

Flares: vital safety equipment, and take more than one. There are a number of good ones on the market. Check any yachting magazine. Also, know how to use it, so buy a couple to practice with—and try them out in the boat.

Gear, camping: this item is covered in Chapter 7. You may want to modify it to lighten the load for going to sea. The important thing is to make sure it is all securely stowed, so that it doesn't unbalance the kayak.

Kit, repair: unfortunately, boats do sometimes leak. The reasons can vary from chafing to colision, either with another vessel or with an underwater obstruction. A simple repair kit stowed where you can get at it is thus essential. Masking tape is good for temporary repairs, but get the type that doesn't mind a wet surface. Scotch tape can also be used for securing a temporary patch, but the area to be covered needs to be dry. Paper towel, sponge, or regular towel for drying area will be needed. Stow in plastic bag to keep moistureproof.

Life jacket: Coast Guard regulation insist upon the use of an approved kapok-type life jacket for seagoing kayaks, and the newer type in which the filling is sealed in waterproof plastic envelopes is very safe. It is safer to modify these by removing the ties and replacing them either with a quick-release Velcro-type fastener, or with a heavy-duty zipper which pulls in either direction to break the cqosure. The reason for this measure is that a jacket can snag in the event of a capsize, and you may want to get out of it in a hurry.

Paddles: a smaller-bladed paddle is preferable if you intend to cover long distances. The key to coastal cruising is to prepare slowly. This means you should test each item in calm water to see how it functions, and to get used to the way it works. You'll find this most useful in getting the bugs out of the system. Your main paddle will have a rigid shaft, and experts recommend using those designed for slalom or white-water work for best control. A British manufacturer recently introduced a grp-shafted paddle of exceptional strength to weight, which is highly spoken of. For your spare set, you'll be using a jointed set, which should be strapped securely to the deck so that you can get at them easily. All blades should be colored fluorescent orange or fire-engine red. Care of paddles is important, and they should be routinely checked both before and after each outing.

Choosing the right length paddle is like choosing the right size skis. Stand with your feet together and hold the paddle vertically in front of you, with one end on the ground. Now stretch an arm fully upward and curl your fingers over the top of the blade. Don't forget to check for your grip on the loom—does it feel comfortable?

An inexpensive paddle may seem like an economy, but, as a general rule, buy the best you can afford. It's usually cheaper in the long run. Repairs can be made easily by using a grp kit. It adds weight, but adds considerable strength, too. The tips of the blades can also be reinforced with a strip of glass cloth and resin.

Rudder: opinions differ, and this is a matter you'll need to decide yourself. If you are going to fit a rudder, the foot-operated type is undoubtedly the best, combined with an over—stern rudder blade which can swivel up for launching. (See diagram.)

Sailing rig: the simplest and easiest to handle is the lateen-type sail, which, with its short mast and relative freedom from cordage, makes it suitably uncluttering for a small boat. While there are versions available which give you a split-sail arrangement—that is, mainsail and small jib, or foresail—you have two sheets to attend to. Why make life difficult for yourself?

The earliest craft to use the wind used a square sail, probably an animal skin, and sailed with the wind from behind. Using the wind, ancient Egyptian vessels would sail up the Nile against the current and then simply drop their sails to come back with it. And it was from this region that the lateen sail was developed—by the Arabs—to power the "baggara" or Arab dhow. The European gaff, and later the Bermudian (or Marconi) rig derive from this. The lugsail as developed by the Chinese seems to be an Eastern system on the same theme as the lateen. And junk-type sails have been successfully used on kayaks.

A quick-release system so that you can drop the sail almost instantly is a must. Most gear comes with this arrangement, or can be easily modified.

For stability, you'll need a keel. For kayaks, you use leeboards of a twin system designed by the Dutch for their cargo barges. These dagger boards, which hang out on either side of the boat, not only keep you from being blown downwind when sailing against the wind, but also add to the stability of your vehicle. Custom-made are best, since you will know the sort of stability you are looking for. The point about them is that they use your vessel as a fulcrum point, and all you have to work out is how much you will need in terms of depth, since the mass of water that they work against is much denser than the air which works—via your sail—against them. However, too stiff a boat is uncomfortably hard to ride, and could break up, since there are very strong forces involved.

To explain this a little further: the wind is a force which you will be using. The water is a force upon which you will be traveling. It is a question of achieving the maximum advantage from these two forces without putting yourself out of equilibrium, i.e., into a capsize. The wind which provides you with your power to travel doesn't care about you as you go upon your way—it has its own errands to attend to. Consequently, it bothers as much about you as you might about a baby roach.

The same thought applies to the water. If you can contrive a way not to bother it, it will play your game. So you can make friends with these two forces, if you will. Which is what leeboards are all about. And both Klepper and Folbot provide these are part of the package which they sell as folding kayaks.

Sailing a kayak is slightly different from sailing a regular boat since you don't have the same beam as a normal (contemporary) sailing boat. But narrow sailing boats have done very well at sea in competent hands. Uffa Fox, the late British yacht designer, made innumerable trips across the English Channel in a sailing kayak while still in his teens; and Baden Powell, founder of the Scout movement, was also making similar experiments at the turn of this century.

If you do decide to use sail, apart from trying it out and seeing whether you feel comfortable with this use of the elements, you should also learn how to stow it fast. When the weather turns nasty, as it can, it's nice to know that you can down-sail quickly and have it stowed in almost the time it takex to restore your main paddle from its stowage perch to your hands. But you won't, of course, be getting yourself into such a situation, since you will always get a good *weather forecast*—on which you will use your judgment—before you set out coastal cruising.

Canoes and kayaks can certainly be sailed. Shown here is a
Klepper folding kayak with a Bermudian type rig. You can
just make out the rudder at the stern, while the lar-
boards--which act as a keel would--are shown mounted
amidships.

Another approach to the stability problem shown here in this
16 ft. Old Town Wahoo. Here the larboards are fitted through
the hull to avoid flexing.

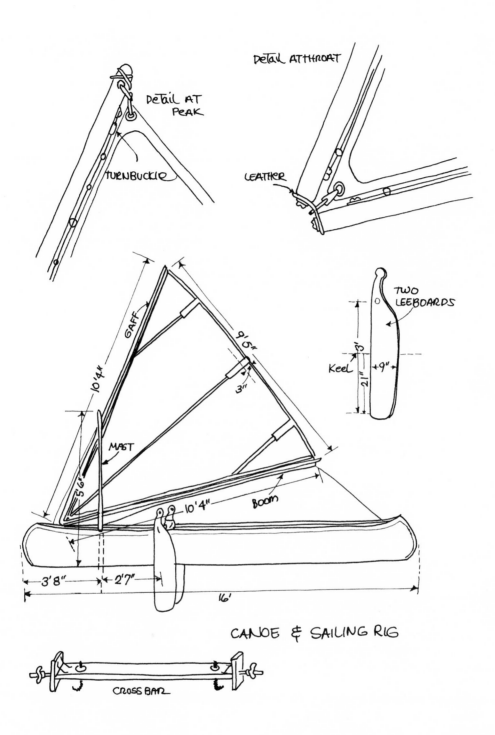

DETAIL AT THROAT

DETAIL AT PEAK

TURNBUCKLE

LEATHER

GAFF

9'5"

3"

10'4"

MAST

5'6"

10'4"

BOOM

TWO LEEBOARDS

Keel

3'

21"

9"

3'8"

2'7"

16'

CANOE & SAILING RIG

CROSS BAR

Canoe's sailing rig. Requirements include a shorty mast and step, leeboards, plus crossbar and rigging. Several manufacturers provide kits to convert open canoes into sailing canoes.

Stowage plans can really help too. A seaworthy boat wants to float at sea, and stowing your gear in the best carrying places makes it easier. The best system so far thought out seems to be to carry in the extreme fore and aft of the canoe you plan to use, your airsponsons—air bags—and possibly foam for flotation. Some like to use both. The objective once again is to achieve balance and stability. And the secret is to achieve this not merely in the fore-and-aft axis, but also across the beam axis, since this makes work much easier for you in terms of balancing your vessel.

Don't try and pack the kitchen sink if you're coastal cruising. Your kayak will ride lower in the water than it should for optimum performance. And while it is one thing to take a slight overload for camping from inland waters, the sea is really no place to put your vessel to such a test. Besides, you can really utilize the additonal buoyancy you'll gain by careful loading when you do go to sea. Apart from anything else, its a handy additional safety factor. (Diagram shows a typical stowage plan for a two-seat kayak for a week's coastal cruising. Reader should compare with layout suggested for inland waterways.)

Whether cruising inland or coastally, a great aid is a stowage diagram used in conjunction with a check list of what you'll be taking with you. A typical check list might run as follows:

Air mattress	Radio (marine band type)
x/antrenching tool	Sailing/storm-weather gear
Cooking/eating gear	Sleeping bag
Food bag with food	Tent
Fuel for stove	Washing gear (don't forget
Ground sheet or fly	toilet tissue and
Lamp (or candle lantern)	paper towels
Portable stove	Water bottle(s)
	Miscellaneous

For a more detailed approach at what you'll need for camping in a canoe or kayak, see Chapter 10.

The secret of any successful coastal cruising is meticulous preparation. If you prepare carefully, you'll find that all will go well. If you are slapdash, you'll inevitably be caught out and you won't enjoy yourself. Which brings us to the importance of weather forecasts.

Weather forecasting is a much more accurate science than it used to be, since the data available in terms of pressure, humidity, and wind can now be confirmed by satellite picture, which shows where the cloud banks are. Weather forecasts are available from a number of sources, from television and radio—low and medium frequencies, i.e., 190-415 and 515-544 kHz, have transcribed weather broad-

casts on selected frequencies; also very high frequency (VHF) in the band from 148-172 MHz—for example, and from the newspaper. Also available are the transcribed weather service reports available to pilots by an automatic telephone system. You dial a number and you'll get an aviation forecast, which can be useful if you know something about the way the weather works, since these are quite detailed forecasts and give a good overall picgure of what is happening weatherwise.

Finally, if none of the above is of any use, you can try your luck with a Flight Service Station. These are to be found at larger airports and are intended for pilot briefing, but if the crews aren't too busy they'll usually help out. Inquire for a reasonable "flight," that is, find a destination airport near where you'll be heading and simply ask for the local weather.

What you're interested in is whether there's likely to be a significant deterioration during your cruise, and if the wind is likely to pipe up. And this information is usually given on NBC's weather program early in the morning each day. Update by using your marine band radio. Don't bother the FSS unless you simply cannot get the information you need any other way.

As a final check, if yur're leaving from a regular marine center, talk with the locals—preferably those who earn their living fishing, sailing, or working on boats.

RESCUE DRILLS

Safety is no accident: so runs a popular truism, and safety at sea depends on being prepared for all eventualities, including the capsize.

There are three drills which must be practiced, and you will be foolish in the extreme if you don't bother to check these out. The first is our old friend the Eskimo roll. Next is the two-man Eskimo rescue. Last, the three-man rescue.

Anyone considering the delights and excitement of coastal cruising should be able to Eskimo roll reflexively. In other words, the rolling technique should be so completely a part of that person's kayaking technique, that no fear, no second thought is essayed in a situation where the roll—boldly undertaken—can obviate a less controlled environment. Water can be cold, as we all know, but the fact that it is should not cause the kayaker to defer his instinct, for you can almost always keep out of trouble with this technique. The exception here is with sail if you experience a knock-down—and truly, you shouldn't be using sail if the wind is too much for your craft.

So the Eskimo roll must be learned thoroughly, in warm water, cold water, and with and without paddle. This means regular practice, and it means some follow-up practice too, after the technique is mastered. If you are planning to coastal cruise some time in the future, it's a good idea to prepare a schedule for training over some weeks before you set out. Make sure that each member of the team has run through a series of these rescues within ten days of taking your trip. Ideally, the team should practice together so that any individual idiosyncrasies can be worked out.

The two-man rescue has also evolved from a similar technique used by Eskimo fisher people. It's especially helpful if you've lost a paddle—in the icy waters around Greenland it's essential. It is not meant for those (hopefully) few occasions when you fall completely out of your kayak, but rather for those times when you're snugged down inside your spray cover which fits both you and the coaming tightly, with your knees secure against your grips.

Here's how it works. Place your kayak at 90 degrees to a friend's and take hold of the bow of that kayak. Lean hard over until your shoulder touches the water. Now pull yourself back upright. It's a little tricky at first since, to begin with, the other boat seems to want to move away from you. But once you master the technique of how to hold the other boat and to pivot—via your arm and shoulder—yourself back up, it becomes much easier. It's the body movement that seems difficult at first. Repeat this several times, and then try with the other arm (you'll have to change the way you're facing, obviously.) It's important to be able to do this both ways.

The next stage is to continue this exercise, but letting yourself get lower and lower in the water until finally you are hanging perpendicularly—upside down. (You'll be pleasantly surprised to discover that you can actually swim your face to one side for a breath of fresh air any time you want: this is *good news.)*

Now that you have mastered this stage, ask your friend to move away. Keep at it, until you can learn to wait without anxiety for him to get to you. In the capsize you'll bang the sides of your boat very frimly to attract attention, waving your hands backward and forward on either side. Practice this also.

This training is one of the best confidence-building exercises there is to avoid panic in the event of capsize.

A second version of this rescue should be used in rough water, and is called the two-man parallel. The rescuing boat comes alongside (parallel) to the capsized kayak, and the rescuer puts his paddle at 90 degrees over his cockpit coaming, with the blade just touching the bottom of the capsized kayak. He next guides the underwater person's hands to the paddle shaft, and the capsized person hauls himself up. The reason this is good in rough water is because there is practically no chance of the rescuer's boat damaging the other kayak, and secondly, by linking the two boats after recovery—rafting is the technical name for this—the capsized person has a chance to regain his breath and recover, safely.

The 3-man rescue is where two kayaks are used to right a capsized kayak in which the crew has fallen out. (If you should be unlucky enough to fall out of your kayak at sea, especially in reasonably heavy water, it is usually better to right the boat as quickly as possible since the airlock can break up and the vessel become waterlogged. The technique here is to inflate your buoyancy jacket to its maximum and go to one side of the kayak at its center, just holding on to keep it from floating away. Now push upward as if you were trying to heave the kayak into the air. This method needs practice for individual boats, but it works. Stay with the kayak until your friends arrive.)

Chapter 10

MAINTENANCE & BUILDING

An ounce of prevention is worth a pound of cure, goes the old adage, and this is certainly true of a regular maintenance program for canoes and kayaks. Apart from protecting your investment, regular maintenance of paddles and hull can save you frustration—and sometimes more—on the stream.

Maintaining your craft is not as large-scale an event as actually building one. Most of it will consist of repairing small leaks, and mending paddles. Occasionally you may come up with a special problem—such as crunching the nose of your kayak—which some ingenuity can solve, as did one East Coast kayaker, who now has the first of the soft-nosed kayaks. His remedy: a multiplicity of aerospace tape formed to make a new nosepiece.

Modern technology has brushed off quite well on aquasport, with fiberglass techniques the most used. The industrial use has been vastly improved over the past few years, and earlier criticisms of grp were for the most part due to poor fabrication technique or simply careless manufacture. With the new glass and resin materials now available, even an averagely skilled handyman can make up a one-holer over a weekend for about $60—provided he's got a mold, of course.

The chemistry involved in new materials is highly sophisticated, but it can be understood quite easily. Take, for instance, some of the new bonding adhesives, or glues as they used to be called. In a metal-to-metal bond, the glue itself becomes part of the join. First it acts as a catalyst in causing a molecular change to take place within the metals, so that, if you like, the hookup occurs at a highly uncomplicated level of atoms. This is enhanced by the pressure used to hold the join together while the bonding adhesive performs its magic.

Much the same molecular hookup occurs when glass cloth is impregnated with resin.

Resins can be simple or complicated. The sort used for making fiberglass repairs is quite simple, needing only to be "activated" and brushed on. For building, more sophisticated types may be used, ranging from regular resins, which are about the same color and viscosity as molasses, to very heavy, almost jellylike resins which are used as an outer coat on hulls.

In order to get the resins to work on the glass fibers, two things are needed: a catalyst, which starts the resin working; and an accelerator, which speeds up the action. But most resins on the market for amateur use are pre-accelerated and thus require only the catalyst to get them going.

Working with glass fiber is not difficult, but you should remember that you are dealing with chemicals which have several undesirable properties when used on human beings. The catalyst, in particular, should always be carefully stored, and any splashed on the skin should be washed off promptly with plenty of water.

The reason fiberglass has such a good strength ratio is that the final product is an amalgam of the tensile strength of the glass, plus the brittle rigidity of resin. But in order to get the maximum strength from the mix, there has to be an exact proportion of one to the other, and there must be as close contact as possible—so that the molecular hookup goes deep.

Glass fiber comes in several versions, from simple chopped strand mat, used mostly for reinforcement, through high-performance woven fabrics and the more open fabrics, to surface mats, which are used for exterior faces, and which improve resistance to crazing and protects the interior layers.

Since this is still a relatively new field, improvements in fabrics are being made on an ongoing basis. As a general rule, fabrics which are woven are more costly than chopped mat, but are stronger and need less resin to process them. A good woven fabric will generally have about twice the strength of a mat, but mats give better rigidity. If you are going to be using fiberglass for building, you should decide before you begin just what your boat will be used for, and what strength-weight ratio, and flexibility are involved. You should also decide on the cost, plus the ability of the constructor. The best way to learn is to make friends with someone who already builds—chances are that if you join a club you'll find one or two people who have already used the material and can show you how to work with it.

You'll also need to get some form of cleaning agent for your equipment, and something to protect your skin, such as a barrier cream, since glass and resin tend to irritate. If you're building, you'll also need a release wax so the laminate can be removed from the mold without damaging either.

The equipment needed is simple. For cutting, a pair of commercial cutting out scissors will do, plus a strong trimming knife with a wide blade. Some builders favor using a chisel for final trimming, in which case a small hammer (rubber headed) might be added. Several builders also use hacksaws or rotary saws for trimming after hardening.

A system of measurement must be worked out for resins and the various additives. Easiest is a spring balance for weighing, and a kitchen measuring cup. You can also use used washing-up liquid containers.

If you buy bulk—and bulk is much less expensive—you can measure off various quantities as you need them. Keep all resin and associated products stored in a dry, clean, fireproof place.

For mixing, sticks of cleaned wood are fine, provided you don't mind working the mixture until thoroughly completed. As a time-saver, you can make up a sort of egg-whisk device with a fairly heavy-gauge piece of wire and use it in a power drill. Some people have even had success with those European-type egg whisks.

Rollers and brushes will be needed for applying resin, and the ordinary good-quality painting type will do. Brushes can usually be bought with the other goods, and are theoretically intended for use with resin. The rollers help squeeze out air and thoroughly mix the resin through the cloth. Remember that unless cleaned promptly, brushes and rollers can very quickly be ruined. Have some cleaning agent available to dunk them in immediately after using. And as soon as the work is completed, take a pail of hot water and work them—and your hands—thoroughly clean. Then give the rollers and brushes another rinse in some more hot water before cleaning them further with kitchen soap, or a liquid detergent. After the soap bath, rinse again and dry thoroughly.

MAINTENANCE PROGRAM

Kayaks and canoes that are expected to work for their owners need a regular maintenance program. Chafing from suspended particles in the water, rubbing and abrasions of the hull which occur in shallow waters, and careless handling are just part of their normal wear and tear. Even careless loading and unloading onto roofracks or trailers can cause damage.

Then there are the more unusual occurrences: the unexpected log lurking just under the water's surface, or a misplaced rock in white water. The jarring thump that accompanies such encounters tells its own story, and, unless competing, the wise paddler makes for a convenient bank and inspects the impact area.

But the maintenance program should begin once you've made or purchased your canoe. The initial customizing and fitting out is the beginning. And most people include a good wax polishing before launching. Wax helps protect the outer skin and keeps the exterior surfaces cleaner, longer. Wax also makes it easier to keep the canoe clean.

On fiberglass boats, scratching is inevitable unless the canoe never leaves the showroom. Depending on the depth of scratches, since very light ones can be left for a more major operation, the area around it should be thoroughly cleaned. Use an acetone-based cleaning agent—the one used for cleaning the brushes may work very well, but read the label first—to clear the area, being sure that, once prepared, it is thoroughly washed off, since it will attack the resin if left. Any loose resin should be removed, and the area to be mended should be roughened with sandpaper. If a rather large area must be treated, the area can be scratched every so often with a file to ensure a closer bonding.

Blow away any loose residue, and dry off with paper towel before proceeding further.

Now you need to decide how much gel coat resin you're going to need to plug the area. Ideally, this should be pigmented so that the color will match. When you're ready to start, mix in the activator and, when mixed in, carefully fill the area with the mix. Use a little more than needed so the new resin mix stands slightly above the normal surface. Now get some Scotch tape and cover the overall area so that the excess resin is squeezed out. This lets the resin contour itself to the line of the hull and also leaves a gloss finish when set.

If the repair was occasioned by one of the thumping noises mentioned earlier, you will do well to inspect both sides of the scratch. It may turn out to be serious, with some structural damage inside. If this is so, use an internal patch—if necessary using glass cloth—as well as the external repair. As a general rule, if the scratch is deep, add a little glass fiber.

Some canoe people prefer to let the bottom of their vessels take a pounding and then do a complete recover. This works quite well, but it is probably better to attach strips of fiberglass to the underside before you begin. It may very slightly detract from performance, but if the strips have been properly finished—burnished and polished after curing—there should be little loss.

Depending on the canoe's condition, a simple gel resin finish can be applied, after thoroughly cleaning and drying, but don't use too much. That is, regard it as a painting job rather than as a covering job. In such circumstances use a good polyurethane house exterior paint or a more expensive yacht finishing paint. Two thin coats should be ample, and the dried (cured) end result should be burnished first and then wax polished. Rubbing down between coats will help the finishing. The compound used by used-car people to brighten up the paintwork of old cars works very well for burnishing. The substance is like a coarse putty which is rubbed in well and then buffed. Then, the wax polish goes on. A power drill helps enormously during these polishing stages.

Let us suppose the worst has happened: the thump has produced a hole. A simple puncture can usually be fixed so that you can get home, but anything more serious will require complicated repair work. A crack through the hull will need a two-stage treatment, with glass mat or fabric and mat applied over the entire area of cracking from the inside. Resin should be forced into the crack before the glass is layed, and then the interior should be let to set.

The exterior will now have some sort of excrescence which needs cleaning and roughing before a gel is added. It's worth taking particular care at this stage, since even a large crack can be made good. Use a file to begin with, and finish with sandpaper.

If you have literally holed the boat, you now have a big project, since some splintering will almost certainly have occurred. What you must do is to cut away from the center of the hole until you get to still solid material. Carefully clean out this area so that there are no lurking whisps around. Try to end up with a V shape so you will have something for the material to hold on to.

For about an inch around this area, file and sand so prepare the adjacent surface inside and out. Next take some Scotch tape—or if the hole is too large to be conveniently covered—some heavy-grade plastic wrap and secure this to the outside with tape. This must be firmly attached so you can push a little against it without its coming adrift.

Depending on where the hole is, you now apply glass cloth and resin. If the hole is in a difficult position, you may have to apply the cloth and resin in a wetted state. The hole should be gradually filled, until the area is filled. A typical way to handle this is to start with a surface mat which is blocked in from about one inch all the way around into the hole. This can be followed by chopped strand mat, and then finished with a neat-woven fabric patch. It is vital to make certain that the proper quantity of resin is used in making the repair.

A more complicated mix would be to use surface mat, backed by woven fabric, then chopped mat, and finally, woven fabric. In order to ensure that the patch works properly, don't skimp on the final patch to cover the working area. There should be a reasonably generous overlap.

To make sure that the glass cloth is thoroughly impregnated with resin, the area can be rollered from the outside if the interior is firmly backed. Then the patch is left to cure, and the exterior is taken care of along lines already described. Where you simply can't get at the interior, you may have to work the backing piece into place from the outside. A simple clamp, as used by automobile-body builders, can be made to hold it secure—a nut and bolt on plywood will do. This is let free once the interior has set, and you just have a small hole where the bolt went to fill in. The interior piece of ply can be extracted via the cockpit, as can the bolt.

On longer strips a simple repair kit should be carried in a waterproof bag, since it is possible—if you've got a tent—to undertake quite difficult repairs in the field. Typical might be:

> Glass: woven fabric, 2 square feet
> mat, 2 square feet
> Resin (viscous, fast setting), 1 pound
> Activator, as required
> Acetone cleaner, 1 pint
> 3 cheap 1-inch brushes
> 1 small roll cardboard
> 1 roll Scotch tape (take heavy-gauge reinforced plus regular)
> 1 roll heavy-gauge kitchen wrap (plastic)
> 1 roll masking tape
> 1 pair scissors
> 1 small file
> Sandpaper
> 1 screwdriver

You could also add a clamp device made up from ¼-inch ply.

Unless you are very unlucky, you should not have to deal with something you can't manage to jury-rig to see you home. Most of your problems will be in the nature of scratching and minor indentations if your canoe has been properly made. Larger cracks and small holes can be patched on the inside and taped on the exterior to get you back safely.

Fiberglass repairs can also be made on wood-hull and canvas-and-wood canoes. Waterproof repair tape also works well for slight damage, and several "wood" putties are on the market for use as filler. The substance is used to plug the hole, and, once set, it can be filed smooth.

If the damage is more serious, it is better to wait for repairs until you get the canoe home. But simple jury-rig using canvas patches which have been waterproofed and then taped inside and out will usually do in the meantime. Another possibility is to use a thin piece of ply in the inside, which is secured by an apoxy glue (it will take about half an hour to dry), and either tape or patch the exterior, with a canvas patch.

Wooden canoes can be protected from abrasives by giving them a fiberglass skin on their undersides.

Temporary patching may also be used on aluminum canoes, but to ensure their staying leakproof you may need to use automobile body filler instead.

ROUTINE MAINTENANCE

Routine maintenance is best considered in three parts: hull, paddles, miscellaneous.

Damage to the hull can also be divided three ways: scratches and minor cracks, which entail work only from the exterior; larger cracks, which may go through the hull, and small holes, and more extensive damage.

Given patience and a little ingenuity, the first two are fairly simple to deal with. In terms of getting back to the original finish, they may be somewhat time-consuming, but the hours will be well spent since it is proper for you to look after your craft.

Larger repairs, especially if you're new to maintenance, may give you a headache if there's no one to talk to, but you can usually figure a way out.

For routine maintenance, always put aside one day for a full inspection when you get back from a trip. You'll most likely have made a quick check on hauling out, but the best system is to make the next morning your inspection time. Make a note of what needs to be done on a piece of paper, and mark off the area that requires attention on the hull with a chinagraph pencil.

Paddles can be inspected at the same time, and you may want to consider the possibility of some preventive maintenance here. Paddle tips frequently suffer from being bashed against rocks, and one way to lengthen their lives is to apply a strip of glass-woven fabric around and over their ends. This should be cut rather carefully to ensure a neat finish.

Before starting the project, clean off the blade with sand or carborundum paper, and then cover with cloth and cut around it. The cloth can be tacked into place to hold it, but you should have some resin underneath for bonding. Make sure it is thoroughly impregnated with resin and, to ensure a good finish, cover with kitchen wrap (waxed kitchen paper also works) and secure with rubber bands. If you have a workshop, you can set up the end in a vise.

Once cured, finish with file and sandpaper, and then burnish and polish. This can also be done to cheaper untipped blades.

Paddles benefit from regular care, and much can be done to make them more comfortable to use. Wooden paddle shafts can be carefully sanded where you grip them, to reduce the chance of blistering. Ingenuity is a key here. Some of the more expensive equipment has a specially shaped grip— you might want to check it out and see if you can adapt the near disk-shaped grip on your own shaft.

Under the heading of miscellaneous items include such essential as kneegrips (functioning properly?), kneestraps (for thigh support in canoes), seat and rear-end support, and so forth. When was the last time you checked the straps (binding) holding your spare paddle? Or when did you check the hip supports in your kayak? Prepare a check list for those items you worked on when readying your canoe, and make sure they're regularly inspected.

A maintenance program is worth carrying out since it ensures that your craft is in shipshape condition almost all the time—except when it is actually under repair. A good maintenance program is one you work out for yourself. Make those check lists, set aside a particular time each week, and carry it all through. It requires some effort to begin with, but in terms of helping you help yourself, it's worth it.

Don't forget to include in your maintenance program an inspection of life-saving equipment (threads wear too), your spray skirt, and so on. Is your helmet strap comfortable? Too loose? Should it be changed?

BUILDING

It's not that difficult to build a canoe. Any person with some ability and patience in handling the average handyman's tools with reasonable accuracy can tackle it. On the other hand, if it's the instant gratification of ownership that you really want, you'll do much better forgetting about the homey odors of varnish and wax, of wood or grp, and simply buy a regular factory-made product.

Homebuilding offers a number of plusses—not least the act of creation itself involved in the manufacture of your toy—and a few headaches. The head- and heartaches are from things that somehow don't come out right, including the time involved to bring the work to completion. You will, of course, need some spare space that can be used for working on the project.

The easy way to go is to use kits. Several are on the market these days, offering excellent value for the person who enjoys the challenge of working on a project, but who finds that time is a life ingredient not to be too generously allotted to making things. Of particular interest is the so-called kayel method of construction, of which a variety of plans are available, and which can be worked up by the individual once the principle is understood.

Under this system, no building boards, frames, or molds are needed. And the construction can even take place in the living room, if you can requisition it from time to time. However, if this is your first venture in building, you would do well to work from published plans.

The kayel system begins with drawings that are full scale and show the actual shape of ply panels used in construction. The measurements are easily placed on the

ply, which is then cut. Joins are fixed in two ways: either by gluing and nailing, or br drilling fine holes and first wiring and then laminating with fiberglass. The plans give complete instructions that must be followed and are easy to work from.

If you already design boats, you will probably have essayed this method of construction, since it is the easiest of them all. And if you would like to start designing boats, this method offers you an easy way to begin. A few thoughts before going into more detail about construction will save you time.

Those who already have made homebuilding a part of their way of life will need no reminding that when the canoe is finished, it is not quite that easy to take it to the water and handle it safely from the word go. Read some of the earlier chapters on technique first, and perhaps then join a club and take part in a regular program of training.

Modern white-water canoes are not easily distinguishable from kayaks. They are decked, and the initial visual clue is that the canoe is wider and that its occupant is using a single paddle. A second clue—if the canoe is empty—is that there is no regular seat, only a butt support and thigh straps. A kayak usually has a molded seat and is equipped with a footrest, kneegrips, and hip supports. Both the canoeist and the kayakist use spray skirts, and both boats can be rolled.

Sprint-racing canoes and kayaks are more obviously distinguished since the former are open like the old Indian canoe. But there the resemblance ends, save in the high kneeling position used by the paddler. Finally, there is the traditional canoe that most of us bring to mind when hearing the term *canoe*.

So these factors should be taken into consideration before it is decided that homebuilding is the answer. The next question—before we get to whether the design will be our own, or whether we'll use someone else's design—is what will be the purpose of the boat? What material will it be made of? Further thought should be given to the benefits of using a kit, since this is a quick way to get a boat built, in that most of the parts are ready to assemble.

Still, the canoe's purpose is perhaps the most important consideration, since the most vital factors in a construction of this sort are stability and speed. Speed, which in canoe terminology really means ease of paddling, is directly related to length. Any boat going through the water creates a wave with its bow, and up to 4 knots the bow wave is rather short and low and hardly creates a hollow behind it. Length soon comes into the equation.

In a manner similar to that occurring when an aircraft

1.

2.

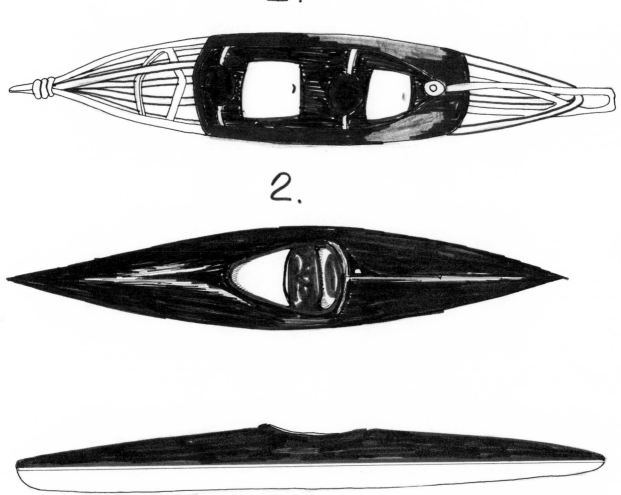

1. The skeletal structure of an Eskimo kayak. The loading area is shown opened. The actual hunting boat is much more skinny and squats close to the water. 2. Today's slalom kayak, with moderate rocker to bow and stern, and symmetrical shape.

There's a lot of talk about the best way to measure your paddle, but the best way is to try out several of various lengths and see which you're most comfortable with. Here Ed. Bliss (Canoe & Kakay Club of NY President) shows how he selects his paddles, starting from the high kneeling position and working it out from there. Note the relative shortness of the shaft--competition paddlers prefer not too long a loom.

A couple of ropes can easily support a canoe for maintenance, provided there's something to steady it with at one end. Work in progress here was making good the seal between hull and top.

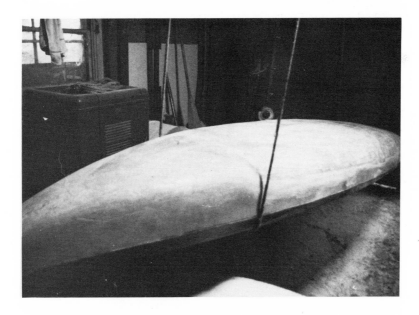

Ropes again provide adequate support for working on the underside of the hull of a canoe. Strips of laminate may be applied to the canoe's bottom where working in shallow waters (or surf) is anticipated. For surf, the entire structure requires strengthening.

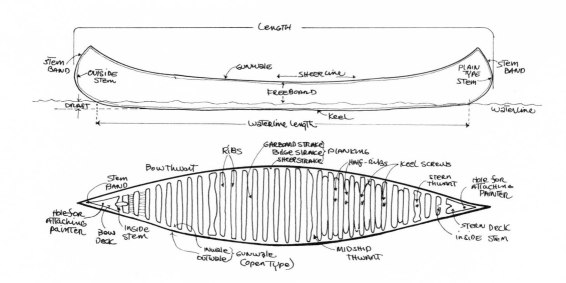

*Above--primitive dugout type canoe. Below--American In-
dian birchbark type open canoe.*

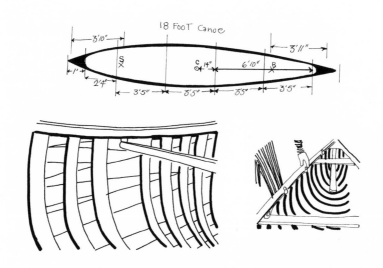

*Locating the thwarts in an 18-foot canoe. The various
stations are shown, and thwarts can be provided at SX for
bow person, BX for stern person. An additional thwart can
be provided at X for either a passenger of for solo paddling.*

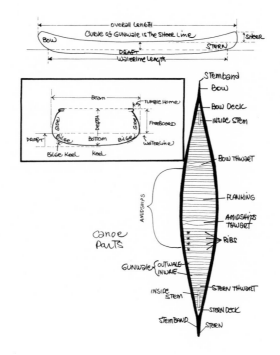

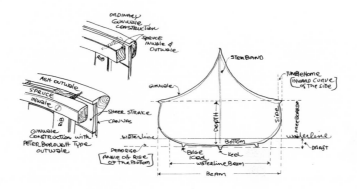

Detail showing relationship of inwale and outwale (gun-wale), shoe and regular keel, and a hull fitted with bilge keels.

approaches the sound barrier, there is a relatively speedy buildup of resistance. Unlike speedboats, canoes rely on a person's arms for power. This means that the planing-type hull—which allows you to plane on the bow wave—cannot be used. As a result, you must design a longer canoe to get more speed (for planing, you use a shorter length and more power.) For the longer the length, the higher the speed at which friction takes its toll in the form of bow-wave resistance.

But longer canoes present problems of their own. First, since there is more material required to put them together, they cost more. Next, questions arise about how you'll store and transport them to the water. Thirdly, while they'll tend to keep to a straight course, they can be difficult to turn unless you use a fairly large rudder—which in turn can add drag. And if you want to make them maneuverable, you may have to give up some of their ability to keep going straight.

Sprint-racing canoes are therefore quite long—about 17 feet, while slalom canoes, which require maneuverability rather than speed, are usually not much more than 13 feet. A touring canoe, not really intended for competition work, will be somewhere between 14 and 15 feet for inland cruising, while for sea cruising, some additional length is carried, since the question of maneuverability is not so crucial while at sea, and the additional length provides for directional stability in waves.

Then there's our old favoriet, the double-ended American canoe, which ranges from around 12 to 18 feet. Here the optimum size for two paddlers is around 16 to 17 feet.

Decisions regarding materials go hand in hand with design. Fairly east-to-follow plans for homebuilding canoes have been around for more than a hundred years, and are getting better. For most homebuilders, it is considerably easier to follow a set of plans than to make up one's own—at least to start with. On the other hand, the type of material you plan to use may dictate the design. It is proposed, therefore, to concentrate on three potential methods of construction. First, the traditional wooden-framed skin-covered canoe; and next, two methods which require a mold, fiberglass, and molded veneer. The kayel method is best dealt with via a kit.

For the serious canoeist, homebuilding in fiberglass offers the most advantages. A mold can be taken off an existing boat which has performed well but which can stand some improvement. The modifications are then applied directly to the mold, and the new version is then laid up. A second possibility is to build a mold directly from one's own design, and then make modifications as performance figures are fed back to the drawing board. Finally, a mold can be made up from someone else's design. The big plus here is that once a mold has been made, it can be used to make up quite a number of boats before it needs to be replaced. And it is quite simple to keep a mold in decent condition, so that it will last a number of years—if the design is that good.

WOOD AND FABRIC CANOE

Perhaps the best thing about building a traditional fabric-covered canoe is that you can build up the round-bottomed hull without the need for the skilled joinery involved in serious woodworking. Also, cost is not too much of a consideration, and the end result is easily made pleasing to the eye without too much skill on the part of the homebuilder.

Before getting out it is necessary to have a plan. You can either make one up from an existing canoe—making sure that the measurements are very precise—or you can purchase a design quite inexpensively. If you are building from another designer's plan, a bill of materials should be included. (A bill of materials tells you exactly what you need in order to produce the finished article.) If you're working from your own design, you will also have to work out your own bill of materials.

Before setting out on the project, study the bill of materials with some care. When dealing with a project of this nature, it is usually possible to work out the stages in which construction will be completed, and thus work out a purchasing schedule which will lessen the strain on your budget—an important consideration these days.

The quality of materials you'll buy is important. The better you can afford, the better the overall quality of your craft. Ply (used for making frames) should be marine quality and resin bonded. If you can't find marine ply locally, an exterior-quality ply will do. Main structural parts of lightweight softwood and sitka spruce—also popular with homebuilders of light aircraft—are favored. White cedar can also be used, if rib construction is preferred. Both hickory and rock elm may be used in place of ash for bent parts. All wooden parts should be fine-sanded and varnished to finish. This will provide a smart and pleasing appearance on completion.

It is unlikely that you'll be using many metal parts, but where metal strip has to be used, brass or gunmetal strip is best. Stainless steel, though even more resistant to corrosion, is rather difficult to work. Aluminum should be chosen with some care, since only a seawater-resistant type should be used. Metals can be sprayed with silicone to help waterproof them, but usage will usually cause this barrier to wear off.

Brass nails and screws are best for fixing wooden joints, and can be assisted—for additional strength—by several of the new adhesives. A less expensive substitute for areas where the risk of abrasion is limited are zinc-plated steel screws. However, these will quickly rust if the zinc plating gets scraped off. Copper tacks should be used for attaching canvas to the frame; or stainless steel staples (to be used from a stallegun) can also be used. Check on prices before making your decision, since in some areas copper may be less expensive, while the stainless-steel staples can be cheaper in others.

For ease of work, a decent-sized work table should be furnished. If you don't have one already, and are thinking of starting up your own woodworking shop, check out a few carpenters' shops and see how they're put together. The main requirements are a straight (i.e., level) work surface, and space for storing the tools you'll use. A vise is almost indispensable.

If you are going to be shaping wood, you'll need something on which to boil a kettle to provide you with steam—and you will need that vise. Modern bending equipment can also be used or (you might be able to arrange with a lumber yard's equipment for this.)

Before you actually begin, make sure you are completely familiar with each stage of the plan. Each item that must be tackled can be tackled more easily if you visualize how to complete it in advance. Time spent in mentally preparing yourself for the task will pay off in time saved doing the work. This is particularly important if the canoe is to be a group project. Each person must know exactly what is what, and each and every stage must be familiar to all workers. There will then be no arguments during construction.

Another time-saver is to see if construction can be broken down into the fabrication of subassemblies. This should be done if at all possible, since working on smaller units makes for greater overall accuracy. There are a number of areas where this policy may be followed with advantage in making fabric-covered canoes. Small parts can be added to frames, or the hog or other parts can be assembled before being built into their place within the framework.

If you are uncertain of your ability to steam frames to shape, one fairly easy alternative is to make the frames themselves, up by lamination. You will need to make up formers to provide the necessary support for the laminate, and the use of plywood templates can save time here. The technique is simplicity itself: merely bend several strips of laminate around a former with a layer of glue (use the modern adhesives) between each. Once set, you can finish these.

By making up each former this way, you can exercise a much greater degree of control over the hull shape of your vessel. And if tumble home is of importance in your design, this is more easily managed by careful crimping of the frame before the adhesive dries.

The only time you are likely to be faced with a dilemma is in the building of a canoe with more than moderate rocker, since this may have to be completed upside down. Here you will need to mount the frames and end posts on a building plank and use temporary spreaders to relate them to the plank. The hog—the central bottom piece to which other parts are attached—will then have to be bent down at each end. This is rather tedious and can be done by using ply of the appropriate thickness and a good circular saw. It is not as elegant a way to solve the problem as others, but it works. Another possibility is to make up the hog out of two pieces which have been fastened, and which may be made up to the curve necessary for rocker.

On the basis that the simplest is usually easiest, the most usual method of building is right way up. Frames and end posts are attached to the hog. Since there are numerous screws to be used for fastening, it is as well to semi-iautomate the process. For this, you require a drill. First of all—from the plans—mark up with a ballpoint where you will need to various screws. Next, take a thinnish drill, rather less in size than the size screw you'll be using, and drill down to almost the length of the screw. Next, take a larger-sized drill, perhaps about two sizes down from the screw you'll be using, and open up about one-eighth of an inch. You'll cut down the time required for inserting screws, and you will also obviate that bane of every homebuilder, the splintering of your wood. Screws should be driven in until they are flush with the surface.

The entire structure should be attached to a decent-weight plank. You can do this either by using clamps or, better, by using screws through holes in the hog. These can be used later if you want to fit a keel or a ballast. Pieces of string can be used to true the lines at the end posts and to check the center lines of the frames. This is quite important, since the structural integrity of the vessel will depend on how well these lines are trued.

The inwale and gunwale can be as simple or as complicated as you want. Depending on the amount of tumble home required—and this will be a matter for careful measurement during fabrication since each side must be a mirror image of the other unless you want an asymmetrical canoe—it is usually best to start your fore-and-aft stringers from the upper center. Work each stage in conjunction with its opposite section on the port side. Go forward one or two frames. Then go backward, one or two frames, so that the whole thing is carefully balanced from the center.

This is the most crucial stage of construction, and if it isn't right, you'll find that more distortion can occur when underway. It's worth taking time over.

If you are fashioning a flattish deck—using chine—the easiest method is to use ply. It can be sanded off and the curve at the chine finished smoothly. The chine joint, however, should be made very secure using both adhesive and either a tack, wire—through drilled holes—or a carefully centered screw. If wire is used for the fastening, it should be smoothed off and filled with wood putty as required.

Varnishing is important, and not less than three coats are needed for a decent finish. All joints should be smoothed, and some prefer to give the first one or two coats before any work is done. If canvas is being used, it is felt by the old school that it should be applied to wet varnish to ensure a more watertight attachment.

As far as the fabric covering is concerned, the most important matter is ensuring a wrinkle-free finish. The key here is warmth, and the best time to do this part of the work is on a warm summer day. If you have to work indoors, suffer some sweat and keep everything warm. If canvas is being used, some builders like to dampen it a little, by using one of those water atomizers for plants. This helps in making a tight fit, but don't overdo the watering, since the canvas could tear when dry.

To toughen the underside, many builders favor placing wooden strip keels and bilge keels. These should be as carefully finished as the framers, to reduce drag. And in the interior, some simply made bottom boards do not merely help spread the load but also add to the finished appearance.

MOLDED VENEER AND FIBERGLASS

Making canoes with molds to assist in shaping the craft is both easier and more difficult than building from scratch. It is easier since once a suitable mold has been made, it can become a master mold from which several canoes can be built. It is more difficult in that the mold itself must be constructed with considerable care. And indeed, making up a mold for the inexperienced may well take as long as fabricating a regular canoe.

Depending on the length of the canoe, it will usually be necessary to make only two molds—a bottom mold for the hull, and an upper mold for the deck. Where symmetrical form is used, it is possible to use a half-mold for the deck and join the two parts at the center of the cockpit area. Still,

a one-piece finish looks better. The two molded portions are then joined along the gunwale line.

There are two ways to go about making molds. The first is from an existing boat which you feel could be improved with some modification. The second is from a plan. In the former, you will take your initial mold directly from the boat and then mount it, before polishing and making changes. In the second, you start by making up sections from the drawings into plywood or hardboard.

Depending on how many sections there are, you'll need hardboard or ply from which to make them, and some lumber on which the structure can be set. A power drill with saw attachment saves considerable time, as does a reasonably fitted workshop. Carbon paper and a pencil or, a ballpoint pen are helpful for marking up the wood, and string is used for seeing that all is aligned properly. In addition, moderately heavyweight cardboard will be required, together with a staplegun and some staples.

The first thing to do is to make up the various sections out of ply or hardboard. While this is going on, you should be deciding whether you are going to make an entire plug of the canoe you are going to be building—this helps considerably in getting joins right once you've taken the molds—or whether you are going to make two plugs. If the latter, considerably more care must be taken in setting up the initial plug, and all measurements must be checked carefully. It's particularly necessary to check the mirror-image quality of each section, but time can be saved by making up simple templates which can measure one side and simply be reversed to measure its opposite.

If you are making a full plug, the centers of each section should be drilled out, and a square hole made to take a piece of lumber of about 2 x 2, or 3 x 1 feet. This should be a decent piece of timber which has already been planed and sanded. It should be knot-free. Each section is fitted into place and pinned with a couple of tacks on each side. You now anchor each section with strong: one piece along the keel line from stem to stern, stapled to each section; one piece from stem to stern around each gunnel; and finally one over the deck. This gives the structure some stability and also enables you to check the flow of the lines.

The next stage is to cover this structure with cardboard. This doesn't have to be too perfect a job, but it is worth taking some time over since you are going to be putting some covering over this in a while. The cardboard can also be stapled into place. The cardboard covering will give you the shape you are about to work with, so make it reasonably efficient. If you can afford it, lightweight nylon fabric works even better, though it is flexible.

The next stage is to lightly wet the cardboard with resin and then lay it up with 1½-ounce mat. This may be difficult to thoroughly wet, and you'll have to work it with a paintbrush for a bit before using rollers on it. This should be left for a day or two to dry out thoroughly, and then polished. All bumps should be sanded down (your power drill makes this quite easy), and any hollows should be filled.

The process is completed again, and, if you wish, you can include an upper layer of woven fabric over the second lot of grass mat. Again let dry, and again fill, grind, and polish. To make a secure plug, a third coating is recommended. You can—if you don't mind going to the extra expense—use woven fabric instead of mat in the third stage, finishing with surface tissue.

During the first stage, should you manage to go through the glass in your enthusiasm for polishing, simply cover with masking tape—this is all right at this stage, but not at the later stages. The plug should be allowed at least an additional two days to cure before you start your final filling and polishing.

Ordinarily automobile body filler works well—as does the automobile body compound for polishing—in finalizing the shape of the plug. Keep one eye on your drawings at this stage and measure everything carefully. If this is a largish canoe, you may be tempted to use a sander for smoothing, but use a pallet knife—it is more accurate. And you can check high and low spots by shining a light on the hull from a distance.

Allow to harden, polish, and repeat the process. Repeat one more time. If your plug is not ready now, it never will be. Run your hand lightly over it, and if it feels about right, it probably is. You are now ready to polish.

The process up to now has taken about a week of work in the evenings. The filling has actually been the longest part, since it has meant going over every item. Now you will need to sand out all the slight marks that have been left over. Don't do this until the filler has completely set or you'll waste your paper.

A series of final coats of resin are now applied. Check with your supplier for the finishing coats available in your area, some brands are available in certain parts of the country and not in others. The Furane people make a product that is well favored, but most companies producing resins include this finishing resin in their product line. You will want about six coats—this will take about four hours to apply, letting each dry before putting on the next.

Leave for about thirty hours to harden and then use wet-and-dry cutting paper on it first—wet. You may have to go down through the resin coat to the filler in some areas,

and you may need more filler. This is your last chance to perfect the plug, and you should take some time on it. When you are happy with it, give it another six coats, and repeat the wet-and-dry process but using a very fine grade of wet-and-dry. By now there should be a dull sheen all over.

The plug is now ready for polishing, with a compounding to begin with. Using an automobile compound, go over the entire surface very lightly, using a soft mop to buff with. Don't use a high-speed drill at this stage—the ordinary handyman's drill is fast enough for the buffing you'll be doing. When the compound is finally worked, you start in on polishing. Use a good high-quality wax polish—and, again you'll need at least six coats. Once completed, you have a plug from which a mold can be taken.

The point of taking such trouble in finishing the plug is that if you are going to get a satisfactory mold you must make sure that the plug is well sealed.

The next job will be to make up a temporary flange so that the upper and lower parts can be separated. Release agents are next applied to the plug, and the mold is then built up, much as was the plug itself. It makes good sense to ensure that the mold is strongly built, since it will last much longer. For this reason, some builders prefer to provide reinforcement to the mold. These can either be thin pieces of metal, woven rovings of glass fiber, or even cardboard tubing. Thin stringers of wood can also be used if needed.

The most difficult parts to form are the joins at the flange, and great care should be taken here to ensure an ultimate good fit. It is here that the builder may decide to use reinforcing so that no twisted lines will occur during fabrication of the canoe.

Once completed, the molds should be allowed to cure for a week in a constant temperature. If the mold is still not stiff enough and tends to twist, it will have to have additional stiffening.

A simple cradle should be worked out so that the mold can be worked on satisfactorily. The mold requires finishing in much the same manner as the plug, and once made up, your first task—before you pull a complete hull—should be to make up a new plug, a sort of master plug. You can also make up master molds, too.

In making up your molds it is suggested that you use a double get coat and not less than 4½-ounce minimum thickness of glass mat and cloth.

TAKING A CANOE FROM THE MOLD

Provided the plug was made properly, and that you took reasonable care in making the mold, the canoe that you'll take from the mold will be acceptable. The more the care that went into each stage, the greater the acceptability of the end product.

In order to get a decent canoe from a mold you must have a proper working area. Ideally, you need to have access to the mold from around it; one way to arrange this is to use slings. The disadvantage is that the canoe will move unless some support is placed at one or both ends.

Your materials should be stowed away from the working area, but so that they are reasonably accessible. You need to have running water—or several containers of water—plus something for washing in. Hot water is essential, as are various chemical-type cleaners. Soap, water, and paper towels are necessary too. Barrier cream, which you put on and rub into your skin before working, is highly recommended. Temperature and humidity control are important if you are aiming at producing a high-quality product, though with some of the newer resins on the market this is not as crucial a matter as it once was.

Before starting, make sure that all the materials you are going to need are to hand. For a single-place fiberglass canoe, you will want about $60 worth of materials, and this should be available and ready when you want to start. Completion time: one weekend.

Brushes and rollers should be clean and ready for work. Glass can be precut—this really saves time—and if patterns are available there is a considerable saving of material that otherwise might be wasted.

Lastly, the mold must be prepared. Wash out with hot water and detergent, rinse with clean water, and finally dry with soft towels.

The next step is to wax lightly and polish with a soft mop. Now release agents are applied, and great care must be taken in application. No unevenness should be apparent, and any pools or runs must be smoothed out immediately. There should be no bare patches at all, and the end result should be an even surface all over the area to be covered. If you have to let it dry overnight, a polythene shroud over the entire mold is a good idea—it keeps dust and stuff out.

Finally, check on all the materials, and once the release agent is dry, you are ready to start.

Gel coat. The function of the gel coat is to provide a strong finish to the outside surface of the shell, to disguise the fibers within. It should not be too thick or it may craze too easily. Neither should it be so thin that the fiberglass mat shows through it. If you are using a pigment for coloring, it should be mixed in before applying to the mold. The pigment should be mixed like flour: that is, use a small amount of resin first, and then add the pigmented resin to the other unpigmented resin to color it.

It is important to watch the resin for any sign of gelling during application. If it does start, it will be useless, since it will not be possible to apply it evenly or thinly and should therefore be thrown away.

Surface tissue. Surface tissue makes for a more professional-looking product, and, if you can afford to use it here, it will pay off. The technique is to apply it to the gel coat, pushing it down into the resin with brushes so that it soaks up the resin rather as paper towels would. Builders working regularly with fiberglass recommend applying resin from the gunwale down, but laying up nylon and glass from the keel (or deck centerline) to the gunwale. A final touch of gel will ensure the full wetting of the tissue, which may be gently rolled. *

Main laminations. When you are buying the various items required, make sure that the person from whom you are buying knows what you are trying to build. A good general-purpose resin is easier to use here, since it is less thick (viscous) than specialist resins. The most important point is to make sure that all glass fabric is thoroughly and evenly wetted. The easiest way to do this is to apply resin from one end of the craft to the other, and perhaps have a helper apply the glass fabric. Once again, the more the fabric (mat) can suck up the resin, the better the final bond. It is sometimes helpful for awkward corners to practice the laying up ahead of time. And here it is worth remembering not to lay one piece of cloth immediately on top of another. They should be overlaid carefully, so that the effect is one of even almost wovenness. Lastly, it is important not to use too much resin, since this will drain down and form a puddle in the keel or centerline area. (There are good cost reasons for not being too generous with resin: first, it costs more; secondly, the end result may be too brittle; finally, you'll end up with a heavier canoe than you need.)

Once the first lamination is completed, strips of reinforcing can be put down. If you have used more resin than was needed, you will find this centering in the keel—or deck centerline—area, and if you work quickly, you can put in your reinforcing strip before the resin starts to gel. If you desire to provide a semicircular shape in thais bilge area, cardboard tubing or rope can be used for forming.

A final lamination may then be applied, followed by another layer of surface tissue. This makes the interior finish more professional, and while it isn't absolutely necessary, if you are going to this trouble to make a canoe, you might as well make a decent-looking one. There's also an insurance

---

* Instead of using surface tissue, nylon fabric is finding increasing acceptability among homebuilders of K-1s and C-1s. it is strong, flexible, and more bump resistant.

factor, in that with surface tissue and an internal gel coat you are providing more protection against bumps and dents and even holes.

If you are working by yourself on this project, take good care that your brushes don't gum up before you've finished a particular task. If there are several working together, this is less likely.

Trimming. Provided you can be really neat, most serious trimming can be done as you go along. If you leave it until the material has hardened, you are in for a difficult—and possibly damaging—time. So keep trimming down to a minimum by careful planning. What needs to be done can usually be completed with a sharp knife or commercial scissors. A wide-bladed chisel is also handy.

Releasing. The longer you leave it— and twenty-four hours should be your minimum—the better the result. And while the laminate may appear quite dry in as little as four or five hours, unless it is properly supported it will have a tendency to develop twists and warps.

To release the mold is quite easy, provided you took good care at the beginning of the project in preparing it. A chisel can be used gently against the join of shell and mold,

and once air has been permitted to enter, the process works more or less on its own without the need for much energy on your part.

If it is very tight, some water will usually free it, together with the use of your fist to thump it about a bit. If you have access to compressed air, it is less messy than water, but you should have none of these problems if the mold was properly prepared.

Cleaning. This is really an ongoing process which must not be skimped at any stage, since this is where expenditure can mount up all too quickly. Brushes and rollers are good for nothing but the garbage pail unless cleaned promptly and allowed to dry. Hot water helps matters; and brushes, hands, and rollers should be worked over with resin remover, and then carefully rinsed out and dried. You may need to boil the equipment to get it clean.

In summary, it is not too difficult to build a canoe or kayak of either wood or fiberglass, provided some experience in making things has been obtained. However, if you do decide to try the fiberglass method, talk to someone who has done it. And get some books on how to use fiberglass efficiently and well.

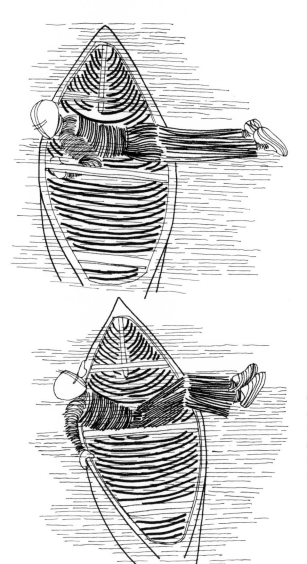

Appendix 1
RESCUE

(A) If capsized some distance from the shore, it is usually best to stay with your canoe since it can provide you with useful buoyancy. Press swamped canoe down and flutter kick your way across the gunwales amidships. (b) Roll yourself over, with your arms and shoulders on one gunwale, and your legs slung across the other.

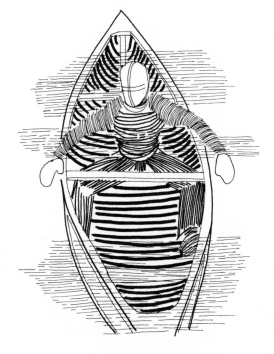

Because of the natural (and artificial) floatation in a canoe, you can handpaddle your way home with a swamped canoe. It will support you too despite its being filled with water, and if you are not in white water--or dangerous conditions--this is the way to go.

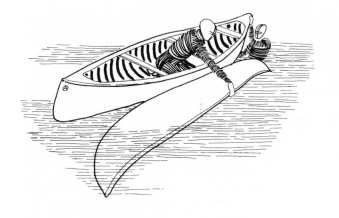

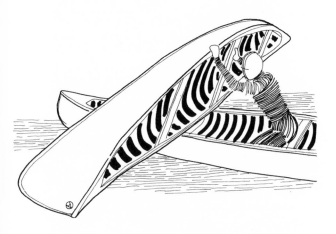

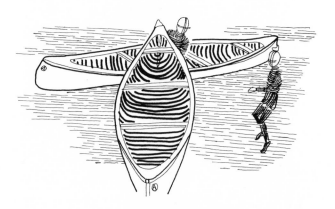

If there is help around, stay in the water and help brace the other canoe as he attempts to get your canoe around (a), and then gets it across his hull to empty it (b), turning it right side up (c) and launching it again (d). Best method of boarding is for other canoeist to brace your vessel alongside his while you board, thus making a platform.

With really tired swimmers it may be all they can do to hold on to the blade in which you may have to pull them in like a fish. (a). Here the paddler opts to brace the canoe (b) while the swimmer slumps himself over the gunwale. It is very important to brace properly for this particular rescue and swamping is all too easy a fate. Note that paddler's weight is mostly on further side of canoe.

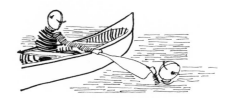

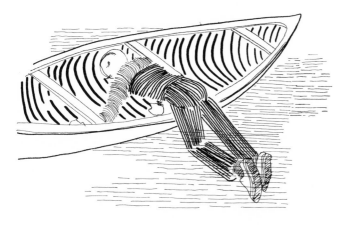

(a) If the capsize has left you outside the canoe and only a little water inside, it is possible to reboard. First grasp the gunwale nearest you. (b) next reach over as far as possible to try to grab the further gunwale with your arm. This canoeist may just make it in before he swamps his canoe if his hands walk fast enough. He did (c) and he swivels himself around to swing his legs inside.

(a) shows canoeist in the water himself with helpless swimmer. He gets him to support himself, before reboarding the craft, and lashing his arms around a thwart (b) is able to paddle him to safety.

A canoe can be used to rescue swimmers in distress. However, approach such persons with great caution at first, since they may well be in shock, if not in panic, and liable to behave irrationally--perhaps tipping you into the water through their anxiety. From top to bottom. Fend them off with a blade, and talk clearly, explaining they should hold on to your paddle blade while they regain their strength. Once they have recovered themselves sufficiently, you may permit them to board. Note that in bottom picture the paddler is seated--to lower the center of gravity--and is also bracing the canoe by paddling. If you are not too far from the shore it may be easier just to give the paddler a tow to the shallows or the shore.

(A) If the person has no more energy left, **you** have to lift. The secret to success here is to make sure that you get as much of the trunk into the canoe. Then (b) get the pelvis and legs into the canoe

Appendix 2
DIAGRAMS

The high kneeling position is mostly used for racing, and the body position is upright and facing slightly toward the paddling side. A sensibly firm kneepad is essential for the high kneeling position, and the knee is placed just off the centerline of the canoe. The toes·of the forward leg are placed toward the centerline also, with the heel out. The left foot is shown braced across the canoe for greater security.

The basic forward stroke which is used when two are paddling for forward motion. The paddle is brought forward and then dipped in and pulled backwards along a line parallel to the boat´s motion. If made single-handedly, the stroke will cause the canoe to turn away from the paddling side.

(ii)
Basic reverse or backwater stroke. Used to slow or halt the canoe, or to move it backward. Used single-handedly, will cause the canoe to turn toward the paddling side. If you´re moving fast, make sure you have a very firm grip of the paddle.

(iii)
The famous J-stroke; the object of which is to drive the canoe forward while correcting the turning tendency.

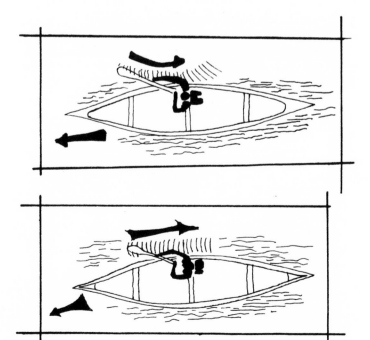

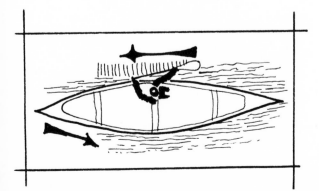

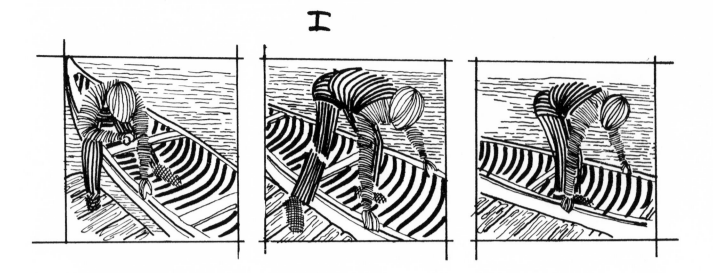

I. Boarding a canoe from a jetty or dock. (a) body weight rests on foot still on jetty, while left moves into boat. Left hand steadies canoe; (b) Both hands now grasp gunwale for security, and weight is then transferred to foot in the canoe; (c) Foot on jetty now is moved into canoe. Either kneel or sit to lower center of gravity.

II. Outside Pivot. (i) Move across canoe from paddling side to begin a reverse quarter sweep (toward the canoe). (ii) as blade comes to hull, lift paddle over to other side, and (iii) make a full 180 degree sweep on normal paddling side (in this instance, the port side). This completes the pivot.

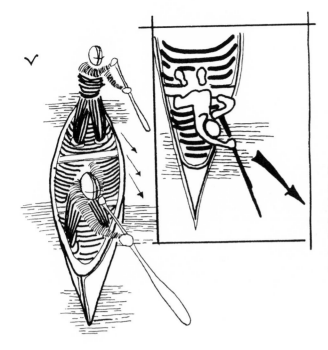

Cross-bow rudder is designed to turn the bow away from the side on which the paddler at the bow has been paddling. This is one of the few occasions when it is accepted that the bow person change sides for paddling. The heel of the right hand may be leaned on the gunwale for extra support. This stroke should be learned at slow speeds--and don't put your left hand in front of your face. You could get a nasty bump.

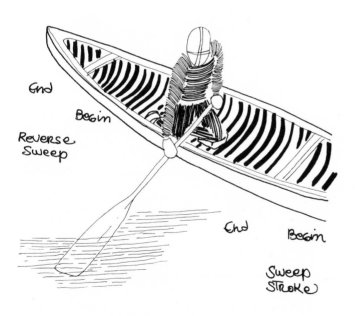

End

Begin

Reverse Sweep

End   Begin

Sweep Stroke

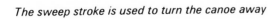

The sweep stroke is used to turn the canoe away

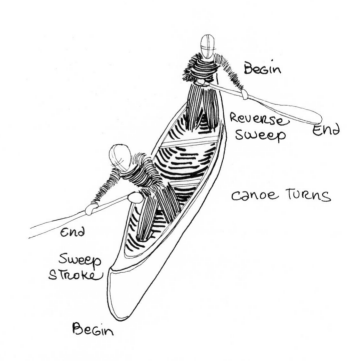

Begin

Reverse Sweep   End

Canoe Turns

End

Sweep Stroke

Begin

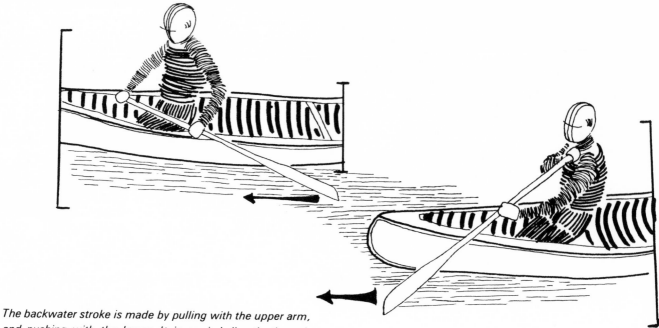

The backwater stroke is made by pulling with the upper arm, and pushing with the lower. It is carried directly through with the blade parallel to the line of the canoe.

In the high kneeling position the canoe is heeled slightly away from the turn it is making.

Shows the completion of the bow stroke, and W.i shows the path of the blade for its return. In (ii) the upper arm is fully extended and the hand should be over the water. The lower hand stops the stroke as it comes to the hip. At (i) the arms are now relaxed, and the blade is carried forward close to the water. The first * marks the point at which the blade is now turned, and the second * nearest the boat is where the new stroke will begin. W.iii shows the end portion of the J-stroke as carried out by the bow person. (Normally the bow person would not be making the J-stroke).

Appendix 3

AMERICAN WHITEWATER AFFILIATES

ALABAMA

N. Alabama River-Runners Association
Carter Martin: 2602 Scenic Dr. S.E.
Huntsville, AL 35801

ALASKA

Knik Kanoers & Kayakers
Ed Swanson: 301 4 Columbia
Anchorage, AK 99504

CALIFORNIA

American Youth Hostels
Santa Clara Valley Club
R.C. Stevens: 5493 Blossom Wood Avenue
San Jose, CA 951 24

Echo Wilderness
Joe Daley: 2424 Russell Street
Berkeley, CA 94705

Feather River   Kayak Club
Mike Schneller: 1 773 Broadway Street
Marysville, CA 95901

Idlewild Yacht Club
Russ Symon, Rep.: 800 Market Street
San Francisco, CA 941 02

Lera Canoe Club
Harold Black: 200 Almond Avenue
Los Altos, CA 94022

Mother Lode Whitewater Experience
Pacific High School: Ken Brunges
581 Continental Drive
San Jose, CA 951 11

Outdoor Adventures
Dave Orlans: 688 Sutter Street
San Francisco, CA 941 02

Sierra Club Loma Prieta Paddlers
Joe Kilner: 1 85 Loucks Avenue
Los Altos, CA 94040

Sierra Club Mother Lode Chapter
Sam Gardali: 91 4 Stanford Avenue
Modesto, CA 95350

Sierra Club River Touring Bay Chapter
Bert Welti: 1 440 Jones, No. 2
San Francisco, CA 941 09

Southern Calif. Canoe Association
Ron Ceurvorst: 3966 S. Menlo Avenue
Los Angeles, CA 90037

Truckee River Kayaks
Box 1592, Tahoe City, CA 95730

Voyageur Canoe & Kayak Club
Leon Hannah: 12814 Arminta Street
N. Hollywood, CA 91605

YMCA of San Joaquin County
640 N. Center Street
Stockton, CA 95202

COLORADO

Aspen Kayak & Canoe
Box 1520, Aspen, CO 81611

Colorado White Water Association
J. Michael Jacobs: 1400 Dayton Street
Aurora, CO 80010

Whitewater Expeditions
Tom Anderson: Box A-122
Ent. Air Force Base, CO 80912

CONNECTICUT

Appalachian Mountain Club
Connecticut Chapter
Christine Papp: 418 Blackstone Village
Meriden, CT 06450

Univ. of Conn. Outing Club
Mary Pfann: Box. 110, Holcom Hall
Univ. of Conn., Storrs, CT 06268

GEORGIA

Dean's Club: John Mathieu
6277 Roswell Road N.E.
Atlanta, GA 30328

Explorer Post 49
Mark Reimer: 2254 Spring Creek Rd.
Decatur, GA 30033

Georgia Canoeing Association
W. D. Crowley, Jr.: Box 7023
Atlanta, GA 30309

IDAHO

Idaho Alpine Club
Dean Hagmann: 1953 Melody
Idaho Falls, ID 83401

ILLINOIS

Belleville Whitewater Club
Linda Seaman, Rep.: No. 3 Oakwood
Belleville, IL 62223

Chicago Whitewater Association
Bruce Weber: 5652 S. California
Chicago, IL 60629

Illinois Paddling Council
Jack Snarr: 2316 Prospect Avenue
Evanston, IL 60201

INDIANA

American Camping Association
Ernest Schmidt: Bradford Woods
Martinsville, IN 46151

Hoosier Canoe Club
Dennis Flickinger: 7224 Tousley Dr.
Indianapolis, IN 46256

Kekionga Voyageurs
E. Heinz Wahl, Rep.:
1818 Kensington Blvd.
Fort Wayne, IN 46805

Prairie Club Canoeists
Charles Stewart: 364 Rose Ellen Dr.
Crown Point, IN 46307

St. Joe Valley Canoe & Kayak Club
Elkhart YMCA
200 B. Jackson, Elkhart, IN 46514

Tukunu Club
Nancy Rea: 952 Riverside Dr.
South Bend, IN 46616

KANSAS

Johnson County Canoe Club
Geo. & Joan Weiter: 7832 Rosewood La.
Prairie Village, KA 66208

KENTUCKY

The Viking Canoe Club
Joe Venhoff: 3108 Rockaway Dr.
Louisville, KY 40216

LOUISIANA

Bayou Haystackers
Marsha Gunter: 624 Moss Street
New Orleans, LA 70119

MAINE

Bates Outing Club
R. Reese: Dept. of Physics
Bates College
Lewiston, ME 04240

MARYLAND

Appalachian River Runners Federation
Joe Monohan: Box 107
McHenry, MD 21541

Canoe Cruisers of Greater Washington, D.C.
6827 Red Top Road No 1-B
Takoma Park, MD 20012

Monacacy Canoe Club
Box 1083, Frederick   MD 21701

Terrapin Trail Club
Univ. of MD.: Kathy Canter
7912 - 15th Avenue, No. 302
Hyattsville, MD 20783

MASSACHUSETTS

Appalachian Mountain Club
Berkshire Chapter
Janice Wolcott: 1004 Stony Hill Rd.
Wilbraham, MA 01095

Appalachian Mountain Club
Boston Chapter
5 Joy Street, Boston, MA 02108

Appalachian Mountain Club
Worcester Chapter
John Dryden: Grafton Road
Milbury, MA 01527

Hampshire College Outdoors Program
Eric M. Evans: Amherst, MA 01002

MICHIGAN

Raw Strength & Courage Kayakers
Mrs. John Dice: 2022 Day Street
Ann Arbor, MI 48104

MISSISSIPPI

Bayou Haystackers
Gary C. Thomann: 112 Grosvenor
Waveland, MS 39576

MISSOURI

Central Missouri State Univ.
Outing Club
Dr. O. Hawksley, Rep.
Wareensburg, MO 64093

Meramec River Canoe Club
Michelle McNalley: 2100 Raynor Road
Kirkwood, MO 63122

Ozark Wilderness Waterways Club
Fork Lane: 6729 Kenwood Avenue
Kansas City, MD 64131

Univ. of Missouri
Recreation Committee
212 Read Hall
Columbia, MO 62501

MONTANA

Montana Kayak Club
Doug Abelin: Box 213
Brady, MT 59416

NEW HAMPSHIRE

Appalachian Mountain Club (NH Chap.)
Wayne H. Huff: 175 St. Anselm's Drive
Manchester, NH 03102

Ledyard Canoe Club
Jay Evans: Hanover, NH 03755

Mad Pemi Canoe Club Inc.
Douglas F. Keating: 93 Realty
Campton, NH 03223

NEW JERSEY

Adventures Unlimited
Homer Hicks: Box 186
Belvedere, NJ 07823

Kayak & Canoe Club of New York
Ed Alexander, Rep.: 6 Winslow Avenue
East Brunswick, NJ 08816

Mohawk Canoe Club
Gerald B. Pidcock, Rep.: Jobstown-Wrightstown Road
Jobstown, NJ 08041

Rutgers University Outdoor Club
Mrs. Rusak: Douglas College Library
New Brunswick, NJ 08903

NEW MEXICO

Albuquerque Whitewater Club
Glenn A. Fowler, Rep.: 804 Warm Sands Drive
Albuquerque, NM 87123

NEW YORK

Adirondack Mountain Club
Genesee Valley Chapter
Doug Smith, Rep.: 769 John Glenn Blvd.
Webster, NY 14580

Adirondack Mountain Club
Schenectady Chapter
Betty Lou Bailey: Schuyler 16
Netherlands Village, Schenectady, NY 12308

Appalachian Mountain Club
New York Chapter
John Meiers: Midlane Road, Box 1956
Syosset, NY 11791

The Boulder Bashers Canoe Club
Robert Evans: 353 Seneca Road
Hornell, NY 14843

Genesee Down River Paddlers
Al Carlin: RD-2 Proctor Road
Wellsville, NY 14895

Ka-Na-Wa-Ke Canoe Club
Arthur Miller: 407 Beattie Street
Syracuse, NY 13224

Niagara Gorge Kayak Club
Doug Bushnell: 41-17th Street
Buffalo, NY 14213

NORTH CAROLINA

Carolina Canoe Club
Tom Erikson: Box 9011
Greensboro, NC 27408

Nantahala Outdoor Center
Payson Kennedy: Star Route, Box 68
Bryson City, NC 28713

OHIO

Columbus Council, AYH
Joe Feiertag: 1421 Inglis Avenue
Columbus, OH 43212

Cuyahoga Canoe Cruising Club
Chas. A. Tummonds: 10465 SR 44, Box T
Mantua, OH 44255

Keel-Haulers Canoe Club
John A. Kobak, Rep.: 1649 Allen Drive
Westlake, OH 44145

Toledo Area Canoe & Kayak
John Dunn: 5837 Elden Street
Sylvania, OH 43560

Wilderness Adventures
Charles Comer: 17 Lonsdale Avenue
Dayton, OH 44519

OREGON

Oregon Kayak & Canoe Club
Box 692, Portland, OR 97205

PENNSYLVANIA

Allegheny Canoe Club
Walter Pilewski: 131 Park Avenue
Franklin, PA 16323

Appalachian Mountain Club
Delaware Valley Chapter
Don H. Pitkin: 923 Springwood Drive
West Chester, PA 19380

Buck Ridge Ski Club
Louis Metzger: 986 Anders Road
Landsdale, PA 19446

Canoe, Kayak & Sailing Craft
Douglass Ettinger: 701 Wood Street
Wilkinsburg, PA 15221

Penn State Outing Clubs
Dr. John R. Sweet: 118 S. Buckhout Street
State College, PA 16801

Philadelphia Canoe Club
Dr. David Knight: 4900 Ridge Avenue
Philadelphia, PA 19128

Wilderness Voyageurs
Lance Martin: Box 97
Ohiopyle, PA 15470

Wildwater Boating Club
Robert L. Martin: LD 179
Bellefonte, PA 16823

RHODE ISLAND

Rhode Island River Boats
Rist Bonnefond: 53 Maplewood Avenue
Misquamicut, RI 02891

SOUTH CAROLINA

Carolina WW Canoeing Association
Jerry L. Paul: 3412 Harvard Avenue
Columbia, SC 29205

Savannah River Paddlers
Explorer Ship 121 & Sea Scout 404
Jim Hall: 1211 Woodbine Road
Aiken, SC 29801

TENNESSEE

Bluff City Canoe Club
L. Migliara: Box 4523
Memphis, TN 38104

Carbide Canoe Club
Herbert Pomerance: 104 Ulena Lane
Oak Ridge, TN 37830

Choto Canoe Club
Anne Phillips: 3811 Woodhill Point
Knoxville, TN 37919

Sewanee Skiing & Outing Club
Hush Caldwell: Univ. of the South
Sewanee, TN 37375

Tennessee Scenic Rivers Association
Box 3104, Nashville, TN 37219

Tennessee Valley Canoe Club
George M. Martere: Box 11125
Chattanooga, TN 37401

Tenn-Tucky Lake Canoe-Camping Club
Calvin Philips, Jr.: 612 Shelby Avenue
Nashville, TN 37206

TEXAS

Down River Club-Dallas
Paul W. McCarty: 1412 Oak Lea
Irving, TX 75061

Explorer Post 151
Tom Sloan, Scoutmaster
2008 Bedford
Midland, TX 79701

Texas Explorers Club
Bob Burleson, Rep.: Box 844
Temple, TX 76501

VERMONT

Canoe Cruisers of Northern Vermont
Mrs. Bruce C. Hodgman: 100 MacDonough Drive
Vergennes, VT 05491

Marlboro College Outdoor Program
Malcolm Moore
Marlboro, VT 05344

VIRGINIA

Blue Ridge Voyageurs
Ralph T. Smith, Rep.: 8119 Hill Crest Drive
Manassas, VA 22110

Canoe Cruisers Association
John Sessler: 1623 Seneca Avenue
McLern, VA 22101

Coastal Canoeists Inc.
Tom Frink: 319-65th Street
Newport News, VA 23607

Explorer Post 999
R. Steve Thomas, Jr.: 3509 N. Colonia l Drive
Hopewell, VA 23860

University of Virginia Outing Club
Box 101 X Newcomb Hall Station
Charlottesville, VA 22901

WASHINGTON

The Tacoma Mountaineers
Kayak & Canoe Comm.
Bob Hammond: 3512 Crystal Springs
Tacoma, WA 98466

Whitewater-Northwest Kayak Club
Box 1081
Spokane, WA 99201

Univ. of Washington Canoe Club
IMA Building: Univ. of Washington
Seattle, WA 98105

WEST VIRGINIA

West Virginia Wildwater Association
Idair Smookler, Rep.: 2737 Daniels Avenue
South Charleston, WV 25303

WISCONSIN

Kayaks Ltd.
John Weil: 5980 Dawson Court
Greendale, WI 53129

Sierra Club (John Muir Chapter)
Jim Senn: 10261 N. Sunnycrest Drive
Mequon, WI 53092

Wisconsin Hoofers Outing Club
Shirley Delsart: 1309 W. Dayton
Madison, WI 53715

Wolf River Canoe Club
R. Charles Steed: Wolf River Lodge
White Lake, WI 54491

CANADA

B.C. Kayak & Canoe Club
1606 W. Broadway
Vancouver, B.C. Canada

Federation Quebecoise de Canot-Kayak Inc.
881 Est. Boul. de Maisonneuve
Montreal 132 PQ, Canada H2L 149

North West Voyageurs
Canadian Youth Hostels Association
10922-88th Avenue
Edmonton, Alberta, Canada T6C-021

AUSTRALIA

Indooroopilly Canoe Club
Box 36, Indooroopilly
Queensland, Australia

Appendix 5

CHARTS, MAPS AND OTHER USEFUL INFORMATION

For any serious canoeing, you should have a chart to tell you where you are. The one's issued by government agencies are best. The Coast & Geodetic Survey publishes Atlantic, Gulf and Pacific Coast charts, plus charts of the Intracoastal Waterway. Their charts go quite deep inland. A catalog is obtainable free, either from your local map store, or from:

      Director, Coast & Geodetic Survey
      ESSA Washington Science Center
      Rockville, Maryland 20852

The Army Corps of Engineers produces river charts, but unfortunately there's no central source of distribution. You should check with your local office of the Corps of Engineers, and if you don't succeed, you can try writing to:

      U.S. Army Corps of Engineers
      Topographic Laboratories
      Fort Belvoir, Virginia 22060

Much quicker is to check the telephone book and call the local district office, however.

The Lake District Survey branch, produces charts of the Great Lakes, and they are located at:

      630 Federal Building & U.S. Court House,
      Detroit, Michigan 48226

Various rivers have River Commissions which also produce charts. The Delaware River Basin Commission produces an excellent series of easily read maps, for example.

Useful information may also be had on a national basis from:

      American Canoe Association
      American White Water Affiliation
      United States Canoe Association

On a regional basis from:

      American Youth Hostels
      American Red Cross
      Appalachian Mountain Club, Boston Mass.

      Appalachian River Runners Federation
      British Columbia Kayak & Canoe Club, Vancouver, B.C.
      Canoe Cruisers Association, Washington, D.C.
      CCA: Slalom Division, Colesville, Maryland
      Chicagoland Canoe Base, Chicago, Ill.
      Colorado White Water Association, Denver, Colo.
      East Tennessee Whitewater Club, Oak Ridge, Tenn.
      Foldboat Club of Southern California, Los Angeles, Calif.
      Kayak and Canoe Club of New York, New York, N.Y.

Ledyard Canoe Club, Hanover, N.H.
Ontario Voyageurs, Toronto, Ont.
Ozark Wilderness Waterways Club, Kansas City, Mo.
Penn State Outing Club, University Park, Pa.
Prairie Club, Chicago, Ill.
Sierra Club, San Francisco, Calif.
Washington Foldboat Club, Seattle, Wash.

Some publications not included in notes for your bookshelf are:

EAST

Adirondack Canoe Routes: Conservation Department, Albany, N.Y. 12200.

Canoe Guide to Western Pennsylvania: American Youth Hostels, 6300 Fifth Avenue, Pittsburgh, Pa. 15232.

Canoeing White Water in North Virginia: Louis Mascia, 3430 Lee Highway, Fairfax, Va. 22030.

Canoe Trips in Florida: American Camping Association.

Delaware River Chart: Delaware River Basin Commission, Box 360, Trenton, N.J. 08603.

Maine Canoeing: Dept. of Economic Development, State House, Augusta, Maine 04330.

Tennessee Division of State Parks: 203 Cordell Hull Building, Nashville, Tenn. 37219.

Unexplored Okefenokee Swamp: Dept. of Industry and Trade, 100 State Capitol, Atlanta, Georgia 30334.

MIDWEST

Canoe Trails of Michigan: Michigan Tourist Council, Lansing, Mich. 48900.

Illinois Canoeing Guide: Dept. of Conservation, Springfield, Ill. 62600.

Indiana Canoe Trails: Conservation Commission, East Seventh and Court Avenues, Des Moines, Iowa 50300.

Wilderness Canoe Trips and Little-Known Minnesota Rivers: Visitor Information Center, Dept. of Economic Development, 57 W 7 St., St. Paul, Minn. 55102.

Missouri Ozark Waterways: Conservation Commission, Jefferson City, Mo. 65101.

Ohio Canoe Trails: Watercraft Division, Dept. of Natural Resources, 802 Ohio Departments Building, Columbus, O. 43215.

Where to Fish in Kansas: Forestry Commission, Box 1028, Pratt, Kan. 67124.

Wisconsin Water Trails: Conservation Dept., Madison, Wis. 53500.

WEST

Contact through the various states' parks commissions can help.

Arizona State Parks Board: State Capitol Building, Phoenix, Ariz. 85007.

California State Park System: P.O. Box 2390, Sacramento, Calif. 95811.

Colorado Dept. of Game, Fish & Parks: 6060 Broadway, Denver, Colo. 80216.

Idaho Dept. of Commerce: State House, Boise, Idaho 83702.

Oregon Travel Information: State Highway Dept., Salem, Oregon 97301.

Texas Parks and Wildlife Dept.: John H. Reagan Building, Austin, Texas 78701.

Utah State Parks Commission: 132 South Second West, Salt Lake City, Utah 84101.

Washington Tourist Promotion Division: General Administration Building, Olympia, Wash. 98501.

Wyoming Recreation Commission: State Office Building, Cheyenne, Wyo. 82001.

CANADA

Excellent unspoiled wilderness draws thousands of American canoeists north each summer. Two of the most popular are the Quetico Provincial Park, which lies to the north (west and east) of Saint Louis County, Minnesota, and comprises some 14,000 square miles, most of it superb;

second is the Algonquin Provincial Park, little more than 100 miles to the northeast of Toronto. Its 3,000 square miles may seem small, but it too is a beautiful area for canoe camping. Southern Saskatchewan has two parks with water; Prince Albert and Nipawin Provincial Park. Alberta and British Columbia too. Write to the local province's Government Travel Bureau for information, or contact Canadian Government Travel Bureau, 150 Kent Street, Ottawa, Ont. The bureau puts out information on canoeing throughout Canada. There are offices in New York (680 Fifth Avenue, NYC 10019) and San Francisco (155 Jackson Street, S.F., Calif. 94111) and in fourteen other cities.

The Hudson's Bay Company (founded in 1670 and still going strong) has moved with the times and now does U-drive canoe rentals. Contact their Northern Stores Department, Hudson's Bay Company, Hudson's Bay House, Winnipeg, Manitoba, for details of their *U-Paddle Canoe* program. You rent a canoe at one post, make your wilderness trip, and drop it off like a rented car at another post.

Canada offers spectacular outdoor scenery, and both people and government have taken considerable care to avoid the spoliation caused by industrial polluters which has occurred in this country. They have taken a firm line with slipshod corporations, which is an indication that we could do the same here. Man is the only living creature to foul his habitat. No self-respecting animal would think of it.

Appendix 6

FOR YOUR BOOKSHELF

Bark Canoes and Skin Boats: Adney & Chappelle. Smithsonian Institution, Washington, D.C.

Basic River Canoeing: Robert McNair.

Canoeing: American Red Cross.

Canoeing: Merit Badge Series. Boy Scouts of America.

Canoes and canoeing: Percy W. Blandford, Lutterworth, England.

Canoeing: William Bliss, Methuen, England.

Canoeing: An All-Star Sports Book. John Malo, Follett, New York.

Canoe Camping: Handel, Carle W., Ronald Sports Library.

Canoe Errant: R. Raven-Hart, Murray, London.

Canoeing for Schools: Sanders, G., British Canoe Union, London.

Coaching Handbook: Sanders, G., edit., British Canoe Union, London.

Canoe Lifeguard Manual: Corps of Canoe Lifeguards.

Fundamentals of Kayaking: Jay Evans, R., Dartmouth Ledyard Canoe Club.

New England Canoe Guide: Appalachian Mountain Club.

Exploring the Little Rivers of New Jersey: James and Margaret Cawley, Rutgers University.

A Thousand Miles in the Rob Roy Canoe on the Rivers and Lakes of Europe: John MacGregor, Reprint. BCU and Canoeing Pubs. London.

Living Canoeing: Alan W. Byde, A & C Black, England.

Cockleshell Heroes: C. E. Lucas Phillips, Heinnemann, London.

Dangerous River: R. M. Patterson, Allen and Unwin, London.

Modern Canoeing: Charles Sutherland, Faber, London.

Wilderness Canoeing: John Malo.

White Water Handbook for Canoe and Kayak: Urban Appalachian Mountain Club, Boston.

White Water Sport: Peter Dwight Whitney, Ronald Press, New York.

MAGAZINES & PERIODICALS:

American White Water: Quarterly. To members of the American Whitewater Affiliation. Subscription is $3.50 to the Affiliation at 456 Hawthorne, San Bruno, Calif. 94066.

Canoe: Bi-monthly. Send $3.50 to Sonderegger Publications, American Canoe Association, 4260 E. Evans Avenue, Denver, Colo. 80222.

New York-New Jersey River Conference Newsletter: Quarterly. Inquiries to One Red Cross Place, Brooklyn, N.Y. 11201.

USCA Newsletter: For members of the United States Canoe Association. Inquiries to: 1818 Kensington Boulevard, Fort Wayne, Indiana 46805.

ON CONSERVATION:

Water Wasteland: Ralph Nader's Study Group Report on Water Pollution. A study of the water polluters and the agencies supposed to police them. $7.95.

Environmental Law Handbook: Norman Landau & Paul Rheingold. What you as a citizen can do about all kinds of pollution. $1.25.

Citizens Guide to Action for Clean Water: Free from the Izaak Walton League, 1326 Waukegan, Glenview Road, Ill. 60025.

Citizen Action Can Get Results: Free, from U.S. Environmental Protection Agency, Washington, D.C. 20460.

71 Things You Can Do to Stop Pollution: Free from KEEP AMERICA BEAUTIFUL, 99 Park Avenue, New York, N.Y. 10016.

CANOEING 101 CANOEING FOR CAMPUS CREDITS

MORE and more colleges are offering wilderness programs for credit. Several of these include courses in canoeing.

The following is not a complete listing, and you should check with the college of your choice to see whether (a) a canoe or canoe-related course is offered, and (b) how many credits such a program is worth. Quite a number of colleges offer these courses but don't give any credits. Some campuses offer more credits than others.

NORTHEAST
Massachusetts
Northern Essex Community College, Haverhill. Canoeing. Carl Beal, Jr., instructor. 2 credits per semester course.

New Hampshire
Plymouth State College, Plymouth. White water. 2 credits.

SOUTHEAST
Alabama
Athens College, Athens. Canoeing. Includes field trips through Arkansas and Florida. Dr. Robert Daly. 3 credits.

Florida
Florida Southern College, Lakeland. Canoeing. (Emphasis on conservation.) Instructor, Samuel W. Luce. 2 credits.

North Carolina
Western Piedmont Community College, Morganton. Canoeing. Bob Benner, instructor. ¼ credit.

MIDWEST
Illinois
Morraine Valley Community College, Palos Hills. Canoeing. Howie Scheidt, instructor. 3 credits.

Indiana
Earlham College, Richmond. Canoeing. Prof. Douglas W. Steeples. 1 credit.

Michigan
Michigan Technical University, Houghton. Special summer courses for persons under eighteen. Write Dr. Cal Gale for details. Includes canoeing.

Minnesota
Southwest Minnesota State College, Marshall. Encounter program includes canoeing in western states and Canada. No detail on credits. Instructor: Dr. Curt Wagner, Jr.

Missouri
Saint Louis University, Saint Louis. Wilderness program includes canoeing. No details on credits. Instructors: William R. Bader and David Bedan.

NORTHWEST
Montana
Rocky Mountain College, Billings. Canoe camping. 1 credit. Rich McKamy and Dick Wallace, instructors.

University of Montana, Missoula. River rafting. No detail of credits. Joel Meier instructs.

South Dakota

Black Hills State College, Spearfish. Environmental Education program includes canoeing. 3 credits. C. R. Popelka and Charles Bare instructors.

Washington

Olympic College, Bremerton. Wilderness Course includes canoeing. No details on credits. Instructor, David W. Sicks.

SOUTHWEST

Arizona

Prescott College, Prescott. Complete outdoors program, but check whether canoeing credited. instructor, Roy Smith.

California

California State University of Fresno. Rafting. Instructor, Roy Ingraham. No detail on credits.

La Verne College, La Verne. River floats and "When Lewis and Clark Met the Mountains" type courses. No detail of credits. Instructor, Roland L. Ortmayer.

Colorado

University of Colorado, Boulder. Rafting. No details of credits if any. Instructors, William Appenzellor and Joe O'Laughlin.

Abaft	Behind, toward, or on the stern, or rear, of a canoe, kayak, or nautical craft. Astern, aft of.
Abeam	At right angles to the center of the fore-and-aft line of a vessel.
Aboard	On or in a craft, on board.
Adrift	Drifting, drfiting without mooring, direction. Untied, broken away.
Afloat	Floating, waterborne. Not grounded.
Aft	At, near, or toward the stern. Behind. The after part of a craft.
Aground	On the river (or sea) bed, touching, as on a reef, beach, shoal, in shallows. Not waterborne.
Ahead	Directly in front of canoe, kayak, other nautical or other craft.
Amidships	Literally, midway between bow and stern. Implies within the craft—see *Abeam*. Also, in bigger vessels, when the tiller (rudder, or wheel) is pointing along the craft's fore-and-aft line.

Astern	Behind the canoe, kayak, or craft. At or toward the rear. Abaft.
Back-Paddle	To paddle backward, to reverse, to paddle with the blade from stern to bow.
Backing (of wind)	When the wind changes in its direction in an anticlockwise motion, i.e., against the sun's movement.
Bail	To remove water from a canoe, kayak, boat by scooping with a bailer (which may be a calabash in a dugout canoe or West Indian sloop), bucket, or even a sponge. To scoop water out of a craft.
Bang Plate	A fixture found on the bows of some canoes, dinghies, and rowboats, to protect the stem; a structure running forward and up at the center of the bow, and to which side pieces are attached. The bang plate is mounted exteriorly to the stem. Also found at stern of some canoes. See also *Stern, Stem band, Sternpost*.
Beam	Width of a canoe at its widest part. For ICF rulings this is measured under the *rubbing strakes (q.v.)*.

Beam Ends	When a craft is flung on its side it is said to be "on her (its) beam ends."
Bearing	A direction referred to in respect of (a) the fore-and-aft line of a craft, and (b) in relation to a point such as true north or magnetic north. To a compass point.
Bear Off, Bear Away	To move away from. To push off from a jetty or other object.
Beat, Beating	To sail a course into or toward the wind. See *to Tack, To.*
Beaufort Scale	Named after a British naval officer who invented it in 1805 the Beaufort Scale is a means of measuring wind velocity, ranging from zero (for winds of less than 1 mph) to 12 (or higher) for winds above 72 mph. These days forecasters call winds in miles per hour, and give average wave heights in forecasts. Small-craft warnings are similarly announced.
Before	In front of.
Bell Buoy	A buoy mounted with a bell which is designed to ring itself by the wave movement of the sea or estuary in which it is sited.
Bend, To	Nautical term meaning to secure one thing to another, usually of rope, or sails.
Bermuda, Bermudian	Sailing rig in which the main sail is three cornered.
Rig	Sometimes called Marconi.
Blade(s)	Term sometimes used to refer to paddles. Also, the flat or curved end of the paddle.
Bollard	A stubby heavy post on a jetty (or a ship) to which a line or lines may be secured.
Boom	A piece of wood or metal (known as a *spar q.v.*) used to extend the lower part of a sail.
Bottom	The underwater part of the hull or craft.
Bow (also Bows of larger craft)	Forward part of canoe, kayak, etc.
Bower	Nautical term for main anchor, carried (not surprisingly) in or at the bow(s).
Bowline	A knot used to form a loop which neither slips nor jams.
Bow Person	Person who paddles from the bow, or front thwart.
Broach, To; Broach To	To swing, or be swung, suddenly into a trough of sea broadside on. To yaw or veer—dangerously—especially in a following sea so that one comes abeam the waves. (To be avoided, since one is quickly out of control.)
Broad Reach	Sailing term referring to when the wind is blowing from behind the centerpoint of the fore-and-aft axis of the boat (abaft the beam). It is between reaching—when the wind is abeam; and running—when the wind is coming from behind.
Bulkhead	Partition in canoes and kayaks where floatation is carried. Usually sealed during manufacture.
Buoy	A distinctively shaped marker, usually colored, anchored at a fixed position to indicate a point on a chart, or to indicate a navigable waterway, or even a wreck. *Mooring buoys* are fixed to ground tackle, and vessels may dock to them in a stream instead of anchoring.
Buoyancy	Material or air bags used to give positive floatation to a craft. Styrofoam blocks make good additional buoyancy material since they can be carved to fit the curves in fiberglass and molded veneer canoes. Many canoes are made with built-in buoyancy, put in during the course of manufacture, so that it is integral with the craft.
By The Head	A craft is said to be by the head when she is loaded deeper forward than aft.
By The Stern	A craft is said to be by the stern when she is loaded deeper aft than forward.
Cable	Rope (or chain) to an anchor. As a measurement of distance 100 fathoms, or 300 yards. Approximately 1/10th of a nautical mile.
Canadian Canoe	Basically a canoe is a vessel powered by a

person using a single, rather than a double, paddle. The original Canadian canoe is like the so-called Red Indian birchbark or North American canoe—that is, a long, light, and narrow boat with both ends sharp and with a slight tumble home to the sides, and usually paddled with a single-bladed paddle. The paddler's position is a kneeling, rather than sitting, one.

Canoe
A general term used to describe a vessel with a pointed stern, not normally differentiating in the way it is paddled and thus encompassing also kayaks, but not rowing boats.

Canoe Stern
Stern of a vessel shaped like a canoe. See also *Counter Stern* and *Transom*.

Carvel
Method of building boats so that the sides are smooth. The planks are laid edge to edge, and the gaps sealed.

Caulk
Waterproofing material or compound to seal the seams between planks.

Centerboard
Also center plate, dagger board, drop keel, dagger plate. A retractable keel, or fin of wood or metal, which can be lowered either through the side or over the side, or through the bottom of a boat to lessen the amount of leeway made when sailing.

Center Of Buoyancy
Center of the immersed volume of a boat or craft.

Center Of Gravity
A single point within a body to which every particle of matter external is gravitationally attracted.
That point of resolution of all weights contained in (within) a canoe, or kayak.

Chafe
To rub; wear caused by friction.

Chart
A map specially prepared for use by navigation or pilotage.

Chine
The joint between the sides and underhull of a boat. Where the sides join the hull in a V-shaped hull, especially.

Cleat
A piece of wood or metal to which ropes may be secured. Usually found on jetties and on sailboats.

Clinker
Method of building boats in which the planks are laid in an overlap, one upon the next. The overlap is known as a land.

Close-hauled
Sailing term, referring to sailing as close into the wind as possible.

Coaming
A raised framework, or vertical structure, designed to prevent anything from entering the area which it surrounds. The cockpit coaming is used to attach the bottom end of a spray skirt and thus make a watertight fitting.

Cockpit
A hole cut in the deck of a canoe or kayak in order to let the paddler sit or kneel inside.
Of *sailboats:* the lower part of the well, from which most of the actual sailing is done.

Compass
A navigational device used for finding direction, the most common of which is the magnetic compass, in which a magnetized needle points to magnetic north.

Counter Stern
Similar to canoe stern in which there is an overhang.

Course
The act of moving in a path from one point to another point. The direction of a craft measured as a clockwise angle from north.

Dead Reckoning
The calculation of the position of a craft, based on the course made, and taking into account any influences of tide, wind, or current.

Dead Water
The water close to the stern of a boat in its wake that looks flat or dead.

Deck
A horizontal partition in a boat; usually refers to that which extends from bow to stern as its upper surface, and which in canoes and kayaks has opening(s) to let the paddler in at the cockpit.

Displacement
The amount of water—usually measured in tons in big ships—displaced by the underwater volume of a vessel or craft.

Draft, Draught
The depth of water that a canoe (or other vessel) draws or displaces when in the

water. The maximum underwater depth of a vessel.

Drag Frictional resistance to forward motion, especially in shallow waters.

Draw, Draw Stroke Descriptive of those strokes in which the effort is used to move the boat sideways through the water; that is, at right angles to its fore-and-aft line.

Drift The unassisted movement of a vessel, caused by currents in the water. Also the rate of a current in knots.

Ebb The falling of a tide.

Eddy A local, spiral, or circular movement of water, not necessarily related to the overall movement of the current around it. These may vary from idiosyncratic daydreams of the water, to quite serious whirlpools.

Even Keel A properly balanced craft, neither by the head nor by the stern.

Fairing, Fairing Up A structure used principally to produce smooth lines and reduce drag. In design, to make the curves smooth and in agreement in different planes.

Fathom A nautical unit of measurement equal to six feet, (i.e., 72 inches) and usually used to measure depths of water.

Feather Refers to the angle of the blade in relation to its opposite in double paddles, and at which angle it is presented to the on-coming air when being brought forward out of the water. A feathered blade presents its narrowest portion—that is, its edge—when brought forward.

Fend, To To ward off, push off. Also *fenders:* cushions that lessen shock, or chafing when two vessels lie alongside one another, or when one vessel lies against a dock or jetty.

Ferry Glide A maneuver in which a canoe or kayak or boat is held almost stationary in the water by back-paddling, and by angling the stern against the current, is carried from one side of a stream to another, sideways. The

amount of angle used in presenting the stern depends on the velocity of the current.

Fiberglass Glass matting, or woven fabric, used in conjunction with special resins to form a homogeneous structure, such as a kayak, canoe, or boat. Fiberglass has a high strength-weight ratio when properly blended, combining the best qualities of glass with resin, without the disadvantages inherent to either one in its natural state.

Flare The concave upward curve of the bow of a vessel, or the overhang on its top side. Also: a *light signal* of the pyrotechnic type, used to attract help when in distress.

Flood The rising, or incoming of a tide.

Fore Forward. Also: forward on the fore side of.

Foul Anchor
Fouled Anchor When the anchor has got stuck, caught up in anything, especially when a turn of its cable is caught around it, it is said to be fouled.

Freeboard Height of the deck or gunwale to waterline.

Furl To gather up, in, sail, and secure it to a spar.

Gale A brisk forceful wind, from 32 mph to 63 mph. Forces 8 and 9 on the Beaufort Scale, from 47 to 55 mph. Gales are not recommended for canoes especially, nor for kayaks as boating weather. See *Beaufort Scale.*

Gear Portmanteau term to describe those items required in a canoe or kayak, or for a camping trip, etc.

Girth Measurement of a hull's circumference at its biggest section, usually the amidship section.

Go About To tack a boat from one side of the wind to the other to change the direction of the wind when sailing into it by moving the bow across the wind and receiving the wind from the opposite side of the boat.

GRP, grp — Glass-reinforced plastic. Fibrous glass reinforced by resin. Fiberglass.

Gunwale, gunnel — Properly, refers to where the deck and topsides meet. More usually refers to the top of the sides of the canoe. The gunwale is actually a longitudinal framer, which is strengthened and supported by a similar stringer known as an *inwale, (q.vi)* and which also supports the ends of the ribs. In canoeing, the gunwale and inwale are more usually one and the same piece.

Halyard — A rope used for hoisting anything, but especially a sail. In lateen-rigged craft, you hoist the sail by hauling the main (sail) halyard.

Hand, To — To furl, e.g., "Hand in the main!" means furl the mainsail. (Very nautical.)

Handsomely — Mostly British usage, meaning gently or slowly (so as not to frighten anyone, or like noblesse oblige--a matter our politicians, bureaucrats and leaders of industry should ponder.) Good manneredly.

Haul, To — To pull a rope. EG "Haul the mainsheet!" See also, *sheet.*

Head, Headsail — Head is the front end of a boat, and headsails are those nearest the bow. A jib is thus a headsail.

Heave, To — To haul or throw. *To heave to* means to stop, or in a mean, heavy sea, to keep a minimum speed required to maintain steerage way.

Heel — The inclination of a vessel, or its list to one side or another.

Fouled Anchor — When the anchor has got stuck, caught up in anything, especially when a turn of its cable is caught around it, it is said to be fouled.

Freeboard — Height of the deck or gunwale to waterline.

Furl — To gather up, in, sail, and secure it to a spar.

Gale — A brisk forceful wind, from 32 mph to 63 mph. Forces 8 and 9 on the Beaufort Scale, from 47 to 55 mph. Gales are not recommended for canoes especially, nor for kayaks as boating weather. See *Beaufort Scale.*

Gear — Portmanteau term to describe those items required in a canoe or kayak, or for a camping trip, etc.

Girth — Measurement of a hull's circumference at its biggest section, usually the amidship section.

Go About — To tack a boat from one side of the wind to the other to change the direction of the wind when sailing into it by moving the bow across the wind and receiving the wind from the opposite side of the boat.

GRP, grp — Glass-reinforced plastic. Fibrous glass reinforced by resin. Fiberglass.

Gunwale, Gunnel — Properly, refers to where the deck and topsides meet. More usually refers to the top of the sides of the canoe. The gunwale is actually a longitudinal framer, which is strengthened and supported by a similar stringer known as an *inwale, (q.v.)* and which also supports the ends of the ribs. In canoeing, the gunwale and inwale are more usually one and the same piece.

Halyard — A rope used for hoisting anything, but especially a sail. In lateen-rigged craft, you hoist the sail by hauling the main (sail) halyard.

Hand, To — To furl, e.g., "Hand in the main!" means furl the mainsail. (Very nautical.)

Handsomely — Mostly British usage, meaning gently or slowly (so as not to frighten anyone, or like noblesse oblige--a matter our politicians, bureaucrats and leaders of industry should ponder.) Good manneredly.

Haul, To — To pull a rope. BG "Haul the mainsheet!" See also, *sheet.*

Head, Headsail — Head is the front end of a boat, and headsails are those nearest the bow. A jib is thus a headsail.

Heave, To — To haul or throw. *To heave to* means to

stop, or in a mean, heavy sea, to keep a minimum speed required to maintain steerage way.

Heel   The inclination of a vessel, or its list to one side or another.

Helm, To Helm   Tiller, or tiller bar, or rudder bar. To helm is also used to indicate steerage, such as to helm down (very nautical) to move the tiller toward the wind so that the bows go to leeward.

Hitch, To   Not to thumb a lift, but to make fast to an object by means of a rope, but not to another rope.

Hog, To; Hogged, Hogging   *To hog* means to scrub thoroughly (nautical); *Hogged* implies that a boat's center is higher than its ends, which in turn usually indicates its back is busted. When this factor is actually part of intended design, it is referred to as *reverse sheer*. *Hogging* is the convex strain on a boat through its fore-and-aft axis.

Hoist, To   To haul anything (but usually sail) aloft (up).

Hull   The body of a vessel, the semienclosing lower portion of a boat, canoe, kayak, which acts as a container for a person.

ICF   International Canoe Federation. See Appendix 2.

Inboard   To be within the hull of a ship, usually nearer to its center.

Irons, In   Sailing term to describe a boat that is bow to the wind with sails flapping, and unwilling to move off the wind in either direction.

Inwale   See *Gunwale.*

Jib   The foremost headsail. Occasionally found in canoe and kayak rigs. Its purpose is to steer wind around the outer side of the mainsail for better power.

Jury   As in "jury-rig" means an ad hoc or makeshift arrangement of sail, to get you home by. Fudged, as in plea-bargaining.

Kayak   An Eskimo (meaning Arctic Indian) canoe made of sealskins stretched over a frame (of wood usually) so as to cover it all except for a small hole in the upper half at the center for its paddler to sit in. Used to describe canoes developed from this craft. See also *Umiack.*

Kedge   A small anchor, usually used with a bigger (main) anchor in larger boats. Canoes and kayaks, should they carry an anchor, can manage very happily with a kedge. To "kedge off" means to remove oneself from being aground into deeper waters by hauling on an anchor to shift the boat. Where the tide is falling one has to do this rather rapidly.

Keel   The lowest fore-and-aft member of the hull and the backbone of a boat. Usually a strip of wood or metal running along the bottom centerline is socalled, though more properly a *false keel,* or deadwood.

King Plank King Post   King plank is the center plank in a deck. King post is a vertical post on deck.

Knee(s)   Wood or metal angle pieces used in framing a vessel. Elbow joints. Elbows.

Knot(s)   A unit of speed of one nautical mile per hour—not a measure of distance which is the nautical mile (6,076.10 feet). A knot (knots, or nautical miles per hour) is also used by aircraft for measuring speed, e.g., the cruise speed of the Blackbird Ace One is 130 kts (Note: *not* knots per hour. Just knots.)

Lanyard   Lashing, or short end of light line (rope).

Lash, To; Lashing   To secure with rope. Lashing is thus a short piece of thin rope, also known as a "tie" or "tye" when used to secure a sail to be stowed.

Lateen   The predecessor of the fore-and-aft sailing rig, the lateen sail was developed by the Arabs. It features a relatively short mast on which are hoisted a large sail attached to yards that rake high abaft the mast. The sail can be rigged to sail effectively to

windward. Because it is simple it is usually favored for canoes and kayaks over the more conventional bermudian rig.

Latitude   Measurement north or south of the equator in degrees, a unit of measurement equal to one 360th part of the circumference of a circle. See also *Longitude*.

Launch, To   To allow to slip into the water, to set afloat.

Leak   The accidental entering of water into a hull via an opening which shouldn't have been there in the first place. ALWAYS CHECK THE HULL FOR DAMAGE BEFORE LAUNCHING.

Lee, Leeward, Leeway   On the side away from the direction the wind is blowing from. *Leeward* (pronounced loo'erd) means downwind. *Leeway*, the drift of a boat downwind.

Leeboards   Boards on the sides of shallow-draft craft which, when lowered on the leeward side of a vessel (they may be lowered on both sides), help reduce the leeward movement of the vessel. See also *Centerboard*, etc.)

Life Vest, Life Jacket   Personal buoyancy device which is worn like a vest (waistcoat). The best sort for canoeists are those that have plenty of space for your arms and don't get in the way. Buoyancy of about 6 kg is recommended in order not to interfere with rolling Eskimo style.

Line   Small cordage or rope used to tie up or tow a canoe. More properly termed *Painter (q.v.)*.

List (see Heel)   Where the inclination from the horizontal plane is due to an adverse change in trim rather than from the effects of external forces.

LOA, LWL   LOA is length overall. LWL is load water line and indicates the length of the waterline along the hull (a) when empty and (b) when loaded.

Long-distance Racing:

LDR   Usually the international term for events downriver of more than 10 miles (for seniors) and 5 miles (for juniors). (See also *Wild Water, Marathon, etc.*)

Longitude   Measurement in degrees (one 360th part of the circumference of a circle) east or west of the prime meridian at Greenwich, England.

Mainsail   The principal sail, set from a mast (in big ships known as the "main" mast). In canoes and kayaks there's usually only one sail involved, and thus no reason to indulge these conceits.

Make Sail   Another good sea-shanty-type expression, meaning to set the sails ("haul 'em up," etc.).

Midsection   Drawing (design) term meaning the section of a craft amidship.

Mold(s)   In fiberglass (or molded veneer), manufacture done on a template called a mold, and upon which the canoe is built. Molds are either female or male. The female mold will produce a male structure, and vice versa. In making canoes there are basically two molds used: the first is to create the hull; the second, the deck. The two are then mated, and you get to use the end result.

Monocoque   A frame construction so designed that each exterior part bears a share of the internal stresses involved in any other part of the frame, and thus does not employ ribs or stringers for support. The dugout canoe is the earliest extant example of this type of construction. Internal bracing is unnecessary since the exterior walls carry loads—modern cars use this quite a lot.

Moorings   Permanent anchors laid in a riverbed, or bed of a harbor, to which a mooring chain is attached. This is buoyed so that a boat coming alongside can pick up the mooring. If you must sleep in your canoe, this is one of the better ways to anchor. Make sure it is a mooring you are picking up and not a fishing trap. (Also, make sure the owner of the mooring doesn't want to anchor too.)

Navigation	The art of bringing a craft from one point to another safely by means of charts and sense.
Oarlock	See *Rowlocks.*
Offsets	A design table, with measurements, from which a craft might be made.
Open	Undecked, of a boat. Of an anchorage, unsheltered.
Outboard	An auxiliary engine. Nautically, beyond a vessel's sides.
Overboard	Over the side. As in: ''He's fallen in the water! Man overboard!''
Painter	Proper term for the light line (cordage) by which a canoe may be moored or towed. The painter is attached to a stem bolt and can be used to tie the boat to anything.
Pintle	A pin or bolt on which some other part may pivot or turn. Especially the metal elbow on which the rudder is hinged and turns.
Plank	Wooden boards (usually) from which the sides of a canoe are formed; in a typical wood-canvas canoe these cover the outside of the ribs, providing a smooth surface to which canvas (or another material) is fitted.
Plug	Occasionally used to refer to a ''mold'' on which a fiberglass or molded veneer canoe is made up.
Pooped, To Be	When running before a heavy sea, large waves overtake the craft, breaking and falling on board the after part.
Port	Left side of a canoe (boat, other craft) looking forward to the bow from astern of it.
Portage	Name given to a place where the canoe has to be shifted from the water and carried around an obstruction in the water, on land. Also used as a verb: E.g., ''We portaged at Marlows' Falls as there simply wasn't enough water to go through.''
Pram	Norwegian-style dinghy with a forward transom.
Punt	Long flat-bottomed boat with transom fore and aft and propelled by a pole. Ends are broad and square. Popular with Victorians, and still found in Britain today.
Race	Local area of disturbed water, usually fast running.
Rapids	A fast moving stretch of water, usually caused by a change in the riverbed.
Reach, To	To sail with the wind free, from the beam.
Rib(s)	Transverse members of the framework of a craft which extend down the sides and across the lower hull and up the other side.
Ride, To	To be at anchor or on moorings.
Rig, To	To set up, especially of sail.
Rocker, Rockered	The rise of the keel line toward the bow and stern, above the amidship section. A rounded or curved keel. Objective of rocker is to obtain increased maneuverability.
Roll	Transverse motion of a craft about its fore-and-aft axis.
Rowlocks, Oarlocks	Square holes for oars, or devices often U-shaped, for holding an oar in place while rowing.
Rubbing Strake	An extra piece of wood (or other material) running around the exterior of a craft just beneath the gunwale, to protect against chafe when lying alongside anything. (Under ICF regulations, beam is measured beneath the rubbing strake.)
Rudder	A flat plate of metal or wood, hinged to a sternpost and used to direct the movement of a craft by changing the direction of its stern.
Run, To; Running	To sail with the wind from astern.
Scull	To propel a boat by means of moving an oar or paddle in a side-to-side motion. A *sculling draw stroke* is a sculling version of a draw stroke.
Sheer	The rise of a boat's side toward the bow

and stern when viewed from abeam, above the amidship section.

Ship, To To take anything in board of a craft.

Shoal A piece of sea or riverbed rising to form shallow water or even a sandbar.

Shoot Of falls and rapids, to go over them.

Skeg The afterpart of a keel, and especially the metal socket that supports the bottom part of the rudder.

Skin Outer covering of a hull, or framework of a craft. These days a skin can refer to a sheath of plastic or fiberglass laid over the regular hull, to provide resistance to chafe and to make for a longer useful life.

Slap Support A stroke made to correct a temporary instability of a canoe or kayak, and in which the flat of the paddle blade is struck against the water to provide the paddler with the support from which a correction to stability can be made.

Sound, To To check the depth of water. The most primitive way is to stick your paddle in vertically.

Spar A piece of metal or wood to which a sail is set.

Spray Deck, Spray Cover, Spray Skirt A spray deck is—not surprisingly—an artificial deck, usually of canvas, and designed to keep the spray out of the hull of a canoe. It may be a full deck—with holes for the paddler(s)—or a part deck. Spray cover is similar to spray skirt, a sealing device installed by the canoeist and which fits around the cockpit coaming and the paddler's waist, to provide a watertight seal and to permit rolling.

Springs Maximum range of the tide cycle, opposite to neaps. *Springs* also refer to mooring ropes on larger craft which lead forward from the bows to a cleat or bollard farther aft and vice versa, known as springs since this is their effect on the hull—to return it to equilibrium after disturbances such as waves, wash, or even wind.

Squall Sudden gust of wind, may also carry driving rain.

Starboard Right-hand side of vessel, when looking forward to the bows from astern.

Stays Mast supports, usually wire, sometimes cordage.

Stem Upright part of the forward part of a canoe. In double enders, each end has a stem. *Stem band:* metal strip attached to the stem to protect the edge from damage. See also *Bang Plate*.

Stem The Tide To sail against a current without losing ground. If you ever get stuck like this, look for slacker waters nearer the shore.

Stern The after part of a vessel. The back or rear of a canoe or kayak.

Stern Person Paddler who paddles from the stern thwart.

Sternpost The after upright member of a frame—same as stem but at other end.

Stringer A rib which is laid down in the fore-and-aft axis of the frame.

Sweep Stroke A turning stroke, made by sweeping the paddle through the water.

Tack, To To work a craft to windward by alternately sailing close-hauled with the wind on the port side, then the starboard, etc., or vice versa. Also, to change from starboard to port, and vice versa, when close-hauled.

Telemark A turning stroke made by leaning on the paddle when the boat is moving forward and pivoting quickly about this point.

Thwart A brace extending across the upper part of a canoe laterally, to provide support for the buttocks. Also known as *spreader* or *crossbar*. In modern competition canoes, thwarts have been exchanged for upright resting posts usually made of carved styrofoam block(s).

Tide Rip, Tide Race Disturbed waters caused by tidal eddies, or the passage of a regular current disturbed by an uneven river- or seabed.

Tight	Watertight.
Tippy	Term used to describe instability of a craft.
Top Hamper	Gear carried above decks. Unnecessary structure above deck.
Top Sides	The sides of a hull above the waterline.
Tow	To pull a canoe or kayak or other craft.
Transom	Stern planking of a square-ended craft.
Trim	Horizontal balance of a vessel.
Tumble Home	Describes a situation where the beam at deck level is narrower than at the waterline in the same section. Most open canoes have this feature which helps to keep them dry.
Umiack	Large open Eskimo boat made of skins stretched over a wooden frame, used mostly by Eskimo women.
Under Way	Having movement through the water.
Veer	When the wind changes clockwise.
Wake	Disturbed water left by a craft passing along; also called wash.
Wake-hang, Wash-hang	To surf on the bow wave of the boat in front of you. This is a free ride for all concerned, since the leading boat doesn't lose any energy in the transaction. Very similar to racing car drivers' ploy of driving in the dead air behind another vehicle.
Waterline	Horizontal length of a vessel at the level of the water when floating.
Waterlogged	Full of water but still afloat.
Weigh, To	Nautical, for pulling up an anchor.
Weir	Low dam built to back up or divert water.
White Horses	Breaking crests of waves.
Wild Water	White water. Used to describe distance events including this type of water.
Windward	Side from which the wind is blowing. Also known as the *weather side*.
Withie, Stake, Or Perch	British usage mostly, referring to stakes that buoy the navigable channel of a small river or creek or tidal marsh.
Yaw	To swing or swerve from an intended course unintentionally.
Young Flood	First movement of a flooding tide.

The American Whitewater Affiliation Safety Code, as revised in 1974 by James C. Sindelar, Executive Director of A.W.A.

Canoe clubs interested in obtaining copies of this code for members can obtain them in lots of 50 at low cost direct from: AMERICAN WHITEWATER AFFILIATION, 264 East Side Drive, Concord, N.H. 03301.

I. PERSONAL PREPAREDNESS AND RESPONSIBILITY
1. BE A COMPETENT SWIMMER with ability to handle yourself underwater.
2. WEAR A LIFEJACKET when approaching, running, or lining rapids.
3. KEEP YOUR CRAFT UNDER CONTROL. Control must be good enough at all times to stop or reach shore before you reach any danger. Do not enter a rapid unless you are reasonably sure you can safely navigate it or swim the entire rapid in event of capsize.
4. BE AWARE OF RIVER HAZARDS AND AVOID THEM. Following are the most frequent KILLERS.
   A. *HIGH WATER*. The river's power and danger, and the difficulty of rescue increase tremendously as the flow rate increases. It is often misleading to judge river level at the put-in. Look at a narrow, critical passage. Could a *sudden* rise from sun on a snow pack rain, or a dam release occur on your trip?

B. *COLD*. Cold quickly robs one's strength, along with his will and ability to save himself. Dress to protect yourself from cold water and weather extremes. When the water temperature is less than 50 degrees F., a diver's wetsuit is essential for safety in event of an upset. Next best is wool clothing under a windproof outer garment such as a splash-proof nylon shell; in this case one should also carry matches and a complete change of clothes in a waterproof package. If, after prolonged exposure a person experiences uncontrollable shaking, has difficulty talking and moving, he must be warmed immediately by whatever means available.
C. *STRAINERS*% Brush, fallen trees, bridge pilings, or anything else which allows river current to sweep through but pins boat and boater against the obstacle. The water pressure on anything trapped this way is overwhelming, and there may be little or no whitewater to warn of danger.
D. *WEIRS, REVERSALS, AND SOUSE HOLES*. The water drops over an obstacle, then curls back on itself in a stationary wave, as is often seen at weirs and dams. The surface water is actually going UPSTREAM, and this action will trap any floating object between the drop and the wave. Once trapped, a swimmer's only

hope is to dive below the surface where current is flowing downstream, or try to swim out the end of the wave.

5. BOATING ALONE is not recommended. The preferred minimum is three craft.

6. HAVE A FRANK KNOWLEDGE OF YOUR BOATING ABILITY. Don't attempt waters beyond this ability. Learn paddling skills and teamwork, if in a multiple-manned craft, to match the river you plan to boat.

7. BE IN GOOD PHYSICAL CONDITION consistent with the difficulties that may be expected.

8. BE PRACTICED IN ESCAPE from an overturned craft, in self rescue, in rescue, and in ARTIFICIAL RESPIRATION. Know first aid.

9. THE ESKIMO ROLL should be mastered by kayakers and canoers planning to run large rivers and/or rivers with continuous rapids where a swimmer would have trouble reaching shore.

10. WEAR A CRASH HELMET where an upset is likely. This is essential in a kayak or covered canoe.

11. BE SUITABLY EQUIPPED. Wear shoes that will protect your feet during a bad swim or a walk for help, yet will not interfere with swimming (tennis shoes recommended). Carry a knife and waterproof matches. If you need eyeglasses, tie them on and carry a spare pair. Do not wear bulky clothing that will interfere with your swimming when water-logged.

II. BOAT AND EQUIPMENT PREPAREDNESS

1. TEST NEW AND UNFAMILIAR EQUIPMENT before relying on it for difficult runs.

2. BE SURE CRAFT IS IN GOOD REPAIR before starting a trip. Eliminate sharp projections that could cause injury during a swim.

3. Inflatable craft should have MULTIPLE AIR CHAMBERS and should be test inflated before starting a trip.

4. HAVE STRONG, ADEQUATELY SIZED PADDLES OR OARS for controlling the craft, and carry sufficient spares for the length of the trip.

5. INSTALL FLOTATION DEVICES in non-inflatable craft, securely fixed, and designed to displace as much water from the craft as possible.

6. BE CERTAIN THERE IS ABSOLUTELY NOTHING TO CAUSE ENTANGLEMENT when coming free from an upset craft, i.e. a spray skirt that won't release or tangles around legs; life jacket buckles, or clothing that might snag; canoe seats that lock on shoe heels; foot braces that fail or allow feet to jam under them; flexible decks that collapse on boater's legs when a kayak is trapped by

water pressure; baggage that dangles in an upset; loose rope in the craft, or badly secured bow/stern lines.

7. PROVIDE ROPES TO ALLOW YOU TO HOLD ONTO YOUR CRAFT in case of upset, and so that it may be rescued. Following are the recommended methods.

A. KAYAKS AND COVERED CANOES should have 6 inch diameter grab loops of ¼ inch rope attached to bow and stern. A stern painter 7 or 8 feet long is optional and may be used if properly secured to prevent entanglement.

B. OPEN CANOES should have bow and stern lines (painters) securely attached consisting of 8 to 10 feet of ¼ or ⅜ inch rope. These lines must be *secured* in such a way that they will not come loose accidently and entangle the boaters during a swim, yet they must be ready for immediate use during an emergency. Attached balls, floats, and knots are NOT recommended.

C. RAFTS AND DORIES should have taut perimeter grab lines threaded through the loops usually provided.

8. RESPECT RULES FOR CRAFT CAPACITY and know how these capacities should be reduced for whitewater use. (Life raft ratings must generally be halved.)

9. CARRY APPROPRIATE REPAIR MATERIALS; tape (heating duct tape) for short trips, complete repair kit for wilderness trips.

10. CAR TOP RACKS MUST BE STRONG and positively attached to the vehicle, and each boat must be tied to each rack. In addition, each end of each boat should be tied to car bumper. Suction cup racks are poor. The entire arrangement should be able to withstand all but the most violent vehicle accident.

III. LEADER'S PREPAREDNESS AND RESPONSIBILITY

1. RIVER CONDITIONS. Have a reasonable knowledge of the difficult parts of the run, or if an exploratory trip, examine maps to estimate the feasibility of the run. Be aware of possible rapid changes in river level, and how these changes can affect the difficulty of the run. If important, determine approximate flow rate or level. If trip involves important tidal currents, secure tide information.

2. PARTICIPANTS. Inform participants of expected river conditions and determine if the prospective boaters are qualified for the trip. All decisions should be founded on group safety and comfort. Difficult decisions on the participation of marginal boaters must be based on total group strength.

3. EQUIPMENT. Plan so that all necessary group equipment is present on the trip; 50 to 100 foot throwing rope, first aid kit with fresh and adquate supplies, extra paddles, repair materials, and survival equipment if appropriate. Check equipment as necessary at the put-in, especially: life jackets, boat flotation, and any item that could prevent complete escape from the boat in case of an upset.

4. ORGANIZATION. Remind each member of individual responsibility in keeping group compact and intact between leader and sweep (capable rear boater). If group is too large, divide into smaller groups, each of appropriate boating strength, and designate group leaders and sweeps.

5. FLOAT PLAN. If trip is into a wilderness area, or for an extended period, your plans should be filed with appropriate authorities, or left with someone who will contact them after a certain time. Establishment of checkpoints along the way at which civilization could be contacted if necessary should be considered. Knowing location of possible help could speed rescue in any case.

IV. IN CASE OF UPSET

1. EVACUATE YOUR BOAT immediately if there is imminent danger of being trapped against logs, brush, or any other form of strainer.

2. RECOVER WITH AN ESKIMO ROLL IF POSSIBLE.

3. IF YOU SWIM, HOLD ONTO YOUR CRAFT. It has much flotation and is easy for rescuers to spot. Get to the upstream end so craft cannot crush you against obstacles.

4. RELEASE YOUR CRAFT IF THIS IMPROVES YOUR SAFETY. If rescue is not imminent and water is numbing cold, or if worse rapids follow, then strike out for the nearest shore.

5. EXTEND YOUR FEET DOWNSTREAM when swimming rapids to fend against rocks. LOOK AHEAD. Avoid possible entrapment situations; rock wedges, fissures, strainers, brush, logs, weirs, reversals, and souse holes.

Watch for eddies and slackwater so that you can be ready to use these when you approach. Use every opportunity to work your way toward shore.

6. If others spill, GO AFTER THE BOATERS. Rescue boats and equipment only if this can be done safely.

V. INTERNATIONAL SCALE OF RIVER DIFFICULTY (If rapids on a river generally fit into one of the following classifications but the water temperature is below 50 degrees F., or if the trip is an extended trip in a wilderness area, the river should be considered one class more difficult than normal.)

CLASS I. Moving water with a few riffles and small waves. Few or no obstructions.

CLASS II. Easy rapids with waves up to 3 feet, and wide, clear channels that are obvious without scouting. Some maneuvering is required.

CLASS III. Rapids with high, irregular waves often capable of swamping an open canoe. Narrow passages that often require complex maneuvering. May require scouting from shore.

CLASS IV. Long, difficult rapids with constricted passages that often require precise maneuvering in very turbulent water. Scouting from shore is often necessary, and conditions make rescue difficult. Generally not possible for open canoes. Boaters in covered canoes and kayaks should be able to Eskimo roll.

CLASS V. Extremely difficult, long, and very violent rapids with highly congested routes which nearly always must be scouted from shore. Rescue conditions are difficult and there is significant hazard to life in event of a mishap. Ability to Eskimo roll is essential for kayaks and canoes.

CLASS VI. Difficulties of class V carried to the extreme of navigability. Nearly impossible and very dangerous. For teams of experts only, after close study and with all precautions taken.